Rebuke and Forever Silence

Rebuke and Forever Silence

Published by Frank M. Johnson, January, 2017

ISBN-13: 978-0692510735
ISBN-10: 0692510737

Printed by CreateSpace, an Amazon.com Company

Available from:
frankmjohnson.net, Amazon.com, CreateSpace.com
and other retail outlets

"For Mia"

Contents

Preface 1

Introduction 3

Chapter 1 9

   The American Colonies 9

   What is America About? 11

   Coming to America 14

   The Virginia Colony 15

   The Dutch Colonies 17

   The Plymouth Colony 18

   The Massachusetts Bay Colony 20

   The Maryland Colony 21

   The Pennsylvania Colony 23

   Under British Rule 24

   Class and Race 26

   The Slave Trade 28

   The Colonies in 1763 36

Chapter 2 41

   A New Nation 41

   The Rumbles of War 44

   The Declaration of Independence 48

   Articles of Confederation 51

   Patriots or Traitors? 52

   Peace and Dilemma 56

   The Constitutional Convention 57

   The Constitution and Slavery 59

   Ratifying the Constitution 60

The Divide Becomes Regional 63

The Virginia Dynasty 65

Like A Fire Bell In The Night 72

The End of a Dynasty 74

The Rise of Sectionalism 75

The End of an Era 82

Chapter 3 85

The Path To War 85

The Taney Court 87

The Rise of Abolitionism 88

Manifest Destiny 105

Gold 109

The Compromise of 1850 111

The Kansas-Nebraska Act 112

Rise of the Republican Party 118

Chapter 4 125

War and Deceit 125

The Republican Plan 127

1860 Republican Convention 142

The 1860 National Election 148

The Secession Crisis 152

The Corwin Amendment 155

Lincoln's War 158

The Emancipation Proclamation 170

The Story Changes 175

Continued Struggles 176

The High Water Mark 180

Lincoln's Dilemma 182

The Election of 1864 190

The Union League 191

The Hard Hand of War 193

The Great Lie 194

Lincoln's Final Term 200

Chapter 5 205

The Aftermath 205

Lincoln the Martyr 207

The Thirteenth Amendment 209

The Fourteenth Amendment 210

Railroads 214

Fate of Native Americans 214

Immigration 216

Republicans and Race Relations 219

Evolution of the Party 223

Appendices 227

Republican Party Platform of 1856 227

Republican Party Platform of 1860 229

1864 National Union Party Platform 232

Bibliography 235

End Notes 237

Preface

My passion for American history developed at a very young age. Early in my high school years, I had taken the required history courses and I suppose that at the time, my views of the War Between the States were in line with most other students my age; the war was about slavery, the Union soldiers were the good guys and the Confederate soldiers were the bad guys. Some of my years in high school were during the period of forced integration. At my school, it was a time of difficult adjustments for both black and white students. In my mid-teens, along with my parents, I made my first visit to a Civil War battlefield at Vicksburg, Mississippi. One of the first stops along the tour was the Vicksburg National Cemetery. On a balmy summer morning, I stood gazing out at an ocean of white markers that seemed endless as they stretched through the early morning fog. I was only a teen but I was awe stricken by the incredible number of graves. I could not imagine what cause could be so great that it would lead to such horrendous carnage. I was not aware at the time that there were no Confederate soldiers in the National Cemetery; thousands of them were lying in unmarked graves in a section of the old city cemetery known as "*Soldier's Rest.*" Even without that knowledge, I was aware that there was much more to the story than I had been taught. Taking required history in college, I soon learned that there was more than one school of thought regarding the war. Things were much more complicated than what I was taught in grade school. I became a dedicated student of American history; especially the years surrounding the War Between the States. It became a constant struggle to find answers to my questions about the war and seemed that for every answer I found, an even greater number of questions would arise. The question that inspired my research for this book arose from my studies of what many historians call "*The Lost Cause.*" I took special note of one particular scholar who proclaimed that the Lost Cause was a legend deriving from the despair of a bitter, defeated people who attempted to down-play a defense of slavery by perpetuating the ideals of the Old South. It was easy to find a multitude of scholars who agreed with him that the Southern cause was a defense of slavery but none of them were obliged to explain who or what the Southerners were defending against. My

1

curiosity was quickly stimulated by reading the 1860 platform of the Republican Party. Not only were Republicans disinterested in abolishing slavery but they were defending it as a right of the States where it existed. To add to the confusion, Republicans were bitterly opposed to slavery being introduced to the new territories in the west. The answer to that quandary was easily found in the words of the Republican leaders; they did not want slavery in the territories because they didn't want blacks in the territories. The war started with Republicans defending slavery in the States where it existed but after three years of death and destruction, the Republican story changed. The focus of this book became a determination of exactly when and why the story changed. After years of intense research it was obvious that the War Between the States had many very complex causes. It was also obvious that the Republican Party's change in its claim for perpetuating the war was driven by the fear of losing an election. The problem with trying to relate this story was that it required the inclusion of over 260 years of American history. While my research is well sourced and well documented, it is my hope that the readers will find the story so incredible that they will challenge my work and do research of their own.

Introduction

1863 was one of the most defining years in American history. Embroiled in the nation's deadliest conflict, the principles and ideals of the founding fathers met their greatest test as the rest of the world watched and waited. The irony of this story is the way historians and researches have reached such opposite conclusions from the same actions and events. The focus of this publication is the manner in which Abraham Lincoln and the Republican Party represented their platform during the 1860 election only to reverse their position in 1864.

Conservative ideologies dominated the first half of the nineteenth century. In Mid-May of 1860, the fledgling Republican Party held its national convention in the city of Chicago. They had failed miserably in the 1856 presidential election when their candidate, former California Senator John C. Frémont, received only 33.1% of the popular vote. He also failed to carry his home state of California.

As the convention began, the front runner was New York Senator William H. Seward. Although Seward had a large following, many Republicans worried that his anti-slavery rhetoric had inspired John Brown's insurrection at Harper's Ferry, Virginia and feared that his stance on slavery could be counterproductive to the goals of the party. Other strong contenders for the nomination were former Free-Soiler Salmon P. Chase along with Edward Bates and Simon Cameron who were former members of the anti-immigration Know Nothing Party. A lesser known and more moderate candidate was former railroad attorney and congressman from Illinois, Abraham Lincoln. His well-publicized debates with Democratic Senator Stephen Douglas gave him credibility as a presidential candidate. Although Lincoln insisted that the white race would always hold a superior position in society, he made it known he was opposed to slavery and dedicated to restricting the expansion of it. Despite being personally opposed to slavery, he contended that the Federal government had no authority to interfere with slavery in the States where it existed. This stance on slavery became a part of the 1860 Platform.

As convention delegates struggled with platform issues, Lincoln's popularity grew and Seward's popularity declined. Other stances taken by Lincoln during his campaign seemed to fall perfectly in line with the sentiments of many delegates. Lincoln favored a strong central government, a trans-continental railroad and believed in promoting immigration through the free distribution of government lands. All of these were prominent issues within the Party. As expected, the struggle by delegates to agree on a Republican Presidential Nominee was intense. After three close votes, Lincoln emerged victorious.

Delegates adopted seventeen resolutions as their 1860 platform. The third resolution contains the title of this book. It begins by proclaiming that the United States as a nation owes its prosperity to the union of states and further resolves that:

> ". . we hold in abhorrence all schemes for disunion, come from whatever source they may. And we congratulate the country that no Republican member of Congress has uttered or countenanced the threats of disunion so often made by Democratic members, without rebuke and with applause from their political associates; and we denounce those threats of disunion, in case of a popular overthrow of their ascendency as denying the vital principles of a free government, and as an avowal of contemplated treason, which it is the imperative duty of an indignant people sternly to **rebuke and forever silence**."

The Republican Party was heir to the Federalist views of Alexander Hamilton. A majority of its members were former Whigs who held strong to Federalist principles. The Whig Party was crushed by the dominance of anti-federalist and conservative beliefs and had lost all of their political influence by the mid-1850s. A divisive issue in the nineteenth century was one that is equally contentious in our society today. Put very mildly, it was the issue of how much power should be vested in the Federal government. A carry-over from bitter struggles which reached a boiling point during the ratification of the United States Constitution, the issue grew hotter with each passing year. To complicate matters, opposing views were becoming increasingly sectional with liberal views being most dominate in the north and conservative views begin most dominate in the south. Decades of ever increasing tensions resulted in the deadliest war in American history. Attempting to tell the story of how the United States reached the point of war is a monumental task. Bringing to light the impact of the war on today's society is just as difficult.

Many historians have concluded that the War Between the States was a glorious struggle for human rights and racial equality while others contend that if slavery had been the only issue, war would have been unlikely. It has become increasingly popular to demean any historian that believes that the War Between the States was anything other than a war about slavery. These historians are often labeled as revisionists, Southern apologists or neo-confederates. Countless books have been written about the so called "*Lost Cause*" of the Confederacy while few examine the cause of the Union during the war; more importantly, the cause of the Republican Party.

The story told in this book is neither new history, nor unpublished history and it is not a revisionist history. It is any many ways, the same history that has been written by most authors. The most crucial difference between this publication and other written histories is its focus on key elements that are often overlooked. A prime example would be the statement that:

> "The first ten amendments to the United States Constitution are known as the Bill of Rights."

Few, if any historians will dispute that this phrase is historically accurate. However, when most Americans are asked to identify the most important word in that statement, they almost unanimously select the word "*Rights*." Americans rarely focus on the word "*Amendments*." They seldom realize that the Constitution had to be amended to include those rights that we hold most dear. Some of our founding fathers were willing to deny us those rights for the sake of a strong central government. This belief is the same liberal federalist belief that was the backbone of the Republican Party in the nineteenth century.

So what was the true agenda of the Republican Party in 1860? They had a master plan for the new territories. It would be populated by white Protestants, perpetuating John Winthrop's "*Model of Christian Charity*" as a "*City upon a Hill*." The 1860 Republican Party Platform outlined the requirements to carry out this plan. They needed a Trans-Continental railroad from the north to California, free land for immigrants, increased tariffs, improved seaports, and have all of this under the complete control of the federal government; a government which they intended to control.

What they did not want in the new territories was Negroes, Mexicans, Indians, Catholics, Jews or Mormons. Every western state and territory already had exclusion laws preventing free blacks and Mexicans from immigrating into the new frontier but the obstacles to such a plan were very clear. They could not allow slavery. As Lincoln stated; If blacks were never introduced in the new territories, there would be no blacks in the new territories. Efforts for the removal of Mormons and Indians from the new territories were already under way but needed to be stepped up. New laws would have to be passed to increase tariffs, build western sea ports and open up government lands to immigrants. Perhaps the greatest threat to the plan was disunion. In 1860, Republicans were clear in their promise to the Southern States that they would not interfere with slavery where it existed and that they would never be threatened with military force.

So what was the meaning of the words "*rebuke and forever silence*?" The Republican Party was determined to remove the word "*Sovereignty*" from the American vocabulary. All resistance to the power of the federal government would have to be crushed.

From 1861 through mid 1863, most of the goals of the Republican Party had been met. The Confederate Army was driven from northern soil at the Battle of Gettysburg. The Confederacy was split by Union control of the Mississippi River after the fall of Vicksburg, Mississippi but suddenly in the fall of 1863, the Republican machine came to a grinding stop. Confederate forces at Chickamauga Creek in Georgia, delivered a devastating blow to the Union army with decisive victory. Diplomatic negotiations with France, Spain and Great Britain were at a standstill, forcing Lincoln to enter into an alliance with Russia. Americans in the north were growing tired of the death and carnage of war and many began to demand a peaceful solution. Lincoln's nemesis, George McLellan announced his candidacy for President as a Peace Democrat. It was at this point that the Republican Party parted ways with Lincoln. The Republican Party could not afford for the war to end without total subjugation of the south. Few people, including Lincoln, believed that he would be re-elected. Republicans chose John C. Frémont, once again as their presidential candidate and Lincoln was forced to call upon the money men of the Union League to gain the nomination of the new National Union Party. Through clever negotiations, Lincoln convinced Frémont to withdraw from the presidential race, leaving the Republican Party with no candidate. General Sherman's burning of Atlanta and devastating the State of Georgia, brought Lincoln back into favor with many of the Republicans and diminished much of the demand for a peaceful resolution to the war. Both Lincoln and the Republican Party had changed their platform and more importantly had changed the story of what the war was fought over. A president who stated during his inaugural address in 1861 that he had neither the lawful right nor the inclination to interfere with slavery where it existed was proclaiming in 1865 that abolishing slavery had been his cause and that:

> *". . . until every drop of blood drawn with the lash shall be paid by another drawn with the sword . . . it must be said, the judgments of the Lord are true and righteous altogether."*

The platform of the Republican Party in 1860 was so radically different that of 1864 that one platform or the other would have to be filled with complete lies. Which platform was a lie and which platform was true, is a subject that continues to be debated.

The beauty of history is that both its villains and its heroes are convicted by their own words and actions. In a complete reversal of their previous platform, the 1864 Republican Party claimed that it was continuing the war effort in an attempt to free the black race from the bonds of slavery and implying that their righteous acts had been ordained by God. What they did not mention is that they were simultaneously cleansing the western frontier of Native Americans and unwanted religious groups; a practice that their party would support well into the twentieth century. They were also ignoring the demands of America's women. There was nothing in the resolves of the Republican Party which provided equality for all Americans.

The following pages contain historical accounts from the Jamestown Colony in 1607 all the way to the present. The events of 1863 were not spontaneous. The trail to the bloodiest conflict in American history is a long one. Understanding how we reached the breaking point requires an understanding of the nation's founders, the war for independence, issues dealing with the United States Constitution, and the motives of the Republican Party. This book makes no attempt to suggest that the readers should adopt a certain opinion. It is filled with accurate accounts of actions taken by America's leaders and tells the story in their own words. These are words as they were spoken not accounts transcribed and transformed by the persuasion of public sentiments. Once you have read the story you will likely have the same heroes as before but you may have to accept some bitter truths about these characters and America as a whole. It is likely that the story will meet with a great deal of *rebuke* in some social or political circles but it is unlikely that the truth will be *forever silenced.*

Chapter 1

The American Colonies

1607 – 1763

The American story is one of many complex twists and turns. To say that the United States of America was created by a group of fledgling colonies uniting against a common enemy would be an over-simplification of the truth. They were new world colonies with old world traditions. Despite having originally been bound together by old world influences, each colony would eventually develop its own new world culture.

While trying to tell the full story of the early colonies in a single publication would be futile, this chapter gives a brief summary of key events which bound the colonists together and yet progressively drove them apart. By the time of the American Revolution, two dominant social and political powers had evolved; the merchant society in the north, led by colonists in Massachusetts and the agrarian society in the south led by colonists in Virginia. It is the struggle between these two great powers that would eventually threaten to divide the nation. Ironically, it was Massachusetts that made the first attempt to secede from the Union. Even as the Colonies united to form a new nation, they were deeply divided in their views and formulas for a new government. In addition, a geographical dividing line continuously developed between northern and southern states. A bitter struggle over political ideology while attempting to adopt the United States Constitution set the stage for the War Between the States, in 1861.

A full appreciation of the incredible story that unfolded in the United States during the War Between the States requires a clear understanding of the men and women that established the first colonies in America. During a speech in 1926, celebrating the 150th anniversary of the Declaration of Independence, President Calvin Coolidge said:

"Our forefathers came to certain conclusions and decided upon certain courses of action which have been a great blessing to the world. Before we can understand their conclusions we must go back and review the course which they followed. We must think the thoughts which they thought."

While investigating the lives and deeds of these people it is important to base our conclusions on facts and dispel any myths that might unfairly bias American history. It seems natural that after hundreds of years, American history could easily become slanted toward accepting certain legends as historical fact, despite evidence to the contrary. It is unlikely that the average American believes that George Washington confessed to his father that he chopped down the cherry tree or that Davy Crockett killed a bear when he was only three, but we accept these accounts as folklore and it is unlikely that stories like these will ever have serious influences on true American history.

All too often, social and political trends cause a slant to history that is not as harmless as the legends of our treasured folk heroes. Many authors, historians and researchers attempt to portray the history of America in a way that would like for it to have been instead the way it actually was. Many annals exploit the passions of present day sentiments by omitting paramount events in the lives of the founders. Frequently, these chronicles are deliberate attempts to distort our perception of the genuine dreams and aspirations of the men and women who built America. They promote a biased belief in the values of immigration, diversity, racial equality and religious freedom which cannot be fully supported by historical facts.

Few would argue that America is the greatest country in the world but the great men and women who made this country what it is today were not perfect people. There are times when a person's greatness is best defined by their ability to deal with their own weaknesses and by rising above their failures. Accepting the unpopular or seemingly wrongful acts of our leaders does not demand that we dismiss or diminish their contributions to the good of the nation. The story of America is a story of the good, the bad and the ugly but it is all a part of making the United States of America what it is today. Deleting any part of the story to conciliate the demands of a popular sentiment could be described as historical genocide.

What is America About?

A popular statement among today's politicians is *"that's not what America is about."* All too frequently, that statement is made by individuals with a limited knowledge of American history, giving little if any regard to the thoughts and ideals of this country's courageous founders. Many of the contemporary versions of American history contend that the first colonists were poor and desperate people, fleeing to the new world to escape poverty, oppression and religious persecution. These contentions may be popular in today's society but they are not supported by historical facts and are unfair representations of the character of the men and women that established the first settlements along America's Atlantic shore.

There is little doubt that the social climate of America today is much different from that of centuries gone by. The persuasions of time and social change often cloud our ability to accept our true history. A prime example of this is found in the symbolism of the Statue of Liberty.

"Lady Liberty" has become one of the greatest iconic images in America. Within the walls of the statue's base is a plaque which contains the words to a sonnet written by Emma Lazarus in 1883, titled *"The New Colossus."* It includes the well-known phrase"

Statue of Liberty

Jet Lowe
U. S. Library of Congress

"Give me your tired, your poor,
Your huddled masses yearning to breathe free,
The wretched refuse of your teeming shore.
Send these, the homeless, tempest-tost to me,
I lift my lamp beside the golden door!"

To many Americans, the statue is a symbol of the nation's commitment to life, liberty and the pursuit of happiness; those unalienable rights embodied in the Declaration of Independence. The association of the statue with the words of the classic sonnet, persuade others to view the statue as a symbol of hope to the oppressed people of the world; a view that many believe was shared by the country's founders. America's history does not fully support that view. In the early colonies of Virginia and New England, religious and racial diversity was almost non-existent. For the first 250 years of America's history, immigration was discouraged by Americans.

In 1865, French professor and political activist Édouard René de Laboulaye initiated a fundraising campaign in France. Laboulaye's original intent was to build a monument to the slain U. S. President Abraham Lincoln.[1] Why Laboulaye felt such a passionate bond with Lincoln is a mystery, considering that Lincoln was attempting to stop a revolution in America while Laboulaye himself was supporting one in France. The only apparent bond was that both men were opposed to slavery. Laboulaye did in fact help fund a gold medal that was presented to the President's widow, Mary Todd Lincoln, in 1866. Laboulaye's deep admiration of Lincoln was not shared by all of his fellow Frenchmen. After resistance to his original plan, Laboulaye and sculptor Frédéric Auguste Bartholdi conceived the idea of the Statue of Liberty and promoted the statue as a gift from France representing some perceived alliance between France and the United States. There is little, if any, historical support of such an alliance prior to World War I. The statue was used by the Republican Party in the late 19th century to promote immigration during a time when heavy restrictions were being placed on immigrants.

Another example of the impact that social change has on true history is the belief that one of America's founding principles was a "separation of church and state." The phrase was first used in a letter by Thomas Jefferson to the Danbury Baptists Association in Connecticut.[2] Although it has been cited many times by the U. S. Supreme Court, it is not a part of the United States Constitution. It was first used by the court during the case of Renyolds v. United States[3] in 1878. This case was brought before the court by English immigrant George Reynolds, who had been caught up in the controversial attempt by the U. S. Congress, to dismantle the Church of Latter Day Saints.

History records that the American colonies were founded by Protestants and that the church and the government were virtually one in the same. In most areas, taxes were levied by the government to support the church.[(4)]   After the American revolution, each state was faced with the question of whether or not the state would continue to raise taxes to support the church.

It would be difficult to deny that the United States Constitution and many of the country's laws are based on what our forefathers believed to be the laws of God rather than the laws of mankind or the laws of nature. Fundamental rights were clearly expressed as a part of God's law. The U. S. Declaration of Independence states:

> *"We hold these truths to be self-evident, that all Men are created equal, that they are endowed by their Creator with certain unalienable rights that among these are Life, Liberty, and the Pursuit of Happiness."*

Over thousands of years of history, the laws of many countries both past and present have shown that a person's rights are no greater than his ability to defend them. These are the laws of man which are clearly alienable. They are the same laws which have divided the world's population into unequal social classes. Laws of nature support survival of the fittest in a world where neither man nor beast is equal. It is only from their religious belief that our forefathers could suggest equality among all people. A complete separation of church and state would require a separation from the laws of God and from the principles of our founders.

There are many more examples which would suggest that current perceptions of America's resolve has been slanted by scholarly interpretations that have little, if any historical basis. They often assert biased principles which cannot accurately be attributed to our founders. An accurate assessment of what America is truly about can only be found in the words and deeds of those men and women who established this great nation. Their views sometimes differed and their beliefs were sometimes complex and conflicting but the basic values of life, liberty and the pursuit of happiness were seemingly shared by all.

Coming to America

The driving forces behind the establishment of colonies along America's Atlantic shore were wealth and opportunity. In short, colonization was a business deal initiated by the monarchs in Europe. The colonists who entered into these contracts were often living more comfortably in Europe than they would be upon arrival in the New World. Many were wealthy and powerful individuals and in some cases were royals, aristocrats and nobles. Often, the original English and Dutch setters are mistakenly regarded as immigrants when in reality they were loyal citizens who decided to relocate to lands claimed by their respective monarchs. They were neither tired nor poor nor homeless. In contrast, they were strong, adventurous and ambitious. Not some huddled mass yearning to breathe but rather a multitude of accomplished, forceful and aspiring individuals who were determined to succeed.

Even the religious leaders were among the elite class in their homelands. Their actions in both Europe and the New World suggest that they were seeking a place and an opportunity for religious dominance rather than running from religious persecution. They were on a mission to set a shining example for the entire world to see. Evidence of their intent can be found in words and deeds of those who led them to the new world. One of the most telling events was John Winthrop's speech, *A Model of Christian Charity*, in which he stated:

"we shall be as a city upon a hill—the eyes of all people are upon us"

"Landing of Governor Winthrop at Salem, 1630." New York Public Library Digital Collections.

Laws that were established in the Colonies were base on what the colonists believed to be "God's Law" according to their protestant convictions. These laws were strict and totally intolerant toward other religious beliefs. Colonists who are often remembered as the persecuted could better be described as the persecutors. Early colonists were required by law to attend religious services and support the church. A violation of church doctrine was not only a sin but also a criminal act. Severe violations of church law were often punishable by death. The success of the colonies depended on everyone being of one mind, having one common goal and only one religious faith.

The Virginia Colony

The first serious attempts by England to establish colonies in North America were initiated during the reign of Queen Elizabeth I. Unfortunately, these attempts ended in failure. These expeditions were business ventures funded by private investors but under the control of the Crown. In 1583, Sir Humphrey Gilbert set sail for North America with five vessels. This was the first of three failed attempts by Gilbert to establish a colony in the New World. Gilbert was lost at sea while attempting to return to England from his third voyage. In 1584, Gilbert's half-brother, Sir Walter Raleigh was granted a seven year royal charter, authorizing him to explore, colonize, and rule any areas not possessed by any Christian Prince, or inhabited by Christian People in return for one-fifth of all the gold and silver that might be mined there.[5] In 1587, Raleigh dispatched 115 colonists, led by John White, to establish a colony in the Chesapeake Bay area. The colony which was eventually located on Roanoke Island in present day North Carolina vanished in 1590 and is remembered today as "The Lost Colony." England made no further attempts to establish a colony in North America until the reign of King James I.

The Virginia Company was a joint stock company chartered by King James I of England in April of 1606, for the purposes of establishing settlements on the Atlantic coast of North America. It created two companies. The first was the Virginia Company of London or The

London Company. The second was the Virginia Company of Plymouth or The Plymouth Company. While it is important that this charter established the first permanent settlements on the Atlantic coast of North America, it is perhaps more important to focus on the two social and political powers that were spawned by the charter. These two great powers, Virginia and New England, would eventually serve not only as the catalyst for a movement that brought the Colonies together as the United States of America but would also establish two very distinct and contrasting societies which would eventually bring the north and south to brutal conflict.

The London Company established the settlement of Jamestown in May of 1607 and served as the capitol of the colony of Virginia until 1699. Virginia's contract included the right of self government provided that they fulfill their obligations to the Crown. Established in 1619, the House of Burgesses became the first elected legislative body in the American Colonies. Burgesses were required to be land owners and members of the Church of England.

The Virginia colony evolved quickly into an agrarian society with large plantations. The most profitable crop was tobacco. When the Virginia Company failed in 1624, King James I of England revoked their charter. Virginia became a Crown Colony and was transferred to royal authority. English authorities soon began to encourage its countrymen to relocate in Virginia. After the execution of Charles I, substantial numbers of his more elite loyalists migrated to Virginia. Many of these followers, sometimes referred to as the "Old Dominion," became the patriarchs of a group known as "The First Families of Virginia." Names of these elite families included Washington, Jefferson, Lee and Randolph.

Although some of the citizens of the Virginia Colony were Puritans, the Church of England was the official church of the colony. Any attempt to introduce differing religious beliefs within the colony was met with fierce opposition. It was not until the passing of the Virginia Statute for Religious Freedom in 1786 that freedom of religion existed in Virginia.[6]

The Dutch Colonies

Although the Dutch Colonies in North America existed for little more than fifty years before falling under the rule of the English Crown, the influences of these early colonists have been felt throughout American history. Most Dutch settlements were established along the Hudson River in what is now New York but some extended into the present states of Pennsylvania, Delaware, New Jersey, Connecticut and Rhode Island. Like the English colonization efforts, Dutch exploration was financed by private investors seeking wealth and opportunity. In 1609, the Dutch East India Company hired English sailor Henry Hudson to search for a northeast passage to Asia. Hudson explored the river which is named in his honor and claimed all of the land along the Hudson River Valley for the East India Company but was unable to establish a permanent colony.

The Dutch West India Company was chartered in 1621 and funded in 1623 by Dutch investors in conjunction with the States General of the Netherlands. The company established a series of settlements and trading posts in the present day Mid-Atlantic States and named the area New Netherland. A settlement called New Amsterdam was established on present day Manhattan Island in 1624. Newly appointed Director General Peter Minuit arrived on the island in 1626 and is credited with purchasing the entire island of Manhattan from local natives for goods valued at 60 guilders (approximately $24.00 at the time). After being suspended from his post as Director General, Minuit lived in Germany for several years. He returned to North America under the authority of the Swedish government. In 1638, Minuit established a Swedish settlement along the lower Delaware River on land previous claimed by the Dutch. The Dutch took control of the settlement in 1655.

From 1647 to 1664, Peter Stuyvesant served as the 7th and last Director General of New Amsterdam. His commitment to the supremacy of the Dutch Reformed Church left little room for religious freedom. He openly opposed Lutherans, Jews, Catholics and Quakers. Continued growth and expansion of New Netherland caused conflicts with both Native Americans and English Colonists. The English took control of New Netherland during the Second Anglo-Dutch War in 1664.

The significance of Dutch colonization in regard to American history is that it was the first representation of diversity among the colonists. Both the English and Dutch colonies were dominated by protestant religious beliefs. The Dutch Reformed Church was the first religion in the new world with no particular relationship with the Church of England. Unlike New England Colonies and the Southern Colonies, the Dutch colonists spoke many languages. During the formative years of the United States, these Mid-Atlantic States did not rise to the dominant social and political ranks of the elite families of Massachusetts or the first families of Virginia but they were often the deciding vote in political confrontations.

The Plymouth Colony

It is probable that in the minds of most Americans, the arrival of the Pilgrim Fathers aboard the Mayflower is the epitome of the American dream. In contrast, the story of the Plymouth Colony is unique among all others. Many historians contend that the Pilgrims came to the New World to escape religious persecution but historical accounts written by their leader, William Bradford, suggest otherwise.

The Puritan separatists who became known as Pilgrims were highly critical of the Church of England. Unlike other Puritans, they did not believe that the church could be purified and advocated a total reform. The group came to prominence during the reign of Queen Elizabeth I. Although the Queen faced constant demands from the Pilgrims for church reform, Elizabeth was not well known for persecution of dissenters. Her successor, James I, took a strong stance against the Catholic Church early in his reign but by the time he had turned his attention toward Puritan dissenters, the Pilgrims had already migrated to Holland, leaving little evidence to suggest that they left England to escape persecution. It appears more likely that it was resentment toward non-acceptance that caused their departure.

The Pilgrim experience in Holland turned out to be worse than what they had experienced in England. In his manuscript *"of Plymouth Plantation,"* William Bradford described the conditions in Holland and the Pilgrims' decision to move to America. He cited many reasons for leaving Holland, including hard work, poor economic conditions, apathy toward their teachings and a fear that the Dutch society might corrupt their youth. Bradford's writings do not conclude that the decision to leave Holland was motivated by religious persecution.

The basic motivations for the Pilgrims' migration to the New World were no different from the other early expeditions. America offered vast amounts of land and opportunity for wealth. In addition, the Pilgrims were driven by yet another passion. Bradford tells that the Pilgrims were motivated by evangelism and had "a great hope and inward zeal of laying good foundations." While it is inspiring to contend that the Pilgrims made a courageous escape from oppression and religious persecution, this contention is misleading and diminishes the importance of their goals and accomplishments. The Puritans were devout Christians, determined to establish new communities to be bound by the laws of God. The influences of their efforts are prominently displayed throughout American history. Despite their disagreements with the Monarchs of England, they maintained their allegiance to the crown for many years.

Before ever setting foot on the shore of North America, the Pilgrims established their government in the form of the "Mayflower Compact" stating:

> *"Having undertaken, for the Glory of God, and advancements of the Christian faith and honor of our King and Country, a voyage to plant the first colony in the Northern parts of Virginia, do by these presents, solemnly and mutually, in the presence of God, and one another, covenant and combine ourselves together into a civil body politic; for our better ordering, and preservation and furtherance of the ends aforesaid; and by virtue hereof to enact, constitute, and frame, such just and equal laws, ordinances, acts, constitutions, and offices, from time to time, as shall be thought most meet and convenient for the general good of the colony; unto which we promise all due submission and obedience."* [7]

The wording of Compact clearly indicates that the Pilgrims traveled to the New World on a mission for the glory of God. Their intent was to establish a society solely governed by the laws of God; setting a shining example for the world to see.

The Massachusetts Bay Colony

The Massachusetts Bay Colony was established under a charter granted to the Massachusetts Bay Company by King Charles I of England. Much like the popular beliefs about the Plymouth Colonists, it is often contended that these colonists came to the New World to escape religious persecution in England. King Charles I. did in fact initiate a series of reforms directed at puritans and other religious groups in 1633 but the Massachusetts Bay Colony was established in 1630. Even though Charles was agitated by the Puritan's constant demands for reform of the Church of England, contending that his agitation was a form of persecution is questionable. It is more likely that the combination of the King's marriage to a Catholic and his failure to support the Protestant cause was a greater influence upon the Puritan's decision to relocate.

A fleet of eleven ships, known as "*The Winthrop Fleet*" carried more than 700 Puritans plus supplies from England to New England during the summer of 1630. This was the beginning of mass migration from England to the Massachusetts Bay Colony that would last for more than a decade. Like the colonists of Plymouth, the Massachusetts Bay colonists were Puritans but they were reformists, believing that the Church of England could be salvaged. The Pilgrim Puritans of the Plymouth Colony did not believe that the church could be reformed and would have to be completely reconstructed. Despite their differences, both groups maintained strong bonds among themselves and with the Church of England. They also maintained their allegiance to the English Crown. A formal border was established between the Massachusetts Bay and Plymouth Colonies in 1639.

Society in the Massachusetts Bay Colony was much like that of other American colonies. The structure of the government and laws were dictated by the church. Their ideals and beliefs were clearly Puritan and they were fiercely intolerant toward other religious beliefs. Their intolerance was a major factor in establishing other colonies in New England. In 1636, Puritan theologian Roger Williams was banished from the Colony for spreading new and dangerous ideas. His banishment led to the establishment of the Providence Plantation and the Rhode Island Colony. In 1637, Puritan clergyman John Wheelwright's banishment was a key factor in the establishment of the New Hampshire Colony. Wheelwright's sister-in-law, Anne

Hutchinson was excommunicated from the church in 1638 and was also banished from the Colony. Further dissent by Puritan clergymen resulted in the establishment of the Connecticut Colony.

Mary Dyer being led to the gallows
By Howard Pyle
Newport Historical Society Collection

The first Quakers in the New World arrived at Boston Harbor in 1656 in the form of two female missionaries; Mary Fisher, a twenty-two year old maidservant and Ann Austin, a middle-aged mother of five. Upon their arrival, Magistrates met them at the dock, seized their printed materials and arrested them. They were stripped naked in public and underwent extensive body searches for signs of witchcraft.[8] The continued persecution of Quakers led to the hanging of Mary Dyer in 1660. King Charles II of England ascended to the throne that same year and in 1661, issued an order forbidding Massachusetts from executing anyone for professing Quaker beliefs. Religious persecution in Massachusetts began to decline when King Charles revoked the Massachusetts Charter in 1684 and later installed a Royal Governor to enforce English Law.

The Maryland Colony

If there was any religious group that could truthfully claim that it fled to the New World to escape religious persecution, it would possibly be the Catholics. As George Calvert was attempting to persuade King James I of England to grant him a new charter in the area of present day Maryland, most of Europe was involved in a series of bloody conflicts known as the "Thirty Years War" which had fragmented the Holy Roman Empire. In 1605, the English Parliament had passed the Popish Recusants Act which forbade Catholics from practicing certain ceremonial acts, allowed magistrates to search their homes, required Catholics to take an oath of allegiance and made it high treason to obey the authority of Rome rather than the authority of the king. The dilemma for Catholics in the American

Colonies was that resentment of the Catholic religion and persecution of Catholic believers was just as great if not greater in the New World than it was in Europe.

George Calvert, 1st Baron Baltimore was a wealthy English politician who once served as Secretary of State under King James I. Like most who received charters for a colony in North America, his original interest was focused on financial gain. He was an investor in both the Virginia Company and the Dutch East India Company. After a failed attempt to establish a permanent colony in Newfoundland, Calvert turned his attentions toward a warmer climate along the Atlantic Coast. His arrival at Jamestown, Virginia in 1629 was met with strong opposition so he returned to England to lobby for a new charter. Unfortunately, his new charter was not granted until shortly after his death. The charter reverted to his first son, Cecil Calvert, 2nd Baron Baltimore. Cecil commissioned his younger brother Leonard to sail to North America and establish the Colony of Maryland where he became the colony's first governor.

For many years, the Colony of Maryland served as a refuge for Catholics despite facing continuous opposition from neighboring Protestants. Puritans migrating from Virginia, where the Church of England was the official church, quickly outnumbered Catholics. In 1645, Puritan leaders took control of the Maryland government. That same year Jesuit missionaries Andrew White and Thomas Copley were arrested for their Catholic preaching and were shipped to England in chains. Catholics received some relief when the Maryland Toleration Act was passed in 1649. While the act gave protection to all Christian faiths, anyone found guilty of denying the divinity of Jesus Christ could be executed for blasphemy. Despite the 1649 act, hostile sentiments toward the Catholic faith remained common in the Maryland Colony for more than two centuries.

The Pennsylvania Colony

Perhaps the most unique story of all the American Colonies is that of Pennsylvania. Here again is a story where it is difficult to distinguish between the persecuted and the persecutors.

William Penn was a wealthy English real estate entrepreneur who converted to Quakerism at the age of twenty-two. While in England, Penn criticized all religions except Quaker. In addition to defying all royal authority and continuously attacking the Church of England, he labeled the Catholic Church as "The Whore of Babylon" and called Puritans "hypocrites and revelers in God." His continued verbal and written abuse of all government and religious authority caused him to be arrested and imprisoned in the Tower of London in 1668. Penn was released after eight months but he refused to stop his attacks on established religions and the King's authority. He was arrested again in 1670 while deliberately challenging laws concerning preaching at public gatherings. Still nothing would deter Penn from his blatant attacks on government and religion.

William Penn addressing King Charles II. "The Birth of Pennsylvania 1680" by Jean Leon Gerome Ferris
U. S. Library of Congress Digital Collection

After his father's death in 1670, William inherited a large fortune which included a debt owed to his father by King Charles II. In 1677, William Penn and a group of prominent Quakers purchased West Jersey (roughly half of the current day State of New Jersey). That same year, approximately 200 English Quakers migrated to the area and later established the town of Burlington. In 1682, East Jersey was purchased by a group led by Scottish Quaker, Robert Barclay.

With a strong Quaker base having been established in America, William Penn went to King Charles II with a proposal that some might consider to be extortion. In essence, Penn offered a release of the debt owed to him by the King plus the promise of a mass migration of Quakers to the new world. The King generously granted Penn a charter for more than 45,000 square miles of land west of the Jersey Colony; a portion of which belonged to Lord Baltimore in Maryland. The enormity of King's grant to William Penn suggests he would pay almost any price to distance himself from the constant agitation of William Penn and the Quakers. Ironically, after William Penn established the Colony of Pennsylvania, he began to welcome people of all nationalities and religious faiths, making Pennsylvania the only colony in North America where racial and religious diversity truly existed during the 17th Century.

Under British Rule

By the year 1729, all of the original charter and proprietary colonies along North America's Atlantic Coast had come under British Rule with the exception of Georgia which was not formed until 1732. Georgia was established under a charter issued by King George II of Great Britain to a group of trustees, led by James Edward Oglethorpe. The last of the trustees sold their lands back to the crown in 1752.

Many people envision early American history as a constant struggle between the colonists and Great Britain. In reality there was very little dissent for the first 150 years of the colonies. The few rebellions that occurred were most often aimed at local authorities who were over-stepping their authority and had little impact on the relationship between the colonists and the British Crown. During most of this time, the colonists were loyal British subjects. Colonists such as

George Washington served honorably in the British Army. Being distanced from the politics and struggles in Europe, they were primarily concerned with local issues. With each passing year they became more vested in the societies that they had developed and the lands which they owned. Their lands now held the graves of their ancestors and the reminders of their struggles to establish a new society. There was an ever increasing attitude of nativism. Although the British government continued to encourage its citizens to settle in the New World, the colonists showed resentment toward new comers.

The estimated population of the British Colonies in 1760 including slaves was approximately 1,593,625. Further dispelling the myth that America has always been a refuge for the world's immigrants, it has been estimated that more than 98% of the total white population in the colonies in 1760 was native born. The two most populated colonies were the Massachusetts Colony, with approximately 202,600 and the Virginia Colony with approximately 339,726. Having more than one third of the total population of British North America, these two colonies had the greatest influence with the British government and set most of the standards for how all of the Colonies were to be governed. Within the two colonies, there was little diversity. Colonists in Massachusetts were predominantly Puritan. Virginia was more committed to the beliefs and customs of the Church of England but both Massachusetts and Virginia were firmly protestant and intolerant of other faiths. The two had many things in common. As a society, they were White, English speaking Christians with strong ties to the British throne but by the time of the American Revolution they had developed sharp contrasts in their economies and in their relations with the British government. Massachusetts along with their neighboring colonies, developed into a society of merchants and urban retailers while Virginia and the southern colonies remained a society of planters in a rural setting. Massachusetts was heavily dependent on foreign trade and trade with Britain while Virginia, for the most part was self sufficient. Methods of taxation and trade policies that were adopted by the British government during the mid-eighteenth century were devastating in the Northern Colonies but had less of an impact in the Southern Colonies. It was these differences that almost divided the colonies during the events leading to the American Revolution

Class and Race

Keeping in mind that English, Dutch and Swedish colonization in the New World was a financial endeavor, it is important to note that the leaders of each group were all elite members of a particular social class as defined by hundreds of years of custom and tradition in Europe. In contrast to many popular beliefs, none of the 13 original colonies were founded by some *"wretched refuse of a teeming shore."*

Those who ranked highest in social classes were the royals and the nobles; a rank which could only be attained by inheritance or royal appointment. Colonial leaders of this class include Lord John Winthrop of the Massachusetts Bay Colony, George Calvert, 1st Lord Baltimore in the Maryland Colony and the Noblemen who were Lords Proprietor of the New Jersey and Carolina Colonies. Clergymen were also among the very elite in most of Europe and because the church and the government sometimes competed for authority, church leaders often came into conflict with the royals. As in all societies, the very wealthy in Europe and in the colonies demanded a certain standing in society and were the very backbone of the colonization ventures. Statesmen and military leaders who served the royals and the government also attained a loft spot on the social ladder. They had proven themselves as being loyal and accomplished individuals that were capable of protecting the interests of both the government and the investors in the New World. The next level on the social scale was determined by a person's education, profession or skills. People beyond these categories were simply commoners or serfs.

There were no free rides to the New World. Colonization ventures were costly. Leaders of these expeditions were members of the elite social class and were often investors. To be a part of one of these ventures, colonists were required to either pay for their passage or have the skills necessary to make a substantial contribution to the success of the new colony. In addition, they were often required to be virtuous and members of good standing in the church. Even the servants that accompanied the wealthier colonists were required to have certain skills that would contribute to the success of the new colony.

The subject of race had little impact on the social classes in the colonies. It was understood that the white race was superior to that of blacks and Native Americans. For the most part, the citizens of each colony believed that they were the chosen people of God. Their lands were theirs by legal contract, the authority of the throne and the blessings of the almighty. While there were many attempts by colonists to live peaceful among the local tribes it was clear to most colonists that Native Americans had no rightful place in their society. Even when Native tribes were able to peacefully co-exist with the colonists, they were never perceived as having a rightful claim to the lands that they inhabited.

The rights of Native Americans are noticeably absent from most of the written histories of America. In addition to excluding our so called "Indians" from our history, we excluded them from the protection of our laws and isolated them from our society for centuries. The phase "*excluding Indians not taxed,*" appears in Article I of the U. S. Constitution and again in the 14th Amendment which was supposed to guarantee equal protection to all Americans. While some Native Americans had received citizenship by way of public or military service, most did not receive citizenship until the passage of the Indian Citizenship Act of 1924. Even then, some Native Americans were excluded and did not receive full rights of citizenship until the 1940s. In areas of Colorado, Indians were not allowed to serve on juries until 1956 and certain tribal members were historically denied the right to vote until 1970.[9] Although many believe that the institution of slavery is the darkest stain on America's past, it is hard to ignore the acts which almost caused the extinction of an entire race; acts which began with our nation's founders.

Though many of the first blacks to settle in the colonies may have been indentured servants, they were never accepted as equals in an all white society. There was a clear distinction between white and black indentured servants. The institution of slavery in America was not born out the need for cheap labor as much as it was the result of the immense profits that could be realized from human trafficking. Population estimates for the colonies in the 17th and 18th centuries suggest that there was a higher demand for free labor in other countries along the triangle trade routes than there was in America during those periods but human trafficking was immensely profitable wherever and whenever slaves could be traded or sold.

The Slave Trade

In a letter to Sir Edwin Sandys (1619/1620), John Rolfe mentions a Dutch ship bringing "20 and odd Negroes" to the Virginia Colony from the West Indies.([10]) According to the Massachusetts' Historical Society, it is likely that the first documented reference to the slave trade in New England can be found in the journal of John Winthrop, when in 1638, he referenced a ship named "Desire," returning from the West Indies with a cargo of cotton, tobacco and negroes. As early as 1644, Boston merchants were importing slaves directly from Africa but for most of the 17th century, the Atlantic slave trade was dominated by the Dutch West India Company and the English Royal African Company. Beginning in 1713, treaties between several European countries, including Spain, Great Britain, France, Portugal, Savoy and the Dutch Republic, ended the English and Dutch dominance of the African slave market. This opened the door for the English colonies in North America to expand their slave trading operations.

The term "*Merchant*" was often synonymous with "*Slave Trader*" in the New England and Mid-Atlantic Colonies. The tiny province of Rhode Island soon was the capital of the slave trade in North America. Citizens would often buy shares in the voyages of slave ships. It has been estimated that more than 200 Rhode Island families were actively involved in the slave trade. Many of the slave traders became the wealthiest men in the colonies. Some of the more prominent family names included, Lopez, Redwood, Mendes, Riveras, Polok, Brown and DeWolf.

Several of these families were Sephardic Jews. The most active slave trader among them was Aaron Lopez. At one time, Lopez owned or controlled at least 30 ships which were involved in the slave trade. By the early 1770s, he had become the wealthiest man in Newport, Rhode Island. Like the other wealthy slave traders of Rhode Island, Lopez was well known for his philanthropy, giving generously to schools, churches and libraries, making Newport a thriving and prosperous community.

Another of the wealthy slave trading families of Rhode Island was the Brown family. The "four brothers," John, Nicholas, Joseph and Moses Brown formed a partnership in the town of Providence, Rhode Island.

John Brown House
Arthur W. LeBoeuf
U. S. Library of Congress

Like their father James and their uncle Obediah, they were heavily involved the triangle trade which included African Slaves. Their successful business made all four brothers immensely wealthy. The leader of the pack was the third brother John. In the events leading up to the American Revolution, John played a leading role in the burning of the British customs schooner, HMS Gaspee, which was a significant factor in causing further hostilities between Great Britain and the colonists. A ship which John ordered to be built in 1768 was first named the Katy and in 1775 was re-named the Providence and became one of the first ships in the Continental Navy. On the eve of the American Revolution, John's brother, Moses abandoned his family's Baptist beliefs and converted to Quakerism. After joining the Religious Society of Friends (Quakers), Moses became a staunch opponent of slavery.

Between 1794 and 1820, the United States enacted several laws designed to put an end to the America's involvement in the Atlantic slave trade. During that time, John Brown was the only one of the four brothers still active in the slave trade. His brother Nicholas had given up the trade in 1767 and diversified his interests. Joseph Brown left the firm in 1784 and died the next year. On August 5, 1797, John Brown became the first person to be tried under the U. S. Slave Trade Act of 1794. His brother Moses was one of those who implicated him. John accused Moses and the Providence Abolition Society of singling him out while offering settlements to others in the slave trade. John lost his case and was forced to forfeit his ship. Despite some minor set-backs to his slave trafficking empire, John Brown was still a wealthy man. He had already begun trading with China in the late 1780s. In his trade with China, he discovered a commodity that was even more profitable than human trafficking; the opium trade.

In recent times, the four Brown brothers have been the focus of a controversy concerning Brown University. All four of the Brown brothers were co-founders of "The College in the English Colony of Rhode Island and Providence Plantations" which was re-named

Brown University in 1804. There can be little doubt that the Brown University was founded and built with money derived from the slave trade. However, six more Ivy League schools share similar connections to slavery.

The only Rhode Island slave trading family to enjoy greater wealth than the four Brown brothers was the DeWolf family. Mark Anthony DeWolf (1726-1793) was the patriarch of the slave trading branch of the family. He had eight sons that were involved in the slave trade. The most successful of these was his seventh son James DeWolf (1764-1837). At the height of his slave trading career, he had imported an estimated 10,000 slaves and was considered to be the second richest man in America. In addition to their vast financial holdings in the American colonies, the family had several plantations in Cuba. The family was also involved in real estate, banking, insurance and the textile industry. In 1791, James DeWolf was indicted for murder when he bound one of his female slaves to a chair and cast her overboard, alleging that she had smallpox and threatened the lives of the rest of the crew and their cargo of slaves. The case was dropped and DeWolf returned immediately to the slave trade.

Linden Place
Arthur W. LeBoeuf
U. S. Library of Congress

The most notorious of the DeWolf family members was James' nephew, George DeWolf. He was another one of the many New England slave traders that became extremely wealthy and continued that trade long after it had become illegal in the United States. His elegant mansion, known as "*Linden Place*" was built in 1810 at an estimated cost of $60,000.00 but was only a fraction of the profits that he had made in a single year of the slave trade. George DeWolf lived a life of luxury at Linden Place until 1825 when the majority of his empire crashed; bankrupting many of his family members and citizens in the town of Bristol, Rhode Island. He fled to his family plantation in Cuba where he lived comfortably for almost two decades. He secretly returned to New England shortly before his death in 1844.

While the slave trade in Rhode Island was the most dominant of all American Colonies, it certainly had no monopoly. Sentiments favorable to the slave trade were likely greater in Massachusetts than any of the other colonies. Puritan beliefs which dominated society in Massachusetts suggested that both Native Americans and Blacks were inferior according to the laws of God. The Puritans, believing that they were God's chosen people, could easily justify slavery. In 1693, renowned theologian Cotton Mather, wrote *"The Rules for the Society of Negroes"* which opened with the sentence:

> *"WE the Miserable Children of Adam, and of Noah, thankfully Admiring and Accepting the Free-Grace of GOD, that Offers to Save us from our Miseries, by the Lord Jesus Christ, freely Resolve, with His Help, to become the Servants of that Glorious LORD. "*

For those of less conscience, the immense profitability of the slave trade overruled any need for justification. Both Native Americans and African slaves were commodities that could be easily traded to satisfy the greedy desires of the New England merchants.

The list of Massachusetts families involved in the slave trade resembled a membership roll of the Colony's elite. Wealth derived from the trade was responsible for most of the development in the colony's towns, including Boston. In 18th century Boston, Faneuil Hall was the center of the town's market place. Today, this Boston landmark is often called *"The Cradle of Liberty."* History records that it was built at the expense of Peter Faneuil, who was at that time, Boston's wealthiest merchant. Truth records that it was paid for by the slave trade.

Like Brown University in Rhode Island, Harvard University benefited greatly from the slave trade. One of the University's greatest benefactors was Isaac Royall, Jr., who at age 20, inherited a tremendous fortune derived from his father's slave trading ventures. After his death in 1781, Harvard Law School was established through a bequest from his estate. The Royall family crest was incorporated in the seal of the Harvard Law School for more than 200 years. In an attempt to hide an unpleasant past, the seal has recently been removed.

From a purely conjectural perspective, it can be contended that slavery existed in Massachusetts longer than any other State in the Union. Although a 1778 draft of the Massachusetts Constitution that legally recognized slavery was rejected by the voters, the State of Massachusetts never completely abolished slavery. The State Constitution which was approved in 1780 contained a declaration of rights which stated "All men are born free and equal" but obtaining status as a free person was still an issue that had to be resolved in the State's courts. In Massachusetts society, neither blacks nor Native Americans were viewed as equal. Indentured servitude existed well into the 19th century. Massachusetts was a state of the very wealthy elite and a very strong and politically active white working class. While much of the white working class was opposed to slavery, it was generally because they did not want to compete with free labor. In a letter to clergyman Jeremy Belknap, John Adams stated:

> "The common white people, or rather the labouring people, were the cause of rendering negroes unprofitable servants. Their scoffs and insults, their continual insinuations, filled the negroes with discontent, made them lazy, idle, proud, vicious, and at length wholly useless to their masters, to such a degree that the abolition of slavery became a measure of economy."[11]

The Rhode Island and Massachusetts Colonies were clearly the leaders in regard to the slave trade but all of New England was complicit. The elegant DeKoven house in Middletown, Connecticut, stands as a reminder of the days when the city was a prosperous port of trade. The home was built in 1791 by Captain Benjamin Williams, who was born on the island of Bermuda and migrated to Connecticut as a young man. He became the owner of many vessels and gained tremendous wealth through trade with the West Indies. Like many of the other "merchants" of New England, little is written about his involvement with the slave trade but it is well documented. The slave trade played a major roll in the economy of Connecticut in the mid to late 18th century. Another prominent Connecticut merchant, Captain John Easton, was said to be "one of the most successful slave-dealers of his time"[12]

The New England province of New Hampshire was noticeably absent from the slave trade. It had only one sea port and the climate was not suitable for major cash crops such as Tobacco but slavery existed in New Hampshire as well. One of the colony's leading citizens and signatory of the United States Declaration of Independence, William Whipple was a slave owner. In addition, Whipple was once a sea captain and acquired substantial wealth from trade in the West Indies. Whipple is remembered for freeing one of his slaves during the American Revolution; expressing his belief that that no man could fight for freedom while holding another in bondage.

Many historians fail to emphasize the role of the Mid-Atlantic colonies in the slave trade. The Colony of New York was originally founded by the Dutch West India Company, an organization that for many years, dominated the Atlantic Slave Trade. When New York became a British Royal Colony in 1664, it was granted to James Duke of York. James, brother of King Charles II, led the British Royal African Company which was also a dominant force in the African Slave Trade from 1664 until the mid 18th Century. Some historians estimate that by 1703, 42% of New York City's households held slaves.[13] In 1705. New York declared that *"punishment by execution will be applied to certain runaway slaves."*

Today, the Wall Street district of New York City is considered to be the world's largest trade center. Wall Street itself is named for a wall that was built by slaves to protect the Dutch settlement of New Amsterdam. Its origins as a trade district included buying, selling and even rental of African and Native American slaves. When the British took control of the settlement, they continued to depend heavily on the slave trade and slave labor. By the time that the wall came down in 1699, the slave trade and the slave population of New York had grown significantly. A New York City law created in 1711, made Wall Street the center for the slave trade:

> *"Be it Ordained by the Mayor Recorder Aldermen and Assistants of the City of New York Convened in Common Council and it is hereby Ordained by the Authority of the same That all Negro and Indian slaves that are lett out to hire within this City do take up their Standing in Order to be hired at the Markett house at the Wall Street Slip untill Such time as they are hired, whereby all Persons may Know where to hire*

slaves as their Occasions Shall require and also Masters discover when their Slaves are so hired and all the Inhabitants of this City are to take Notice hereof Accordingly.[14]

In 1712, a group of slaves were part of a revolt that left nine whites dead and six wounded. Estimates of the number of Blacks arrested range from 27 to 70. Some reports claim that 6 committed suicide and 21 were convicted and executed.

The Slave Market at the corner of Wall and Pearl Streets continued to thrive until approximately 1762. The Wall Street Slave Market held auctions weekly and during some periods, daily. Local newspapers were filled with advertisements relating to slaves being offered for sale and announcements about the arrival of new slave shipments.

For Sale,

A LIKELY, HEALTHY, YOUNG
NEGRO WENCH,

BETWEEN fifteen and fixteen Years old: She has been ufed to the Farming Bufinefs. Sold for want of Employ.—Enquire at No. 81, William-ftreet.

New-York, March 30, 1789.

Sale in New York: New York Public Library, Digital Collections

One of the most prominent slave trading families of New York was the Livingston family. Robert Livingston the Elder was that patriarch of the family and First Lord of the 160,000 acre Livingston Manor along the Hudson River. After Robert's death in 1728, his son Philip inherited a number of his father's slaves, the Livingston Manor and the family business. Philip developed his business into one of the largest slave trading operation in the State. Philip was one of the four men from New York to sign the Declaration of Independence, all four of which were slave owners.[15] In recent times, Yale University has come under scrutiny because of Philip Livingston's donation to the University which created the first endowed professorship at Yale.

Free blacks lived in 18th century New York at the risk of loosing their freedom. Blacks were automatically assumed to be slaves and being able to prove that you were a free man was difficult and local authorities handled the problem as they saw fit. The arrest of free blacks was a common occurrence.[16]

In regard to slavery, the New Jersey Province had much the same history as that of New York. The area was originally settled by the Dutch who imported slaves for labor. When the British took control, slavery was heavily promoted. The Lord's Proprietors of the Province, Lord John Berkeley and Sir George Carteret offered free land to settlers who would import slaves.[17] The center for arrival and sale of slaves in New Jersey was present day Camden. Philadelphia newspapers were filled with advertisements offering the sale of slaves. The advertisements often boasted the slaves that were offered for sale in New Jersey were of higher quality and more robust than other slaves because they were imported directly from Africa. It is not surprising that many New Jersey families became extremely wealthy from their involvement in the slave trade. What would surprise many Americans is that a substantial number of these wealthy families were Quakers even though the Quakers or Religious Society of Friends are most often recorded in American history as being opposed to slavery; not promoters of it. The first United States Census which was taken in 1790 lists New Jersey as having a black slave population of 11,423; more than any northern state except New York.

Across the Delaware River from slave markets of Camden, New Jersey, was the City of Philadelphia. The Port of Philadelphia was another major Atlantic trading hub known for its involvement in the slave trade. Like New Jersey, many of the wealthy traders and buyers were Quakers in the early days of the trade. Eventually many of the Quakers would give way to the conflict between their religious beliefs and the institution of slavery and join the abolitionist movement. The transition was much like that of their founder William Penn and Philadelphia's favorite son, Benjamin Franklin; both were slaveholders at one point in their lives.

The London Coffee House was a popular place in the Philadelphia market district. Here slaves could be inspected and bought at auction. It was a venue where merchants and ship's captains could conduct their business while surrounded by the city's social elite. Slave ownership in the Province of Pennsylvania was much lower than that of neighboring colonies but for many years the slave trade was a vital part of the Pennsylvania economy and was a source of great wealth for many of its citizens.

The Colony of Delaware began as the very small settlement of New Sweden. Although the Swedes were attempting to become a regional power, they were not heavily involved in the slave trade. Not having a source for African slaves, the settlers of New Sweden turned more toward Native American slaves. Importation of African slaves to the area increased when the Dutch took control of the region but declined when the British occupied the territory in 1664. It began to increase again in the 18th century with the expansion of tobacco growing in the area. In 1663 more than 20% percent of Delaware's population was enslaved. According to the 1790 United States Census, the slave population of Delaware was 8,887 and by 1860 had declined to 1,798. Delaware never officially abolished slavery. Some Delaware citizens continued to hold slaves until the passage of the 13th Amendment to the U. S. Constitution in 1865.

The Colonies in 1763

The year of 1763 was a significant turning point in the history of America. It marked the beginning of the end of the colonist's loyalty to the British Crown. At that point in time, the vast majority of the population was native born, with the exception of imported African slaves. King George III of Great Britain ascended to the throne in 1761, at a time when Great Britain was struggling to maintain control of the colonies.

In the relationship between the thirteen colonies, much of what had once bound them together had dwindled but a few common factors still remained. An overwhelming majority of the colonists were white, English speaking Protestants who were native born Americans. By 1763, social, political and economical differences divided the colonies into three distinct groups. The first group consisted of the colonies of Massachusetts, New Hampshire, Connecticut and Rhode Island

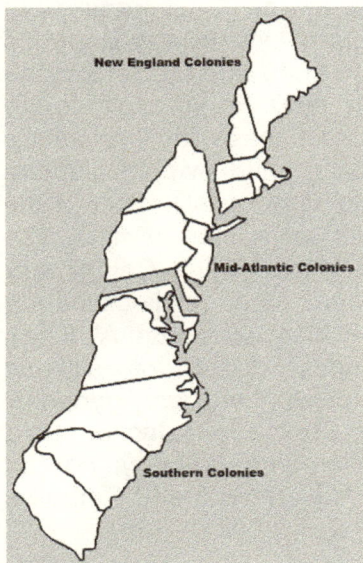

making up the New England Colonies. The second group consisted of the colonies of Delaware, New York, Pennsylvania and New Jersey making up the Mid-Atlantic Colonies. The third group consisted of Maryland, Virginia, North Carolina, South Carolina and Georgia making up the Southern Colonies.

In New England, colonists were divided into two social classes. The upper class merchants were generally the dominant force in government and politics. Many had amassed great fortunes and were among the wealthiest colonists in all of North American. The common laborers made up a second social class. Although they were clearly separated in society, both groups were still heavily influenced by the Puritan beliefs which established the first colony in Massachusetts. Even those colonies that were established by a conflict with Puritan beliefs, held fast to the basic Protestant principles which were the basis of all laws and government in New England.

Most of the Mid-Atlantic colonies were originally founded by the Dutch, thus the Dutch Reformed Church had a considerable influence on society and culture in these colonies. Another major religious influence in the region was that of the Quakers. Unlike other denominations, the Quakers were more tolerant toward other religious beliefs. This allowed the Mid-Atlantic colonies to be more religiously diverse than the other regions but remained dominantly Protestant. In most colonies, Catholics and Jews were not allowed to vote. The economy, political ideology and social classes in the Mid-Atlantic colonies were also more diverse. Having major seaports in all four colonies, they had their share of wealthy merchants; much like those in New England. Because much of the region was suitable for farming, Mid-Atlantic colonies had their share of wealthy planters; much like those in the South.

Society throughout the South was heavily influenced by the Virginia Colony. Aside from being the oldest of the British Colonies, it was the home of a group of social elitists known as the "First Families of Virginia," many of which migrated to the colony during a period between the execution of King Charles I in 1649 and the restoration of King Charles II to the English throne in 1660. Their loyalty to the throne of England caused Charles II to view these families as his "Old Dominion." These nobles were wealthy land owning planters and were the core of the "Gentry" class of Virginia; still most of the colonists of Virginia were common laborers or yeomen farmers. The Church of England was the official religion of the Virginia Colony until the American Revolution. Intolerance toward other religious beliefs was as just as great in Virginia as it was in Massachusetts. Although other Southern Colonies granted a modest degree of religious freedom from time to time, the Church of England was generally accepted as the official religion of the Southern Colonies. Lord Baltimore had established Catholic settlements in Maryland but Protestants eventually took control of the government and Catholics could no longer worship in public.

The first tear in the fabric of loyalty to the throne was a proclamation by King George III in 1763, forbidding further colonization in the new territories acquired from France. The Royal Proclamation of 1763 was an attempt by the British government to control the cost of defending and governing the American colonies. The colony most affected by the act was Virginia; a place where wealth and status was measured by the ownership of land. Several of Virginia's elite had already acquired land west of the boundary by way of the land company known as the Ohio Company of Virginia. In addition, colonists in the Carolinas were eager to claim lands west of the Appalachians. Despite the agitation caused by the Act, most of the Southern Colonists maintained their allegiance to the British crown. Over the next twelve years, a series of laws and acts by the British government would lead to rebellion in the North but it was a rebellion that colonists in the South were reluctant to join.

A point often overlooked in American history is that 1763 was a year in which jealousy and resentment between the colonists in the North and colonists in the South began to accelerate. Differences between political and religious ideologies combined with issues of population, geography, economy, and social class were all contributing factors.

The chief antagonists in the conflict were the colonies of Massachusetts and Virginia. Massachusetts grew increasingly hostile toward the British government while Virginia maintained its loyalty to the crown.

Much has been written about the so-called "*Cavalier Myth*" which suggests that the Southerner planter class believed that they descended from English aristocrats, elevating them to a higher social class than the wealthy merchants of the North who were considered to have been born of commoners. It may or may not be true that such a class existed but there is little doubt that extreme resentments concerning social class existed between the northern and southern colonies.

In 1763, Virginia had the largest population of any colony in North America. Virginia was first of the British Colonies and the first to become a Royal Colony. The colonist's loyalty to the throne is well documented. After King Charles I was beheaded in 1649, Virginia opposed the new government under Oliver Cromwell and welcomed the restoration of the throne to King Charles II in 1660. The Church of England remained the official church of the Colony and played a significant role in the Colony's government which supported the church financially. With a multitude of plantations and long growing seasons, the agrarian based economy of Virginia, allowed the colonists to be virtually self supporting.

In 1763, Massachusetts had second largest population of any Colony in North America. The colonist's devout Puritan beliefs were the basis for their government, their laws and their way of life. Although the colonists were opposed to the absolute authority of English monarchs, their merchant based society depended largely on trade with England.

The Mid-Atlantic colonies held no particular allegiance to the crown or to the colonies in other regions. Although the colonists were devout Protestants, there was no predominant church. Having plantations and major seaports, the Mid-Atlantic colonists had the best of both worlds.

The merchants in the North, who had previously made their fortunes by selling slaves in South America and the West Indies, were now selling slaves in the southern colonies at an alarming rate. So much so that on April 1, 1772, the Virginia House of Burgesses petitioned the throne to abolish the slave trade or give the colonies the right to do so.[18] Leaders in the colony of Virginia expressed that they were being victimized by the greed of the Northern Merchants.

For Native Americans, 1763 was no different than the last 150 years. Native tribes continued to be driven from their lands. With the French being eliminated after the Treaty of Paris, tribes were all alone in their fight against the British.

So what was America about in 1763? As a nation, America did not exist in 1763. Beyond the fact that all of the colonies were subject to British rule, there were no absolutes which could be used to define them as one unit. Over all, diversity was not an issue within the colonies. Differences in language, heritage and culture were more of a regional concern. Colonists in those regions tended to segregate themselves according to those differences. Protestantism dominated the culture and societies of all 13 colonies but it was not exclusive. All of the colonies persecuted Catholics and Jews but the severity of the persecution varied extensively from one region to the next. Massachusetts was splintered into four separate colonies over differing Protestant philosophies concerning church doctrine and conformity. Mid-Atlantic colonists, shared no dominate protestant belief. Virginia and the rest of the southern colonies were closely aligned with the Church of England but there were significant numbers of dissenters within their societies. An evangelical and revitalization movement known as the "First Great Awakening" had shaken the foundations of many established beliefs in almost all of the colonies in the mid-eighteenth century.

Immigration was not an issue in 1763 and the native born colonists were reluctant to accept new comers in their communities. As the population of each colony grew, an increasing number of Native Americans were driven from their lands. Major seaports in the New England and Mid-Atlantic Colonies competed heavily against each other in slave trade. North America's colonies were on the verge of a hostile split with Great Britain at a time when the regional differences made it difficult to find a common bond to unite them.

40

Chapter 2

A New Nation

1764 – 1837

Beginning in 1764, a series of acts initiated by King George III created hostilities between the American colonies and Great Britain which would lead to the American Revolution. Great Britain was struggling to maintain control of its North American Colonies which now had a population of more than two million. Loyalty to the British crown was diminishing. Colonists, having been born in North America, now had their own culture and their own heritage.

Early actions by the King had their most damaging effects on the major port cities in New England and the Middle Colonies. Merchants in these areas were among the earliest to rebel against British authority. Most of the colonists in the South, viewed the hostilities as a Northern problem for many years. Had it not been for the British dissolution of the House of Burgesses and Patrick Henry's rousing *"give me liberty or give me death"* speech, it is possible that Virginia might not have joined in the American Revolution. While Virginia had its share of well known patriots in favor of independence, it also had its share of loyalists. Loyalty to the Crown was common in other Southern Colonies as well. Many of the upland farmers of South Carolina, found little difference between the planter class aristocracy in its colony and the abusive force of British rule.

Colonial loyalty to Great Britain during the American Revolution is a subject often avoided by historians but it was widespread; particularly in the South. It sometimes divided the most elite families such as the Randolphs in Virginia and the Arnolds of New England. Benjamin Franklin's son William was a steadfast loyalist exiled to England before the end of the American Revolution. Founding father, John Dickinson of Pennsylvania and Delaware, refused to sign the Declaration of Independence yet supported the colonies during the war. Thousands of blacks, both free and enslaved, supported the British during the revolution. Most historians estimate the number of British Loyalists in the colonies to be about one out of every five.

41

Regardless of the actual numbers, the hostilities between the two factions were fierce. Each group considered the others to be traitors. Ironically, as the colonies united against Great Britain, they were actually destroying the only remaining political bond that they had in common.

Importation of African slaves to North America slowed during the revolution but many of the northern merchants had holdings in Cuba and the West Indies so their slave trading activities continued. Several colonies, including Virginia, attempted to take advantage of the situation and tried unsuccessfully to end the slave trade all together. As the war drew to an end, human trafficking was once again a source of great wealth.

With the Treaty of Paris in 1783, the thirteen colonies managed to free themselves from British rule. The government of the United States of America was operating under the rules established by the Articles of Confederation. Being clearly styled as a confederation, sovereignty of the states took precedent in the new government. Soon after independence, the short-comings of the Articles became painfully obvious. In February of 1787, the Confederation Congress called for a convention of states delegates for the "*sole and express purpose of revising the Articles of Confederation.*"[19] Had the delegates simply revised the Articles, the nation might never have experienced a War Between the States. A bitter, two year political struggle between Federalist and Anti-Federalist factions resulted in the dissolution of the former confederation and replacing it with a new republic.

The greatest point of contention between the two factions was the power of the central government. Federalists promoted a strong central government with extensive authority over the States. Anti-Federalists feared that delegating excessive powers to the Federal government would return the States to the conditions that existed under British rule. Both during and after the convention, Anti-Federalists demanded that certain rights be guaranteed by the Constitution. When the new Constitution was completed, the Federalist had won the argument but the battle was not over. The new Constitution did not guarantee the personal freedoms that are held so dear in America today and it did not place limits on the powers of the Federal Government. Anti-Federalist demanded that a "*Bill of Rights*" be added to the Constitution. In an attempt to speed up the ratification process by pacifying the Anti-Federalists, James Madison introduced thirty-nine amendments to the Constitution; ten of which were approved and became what we know as the "*Bill of Rights.*" Federalist and Anti-Federalist factions existed in all of the States but the majority of the leaders were divided geographically. The more prominent members of the Federalist Party were led by Massachusetts in the North while many of the prominent members of the Anti-Federalist Party were led by Virginia in the South. The balance of power was often tilted by representatives from the Mid-Atlantic States; primarily New York. This phenomenon is often present in the politics of America today.

By the turn of the 19th century, The Federalist Party appeared to have everything going their way but the election of 1800 shifted the balance of power to the newly formed Democratic-Republican Party. It was also the beginning a 24 year reign of U. S. Presidents from the State of Virginia. The Federalists who had fought so diligently for the power of the Federal Government was now seeing that power turned against them. The unbridled hatred between political factions in Massachusetts and Virginia had Federalists in New England calling for secession during the war of 1812.

When Massachusetts native, John Quincy Adams became president in 1825, hatred between Northern and Southern politicians only escalated. The election of 1824 had to be decided by the House of Representatives under the provisions of the Constitution. Adams was given a victory in the election over rival Andrew Jackson even though Jackson had received the most electoral and popular votes of any of the four candidates. What Southerners called "*The Corrupt Bargain,*" led to a campaign of revenge by Jackson and his supporters.

Jackson defeated Adams in the 1828 election by a substantial margin. He was the first U. S. President who had not been born in Virginia or Massachusetts. He defeated Henry Clay and two other candidates in the 1832 Presidential election in a landslide victory. During Andrew Jackson's eight years as President, no one escaped his wrath. His hatred for Northerners and the social elite in Washington was well documented. His policies also included the removal of thousands of Native Americans from their homelands. Though Jackson was Southern born and owned hundreds of slaves, his sentiments toward Southern leaders were often hostile as well. The term "*abuse of power*" is probably better exemplified by Andrew

Jackson than any other President in American history. The seventy-three year period that began with hostilities against British authority in 1764 and ended with the Presidency of Andrew Jackson in 1837 found the United States of America sitting on a social and political powder keg; just waiting to explode.

The Rumbles of War

The story of the British North American Colonies ended much in the same way that it had begun. The colonies were founded upon the prospect of great personal wealth and opportunity. By the 1760s, a large number of American colonists had amassed great fortunes but King George III was now threatening those fortunes. The irony of the events leading up to the American Revolution is that the colonists who were most belligerent toward British rule were the same colonists who were most dependent on trade with Great Britain.

Among the first major acts of contention was the Stamp Act of 1765. While it produced very little revenue and was soon repealed, it was viewed by many colonists as "*taxation with representation.*" In addition to triggering public protests in New England, the act was responsible for initiating the first joint assembly of colonies to challenge British authority. The assembly known as the Stamp Act Congress consisted of twenty-seven delegates from nine colonies and resulted in a "*Declaration of Rights and Grievances*" being sent to the King and the British Parliament. It is important to note that only the colonies with major seaports were represented. There were no delegates from New Hampshire, Virginia, North Carolina or Georgia. It is also important to note that despite their protests, delegates William Bayard of New York and Timothy Ruggles of Massachusetts remained loyal to Great Britain during the American Revolution.

From 1765 to 1770, the British Parliament continued to establish policies that infuriated colonists. Secret societies such as the "*Sons of Liberty*" were forming throughout New England and the Middle colonies. In 1770, the growing hostilities went beyond protest and developed into bloodshed. During an event that became known as the "*Boston Massacre,*" British soldiers killed five and wounded six colonists. In June of 1772, Rhode Island colonists led by wealthy slave trader, John Brown and his former Captain Abraham Whipple, burned the British revenue ship, HMS Gaspee. On December 16, 1773, Massachusetts colonists disguised as Mohawks, destroyed a shipment of tea belonging to the British East India Company. In retaliation, the British Parliament passed a series of punitive laws, which became known as the *"Intolerable Acts."* Once again, the British Parliament had incited the wrath of the wealthy merchant class in the colonies.

1774 marked a full decade since hostilities had begun between the colonists and the government of Great Britain. At this point, the majority of the conflicts occurred in the New England and Middle Colonies. Most of the Southern colonists continued their loyalty to the crown. The city of Charleston, in South Carolina was the exception. With a population of more than 11,000 it was now the fourth largest port in the colonies. Charleston had strong ties to the merchants in the North and an abundance of wealthy merchants who were complicit in the importation of slaves.

Many historians consider the *"Boston Massacre"* to be the breaking point between the colonies and Great Britain but the skirmish was in New England and had less of an impact on southern colonists. A more decisive chain of events began in June of 1774. The Virginia House of Burgesses proclaimed that June 1, 1774, would be a day of *"fasting, humiliation, and prayer."* It was the first appreciable act where Virginia demonstrated a bond with the Northern colonies concerning opposition to British Authority. Lord Dunmore, Royal Governor of Virginia, responded by dissolving the Virginia House of Burgesses. For the first time, not only was the British government opposed by the wealthy merchant class in its Northern colonies but had also alienated the *"First Families of Virginia."* The Virginia gentry who had once been called King Charles' "Old Dominion" were threatening to denounce their loyalty to Great Britain. Despite orders by Lord Dunmore, members of the House of Burgesses continued to meet. On August 1, 1774, they elected Payton Randolph as president and banned trade with Great Britain

Colonists responded to the *"Intolerable Acts"* by calling for delegates to attend a meeting of the First Continental Congress at Philadelphia, Pennsylvania in the fall of 1774. Georgia did not send delegates to the meeting. On October 14, 1774, the First Continental Congress adopted a statement called the Declaration and Resolves of the First Continental Congress. Included in the document was a plan to boycott British trade until the colonist's grievances were redressed. The resolves adopted by the Continental Congress emphasized that colonists were British citizens *"entitled to all the rights, liberties, and immunities of free and natural-born subjects, within the realm of England."*[20]. This statement clearly shows that despite the recent hostilities, the colonists were willing to continue as British citizens provided they were given equal treatment and allowed to participate in their own government. The resolves were largely ignored by the British Parliament and no formal reply was given by King George III. In a letter to Lord North, the King stated:

"The die is now cast; the colonies must either submit or triumph"

As hostilities carried into 1775, many colonists were still torn between their passions for independence and their loyalty to Great Britain. Loyalists, commonly called *"Tories,"* could be found in all of the colonies. Few colonists were allowed the concession of neutrality. Colonists who favored independence over British rule were called traitors by the loyalists and adversely, loyalists were considered to be traitors to the cause of independence. Traitor had become the ugliest word in the English language and has continued to be used as a divisive tool in America's political and social culture throughout history. Using the word traitor to label those with differing political views was as prevalent in the War Between the States as it had been in the American Revolution.

At the time of the American Revolution, Virginia was the largest colony in both land mass and population. It accounted for more than 20% of the entire population of the American Colonies. The social and political influences of Virginia and its first families were equally as large. Without Virginia, it is unlikely that a revolution could have succeeded. Many of Virginia's social elite had been considering independence since 1763 while others were determined that Virginia would remain as a Royal Colony. The Randolph family was considered to be wealthiest and the most powerful family in Colonial Virginia. Sir John Randolph was well respected in Great Britain and was the only native of Colonial Virginia to receive a knighthood. His two sons, Payton and John, were bitterly divided between Loyalist sentiments and the independence movement. Payton would go on to be the president of both the First and Second Continental Congress but John boycotted the Congress and was eventually forced to flee to Scotland. Among the elite Virginians who supported independence were, Thomas Jefferson, Richard Henry Lee, Patrick Henry and George Washington but many prominent Virginians remained loyal to the British Crown.

Possibly the most important native of Virginia in the cause for independence was Patrick Henry. It was Henry's passionate speech at Virginia's second convention in Richmond on March 23, 1775, which convinced Virginia's delegates to support the American Revolution. In an address to the Convention's president, Patrick Henry proposed that Virginia raise a militia to support the cause of independence. His opponents preferred that the convention move with caution and contended that Virginia should wait for a response from Great Britain concerning their latest proposal for reconciliation. Henry's brief but powerful oration quieted the opposition. Without the forceful persuasion of Patrick Henry, it is likely that Virginia and most of the Southern Colonies would have remained loyal to Great Britain. He ended his famous address with the statement:

"Give me Liberty, or Give me Death!"
Published by Currier & Ives 1876
U. S. Library of Congress

> *"It is in vain, sir, to extenuate the matter. Gentlemen may cry, Peace, Peace but there is no peace. The war is actually begun! The next gale that sweeps from the north will bring to our ears the clash of resounding arms! Our brethren are already in the field! Why stand we here idle? What is it that gentlemen wish? What would they have? Is life so dear, or peace so sweet, as to be purchased at the price of chains and slavery? Forbid it, Almighty God! I know not what course others may take; but as for me, give me liberty or give me death!"*

With America's largest and most powerful colony in support, the march toward independence continued. On April 19, 1775, in Middlesex County, Province of Massachusetts Bay, the American Revolution began in earnest with significant battles taking place at Lexington and Concord. In the summer of 1775, the Second Continental Congress began its meetings.

The Declaration of Independence

By early summer of 1776, every colony had adopted some form of resolution defying British rule but there was still no unanimous agreement between the colonies concerning a new form of government. The Second Continental Congress appointed a committee of five men to draft a proposal for declaring the colonies' independence from Great Britain. The leading architect of the document was Thomas Jefferson of Virginia. After changes in Jefferson's original draft were made by John Adams and Benjamin Franklin, the committee presented the document to the "*Committee of the Whole*" on June 28, 1776. In reality, the independence of the colonies was declared by Congress on July 2, 1776. In a letter to his wife Abigail on July 3, 1776, John Adams stated:

> *"The Second Day of July, 1776, will be the most memorable Epocha, in the History of America."* [21]

On July 3, several passages in the document were rejected by the Committee of the Whole. One was a passage criticizing the British people and another was a passage that denounced both slavery and the slave trade; both of these passages were removed from the original draft. Many of the delegates expressed a desire to retain reasonable relations with British citizens. Some delegates were still hoping that there could be some form of reconciliation with the British government and considered Jefferson's harsh words toward the British people to be inflammatory and unnecessary. In addition, many of the delegates and their families were complicit in slavery and feared that condemning Great Britain over the slavery issue would cast a shadow of guilt on their own transgressions. Three members of the Committee of Five, Thomas Jefferson, Benjamin Franklin and Philip Livingston, were current or former slave holders. In all, at least 41 of the 56 signers of the Declaration of Independence were complicit in the evils of slavery. Despite early attempts to discourage the importation of slaves, Philadelphia was still an active market for human trafficking. Notwithstanding Jefferson's protest to the changes in his original draft, the document became the "*United States Declaration of Independence.*"

The declaration, in itself was as complex as its author and was more of a perpetuation of the sentiments of the colonists than a statement of fact. It opened with the well known sentence:

"When in the Course of human events, it becomes necessary for one people to dissolve the political bands which have connected them with another, and to assume among the powers of the earth, the separate and equal station to which the Laws of Nature and of Nature's God entitle them, a decent respect to the opinions of mankind requires that they should declare the causes which impel them to the separation.

Jefferson clearly expresses that the colonies were entitled to form a new government according to the Laws of Nature and the Laws of God. Knowing that Jefferson was a strong proponent of what he called "*a wall of separation between Church & State*," many people believed this statement to be in conflict with his views concerning government and religion. Jefferson's writings and speeches suggest that he was more concerned about the governments influence on religion than the influence of religion upon government. He never wavered in his contention that "*the God who gave us life, gave us liberty at the same time.*"

In addition to the religious aspects, the first sentence of the Declaration implies that citizens of all nations possess a natural right to separate themselves from a government in which they no longer believe and to form a new one. With certain paragraphs having been removed from the original text, the first sentence of the second paragraph suggests a conflict between the declaration and its stated principles:

"We hold these truths to be self-evident, that all men are created equal, that they are endowed by their Creator with certain unalienable rights; that among these are life, liberty and the pursuit of happiness."

With a new nation being formed without objection to slavery, it appears that the words "*all men*" did not include blacks or Native Americans. Had the delegates not insisted on the removal of the passage containing Jefferson's condemnation of slavery, the sentence would have made better sense. Once again, the founding fathers had failed to take advantage of an opportunity to end slavery

49

in North America. Thomas Jefferson headed a delegation of Virginia leaders who had been trying for years to abolish or at least inhibit the slave trade. Not only was Virginia the largest, most powerful and most populous colony, at the time of the revolution, it held the largest number of slaves. Jefferson and others expressed that the rapid growth slavery in Virginia posed a threat to society. It is clear that the majority of the delegates wanted to avoid the subject of slavery altogether. Failing to take advantage of the Virginia delegations desire to bring the slave trade to an end was essentially condemning the new nation to the continued growth of an institution in direct conflict with its own principles.

After expressing that a just form of government derives its powers from the consent of the governed, the declaration warns that *"Governments long established should not be changed for light and transient causes"* but professes that *"when a long train of abuses and usurpations"* continue, it is not only the *"right"* but also the *"duty"* of the citizens to *"throw off such Government."* Ironically, these rights were deemed unconstitutional and denied to the American people by a ruling of the United States Supreme Court in 1869[22] with Chief Justice Salmon P. Chase stating that the United States government was and is:

> *"an indestructible Union, composed of indestructible states."*

It should be noted that Salmon Chase was one of President Abraham Lincoln's cabinet members when West Virginia was allowed to secede from the *"indestructible"* State of Virginia.

The Declaration of Independence continued with a list of the causes which impelled the colonies to the separation. The last mentioned cause was an accusation that Great Britain had *"excited domestic insurrection"* by committing acts which let to attacks by Native American tribes. The declaration describes these tribes as:

> *"merciless Indian savage, whose known rule of warfare is an undistinguished destruction, of all ages, sexes and conditions."*

The phrase is a testament to the attitudes toward Native Americans at that time; an attitude which would continue to be acceptable among future generations.

After a long list of grievances, the document ended with an appeal to the Supreme Judge of the world for the rectitude of the Colonies' intentions and "*reliance on the protection of divine providence.*"

Articles of Confederation

Following the Declaration of Independence, the Second Continental Congress appointed a committee to draft an agreement between the new States. An approved version was sent the States for ratification in 1777 after several drafts and four years of debates, the Articles were finally ratified and went into effect on March 1, 1781. The agreement was formally known as the "*Articles of Confederation and Perpetual Union*" and served as the basis for the government of the United States from 1781 until it was replaced by the United States Constitution in 1789. Simple in structure, the document contained 13 Articles. Article I, stated only that:

> "*The Stile of this Confederacy shall be "The United States of America."*

Article II, expresses one of the most important yet most contentious principles in the history of the United States. It reads:

> "*Each state retains its sovereignty, freedom, and independence, and every power, jurisdiction, and right, which is not by this confederation expressly delegated to the United States, in Congress assembled.*"

The operative word in this sentence is the word "*sovereignty.*" State sovereignty is what the Federalists sought most to exclude from the Constitution. It is exactly what the 1860 Republican Party Platform eluded to when it stated that "*it is the imperative duty of an indignant people sternly to rebuke and forever silence.*" Popular sovereignty was described in this 1860 platform as "*a demonstration of deception and fraud.*" In the Constitution and the subsequent Bill of Rights, the word sovereignty was replaced with the word "*powers.*" The Federalist would later contend that powers delegated to the Federal government need not be expressed in the Constitution but merely implied.

51

Article III, tells that the States are hereby entered into a *"league of friendship"* with common goals while the remaining ten articles deal with the power and structure of the government and the admission of Canada. It also declared that the Articles were perpetual and could only be altered with the approval of Congress and ratification by all state legislatures.

The most obvious weaknesses of the new government were that it lacked the power to tax, could not raise an army or navy, had no power to enforce its laws and allowed states to place tariffs on each other. Having only one House of Congress and not having a President or Supreme Court may or may not have been a good thing. While it is doubtful that the provisions of Articles of Confederation could ever successfully support the common goals of the colonies the intentions of the delegates were clear. It is important to note that this *"league of friendship"* consisted of colonies from three regions that were clearly divided by culture, differing economies, political ideology and religious beliefs. They had become thirteen *"sovereign"* nations, joining their efforts for the good of all.

Patriots or Traitors?

In February of 1778, the United States signed a Treaty of Alliance with France. Later that year, the British government attempted to negotiate with the States by offering complete self government and representation in the British Parliament. If the same offer had been made prior to the Declaration of Independence it is likely that most of the Colonies would have accepted but the offer came too late. Beyond that point, nothing less than total independence was acceptable.

The surrender of British General Charles Cornwallis at Yorktown, Virginia on October 19, 1781, was the last land battle of the American Revolution. Five days after the surrender, the British Fleet which had been sent to rescue the British Army arrived. The fleet rescued many fleeing loyalists and then set sail. Naval conflicts continued for more than a year but the United States had already won their treasured independence which was formalized by the signing of the Treaty of Paris on September 3, 1783.

Thousands of Americans, who had remained loyal to the British during the war, lost their homes and were now exiled to other parts of the British Commonwealth. Men and women who had once considered themselves to be loyal patriots of their colony, were now outcasts and labeled as traitors. Many of them were from the wealthiest most elite families in North America. Benedict Arnold, who descended from one of the most prominent families in New England, served honorably as an American General but switched his loyalty to Great Britain during the war; he died in exile in England. William Franklin, the acknowledged illegitimate son of Benjamin Franklin, served Great Britain as the last royal Governor of New Jersey. He fled to England in 1782, never to return. John Randolph, whose brother Payton, was the first President of the Continental Congress, remained loyal to Great Britain all of his life. After his death in London in 1784, his remains were returned to his native Virginia to be buried with his father and brother in the Chapel at William and Mary College.

American history gives little notice to those who remained loyal to Great Britain during the war. In the American Revolution, as in all revolutions, it is the victor who ultimately decides who were the patriots and who were the traitors. The story would be no different at the close of the War Between the States.

Another comparison that can be drawn between the American Revolution and the War Between the States is using the prospect of freedom to entice slaves to support the war effort. It was used by both sides in the American Revolution and again by both sides in the War Between the States. In his own words, Abraham Lincoln admits that his Emancipation Proclamation was a war effort issued under his authority as Commander-in-Chief of the U. S. Military. Unfortunately, the right of equality, as described in the Declaration of Independence, did not accompany the offers of freedom. No exact number of former slaves in the military can be determined in either conflict. Many historians contend that numbers of blacks who joined the fight for independence were as few as five thousand. Others estimated the numbers to be between twelve and fifteen thousand. Estimates of the numbers of blacks who served in the British Army, often reach beyond ten thousand. While the vast majority of black soldiers on both sides during the American Revolution were former slaves, there were also free blacks who enlisted for service as well. For enslaved Americans, the decision between loyalty and independence was overshadowed by their desire for freedom.

Crispus Attucks was among the five Americans killed at the Boston Massacre. Historians have often disagreed on whether Crispus Attucks was a free man or an escaped slave but they most often agree that he was of both Native American and African descent. He is considered by many to be the first casualty in the American Revolution. Eleven year old Christopher Seider, was shot more than a week earlier and was likely the first person killed during the rebellion but his death was considered to be more of an accident than an act of war. He was killed by a British customs agent who fired into a crowd of boys who were throwing rocks at his home. His death

Boston Massacre, death of Crispus Attucks
National Archives & Records Administration

however, fueled outrage, leading up to the armed conflict on March 5, 1770, where Crispus Attucks lost his life. While Attucks may have been the first, he certainly was not the last black man to fight or die for the cause of American independence. Acts of courage by black soldiers such as Prince Estabrook at Lexington, Salem Poor at Bunker Hill and Marine, John Martin, aboard the brig *USS Reprisal*, were not uncommon. To American loyalists, their actions were as treasonous as their white counterparts. To the Americans fighting for independence, they were acts of patriotism.

Recruitment of blacks into the Continental Army was an "*on again-off again*" situation. Unlike many of the wars fought by American soldiers, blacks were most often integrated among white troops and in many cases, received the same pay but the rewards for being a black patriot were few. Possibly the highest rank attained by a black soldier in the Continental Army was the rank of corporal.

British recruitment of black soldiers was much more aggressive than that of the colonies. Virginia Royal Governor, Lord Dunmore, played a leading role in recruiting slaves by offering freedom in exchange. A proclamation which was signed by Dunmore on November 7, 1775 and formally proclaimed on November, 14th; it required:

> *"every person capable of bearing Arms, to resort to His Majesty's Standard, or be looked upon as traitors to His Majesty's Crown and Government."*

The proclamation also declared that:

> *"all indentured servants, negroes, or others (including rebels), free that are able and willing to bear arms, they joining His Majesty's Troops as soon as may be, for the more speedily reducing this Colony (Virginia) to a proper Sense of their Duty, to His Majesty's Crown and Dignity."*

Dunmore's proclamation further enraged the colonists of Virginia. It failed to successfully recruit rebels but succeeded in recruiting a significant number of slaves. Dunmore organized more than 800 blacks into a unit known as the *"Royal Ethiopian Regiment."* Other black loyalist units included the *"Black Pioneers, Black Brigade, the Associators, Jersey Shore Volunteers, King's American Dragoons, Jamaica Rangers, and the Mosquito Shore Volunteers."* One notable black loyalist was Titus Cornelius. Because of his fighting skills and leadership in the Royal Ethiopian Regiment and the Black Brigade, he was referred to as *"Colonel Tye,"* even though no black was known to have been a commissioned officer in the British military.

The fate of the black loyalists was much the same as whites. After the Battle of Yorktown, General Cornwallis abandoned his black troops. Several other British commanders were less willing to do the same. A manuscript known as *"The Book of Negroes,"* recorded the names of more than 3,000 black loyalists that escaped to the British lines and were evacuated to Nova Scotia as free people of color. They established black settlements such as Birchtown, Brindley and Tracadie. Despite being free, the former loyalists experienced much the same poverty and racial discrimination in Nova Scotia as they had in the former colonies. Hundreds of them would later relocate to Africa.

Peace and Dilemma

The surrender of British General Charles Cornwallis on October 19, 1781, effectively ended the Revolutionary war within the boundaries of the former American Colonies but hostilities continued at sea. King George III wanted to continue the fight but lacked the support of Parliament and was forced to agree to peace negotiations.

Beginning in April of 1782, representatives from the United States and Great Britain started their negotiations and continued through the summer. The two parties signed an agreement in Paris France on September 3, 1783 with Great Britain formally recognizing the sovereignty of the 13 former British Colonies, stating:

> *"His Brittanic Majesty acknowledges the said United States, viz., New Hampshire, Massachusetts Bay, Rhode Island and Providence Plantations, Connecticut, New York, New Jersey, Pennsylvania, Maryland, Virginia, North Carolina, South Carolina and Georgia, to be free sovereign and independent states, that he treats with them as such, and for himself, his heirs, and successors, relinquishes all claims to the government, propriety, and territorial rights of the same and every part thereof".* [23]

The United States of America, still operating under the Articles of Confederation, discovered quickly that its unsettled government had little power to finance itself. Many statesmen began to question if the sovereign States could continue to maintain its *"league of friendship"* without a stronger central government.

Alexander Hamilton was among the most outspoken leaders of those who were calling for amendments to the Articles of Confederation. Many historians portray Hamilton as prestigious patriot. In addition to his fame as a military leader, he is often touted for his contributions to the Constitution of the United States, the Federalist Party and America's banking system. Unfortunately, some of Hamilton's most celebrated accomplishments have led to a prominent division in our governmental ideology and the interpretation of powers delegated to the Federal government.

In September of 1786, Alexander Hamilton, helped to organize a convention in Annapolis, Maryland which was formally declared to be a *"Meeting of Commissioners to Remedy Defects of the Federal Government"*. The convention consisted of delegates from the states of Virginia, New Jersey, New York, Pennsylvania and Delaware. The states of New Hampshire, Massachusetts, Rhode Island, and North Carolina had appointed delegates but they failed to arrive in time for the meeting. Connecticut, Maryland, South Carolina, and Georgia did not appoint delegates. With few delegates present, the convention had little authority but sent its final report to Congress and called for a broader convention. Continued uprisings such as the Shay's Rebellion added a sense of urgency in calling for a new convention.

The Constitutional Convention

The Constitutional Convention held in Philadelphia, Pennsylvania from May 25, through September 17, 1787 could easily be described as a bloodless war. Because the proceedings were held in secret, Thomas Jefferson commented:

> *"I am sorry they began their deliberations by so abominable a precedent as that of tying of the tongues of their members. Nothing can justify this example but the innocence of their intentions and ignorance of the value of public discussions."*

The original intent of the Philadelphia Convention was to revise the Articles of Confederation but Alexander Hamilton and his supporters convinced the majority of the delegates that a totally new form of government was necessary. Many of the delegates held fast to principals of the Articles of Confederation. As a result, delegates John Mercer of Maryland and Caleb Strong of Massachusetts left the convention in protest. Patrick Henry, a delegate from Virginia, was suspicious of the proceedings and refused to attend.

After electing George Washington to preside over the convention, the delegates spent almost four months in continuous dispute. The first plan for a new government was presented by Virginia governor Edmund Randolph on May 29, 1787 and was based on a model designed by James Madison. Although the Virginia plan contained most of the elements that would eventually become the Constitution of the United States, the proposal that both houses of legislature were to be based proportionate to population, clearly favored large states such as Virginia. As a result, New Jersey delegate William Paterson proposed a plan whereby each state had equal representation in Congress, as it had been under the Articles of Confederation. Still another plan was offered by South Carolina delegate Charles Pinckney which would basically keep the nation as a Confederation with a treaty between States.

On June 18, 1787, Alexander Hamilton offered his own plan. The Hamilton Plan would completely eliminate state sovereignty and consolidate the states into a single nation. It proposed an upper and lower house of congress. Representatives of the lower house would be elected by the people for at term of three years. Representatives of the upper house would chosen by electors for a life term. The Hamilton plan also allowed for a governor who would be chosen by electors for a life term. The governor would have the authority of absolute veto over all bills. Delegates rejected Hamilton's plan because it too closely resembled the government of Great Britain and violated the rights of the States.

Hamilton was relentless in his efforts to create a strong central government. It was a defining moment for America's political ideology. Those who supported Hamilton's efforts were liberals who became know as Federalists. Those who opposed him were conservatives who became known as Anti-Federalists. Although the names are different, current political ideologies in the United States are the same as they were in 1787. In short, liberals believe that a strong government can solve all the problems of the people while conservatives believe that the people can solve all of the problems of the government. At the time of the convention, the majority of the delegates favored the Federalists. Although he would soon change his views, even James Madison was a Federalist. Madison, along with Alexander Hamilton and John Jay wrote a series of 85 articles and essays known today as the *"Federalist Papers."* The papers strongly influenced the ratification process of the Constitution.

Perhaps the greatest stumbling block in adopting the Constitution was the issue of representation in Congress. Highly populated states such as Virginia, could easily dominate congress if representation was based solely on population. Delegate Roger Sherman from

Connecticut, introduced a plan called the Connecticut Compromise which would eventually provide for the structure of Congress as we know it today. After being slightly modified by Benjamin Franklin, the plan allowed for members of the House of Representatives to be elected based on population and the members of the Senate to be elected with equal representation from each state.

The Constitution and Slavery

It is important to remember that the document which created the United States of America is the Declaration of Independence. Both the Articles of Confederation and the United States Constitution served only as by-laws and were extensions of that charter. The removal of Thomas Jefferson's condemnation of slavery from the original text of the Declaration of Independence came back to haunt the delegates at the Constitutional Convention. Although some states had begun the process of gradual emancipation, at the time of the Convention, slavery existed in all 13 States. Slavery during the 11 years between the Declaration of Independence and the Convention at Philadelphia had grown at a substantial rate. By 1787, some states had passed laws regulating importation of African Slaves but the laws had little impact on the number American ships delivering slaves to the West Indies. For wealthy merchants in New England and the Mid-Atlantic States, the slave trade was bigger than ever.

In addition to the slave trade, slave ownership was on the rise. At the time of the Convention approximately 1 out of every 3 families in the South owned slaves. In addition, the numbers of slaves in Northern States were about 60,000 with more than 20,000 in the State of New York alone. It became apparent in the early days of the convention that there would be little if any discussion about slavery. The problem that had to be address was how more than 600,000 slaves would affect representation in Congress. As expected, Southern States insisted that their slaves be counted for the purpose of representation but faced the reality that if Congress decided to asses taxes on property, their slaves would be subject to taxation also. With the combined totals of free persons and slaves, the population of the five Southern States was essentially equal to the remaining eight

Northern States combined. It is unlikely that the eight Northern States would have ever allowed that type of representation. The end result was the measure known as the three-fifths compromise, stating:

> "*Representatives and direct Taxes shall be apportioned among the several States which may be included within this Union, according to their respective Numbers, which shall be determined by adding to the whole Number of free Persons, including those bound to Service for a Term of Years, and excluding Indians not taxed, three fifths of all other Persons.*"

Like the actions of those who approved the Declaration of Independence, delegates to the Constitutional Convention failed to deal with the issues of slavery. Once again America's leaders missed an opportunity to resolve a problem that would plague the country for centuries to come. In addition, they had established a division between states that they had intended to unite. By the time the Convention ended, that division would become even greater.

Ratifying the Constitution

One of the greatest misconceptions in the contemporary view of the United States Constitution is the popular yet misguided belief that this treasured document bound the new nation together in a glorious union. While it is unlikely that the delegates meeting in Philadelphia expected to emerge from the convention with a plan for a perfect government, many expressed concerns that they might be leaving with less than they came with. What had been represented as a meeting to strengthen the Articles of Confederation, turned out to be a power grab by some of the wealthiest and most influential men in America. At the conclusion of the Philadelphia Convention all dreams of a *"league of friendship"* between the States lay dead on the steps of Independence Hall.

Many historians contend that the America's two-party political system began in the 1790's. It is clear that two very distinct and contrasting political ideologies existed at the time of the convention. Federalists were dedicated to establishing a very strong central government allowing very limited rights to the States. Their opponents, the Anti-

Federalists were proponents of limiting the powers of the central government, defending the sovereignty of the States and demanding that certain basic rights be guaranteed to its citizens. The Federalist held the upper hand with the final draft of the Constitution which made no mention of the word sovereignty.

Perhaps the most important lesson to be learned from the struggles to ratify the Constitution is that "*We the People*" were not guaranteed the free exercise of religion, freedom of speech, freedom of the press, the right to keep and bear arms nor the right to peaceably assemble. These guarantees along the other rights and freedoms that we hold so dear were only attained by amending the original Constitution. It was no accident that these guarantees were not included in the original document. The Federalists were fully aware that with every right guaranteed to the people, would in as much diminish the power of government. Alexander Hamilton fiercely opposed amending the Constitution to allow for a bill of rights. He argued that bills of rights were stipulations between kings and their subjects and had no significance in a Constitution. Hamilton further stated that not only was a bill of rights unnecessary but would even be dangerous.[24] Between October, 1787 and August, 1788, Alexander Hamilton, James Madison and John Jay drafted their "*Federalist Papers*," representing a radical view of the need for a strong central government.

Bitter debates between the Federalist and Anti-Federalist factions threatened to splinter the new nation. The bitterness was so intense that it could have easily evolved into war had the problem been a sectional one; but ideological differences existed in virtually every state. By January 9, 1788, the states of Delaware, Pennsylvania, New Jersey, Georgia and Connecticut had ratified the Constitution but the count was four short of the required nine states needed to become law. The first real test came with the State of Massachusetts. The Massachusetts Ratifying Convention met from January 9 through February 5, 1788. The delegates remained deadlocked until Governor John Hancock arrived at the end of the month with a proposal that certain amendments, including a bill of rights be annexed to the ratification. The compromise was sufficient to satisfy many of the Anti-Federalists and Massachusetts ratified the Constitution by a narrow vote of 187 to 168. Ratification based on contingent amendments became the model for conventions in other states.

Also proposing certain amendments, Maryland became the seventh state to ratify the Constitution on April 28, 1788. Despite the fact that Maryland delegates Luther Martin and John Mercer made an early departure from the Philadelphia Convention to challenge ratification of the Constitution, the Maryland Ratifying Convention conditionally approved the new Constitution with little opposition from the Anti-Federalists.

South Carolina, demanding amendments which included a guarantee of state sovereignty, ratified the Constitution on May 23, 1788. On June 21, 1788, New Hampshire became the ninth state to ratify the Constitution. The requirements for putting the new United States government into place had been met but four states remained in contentious debate.

Once again, old Virginia stood at the brink of separating from a union that it had helped to establish. Judge Edmund Pendleton, president of the Virginia Ratifying Convention, was a leader among the Federalist faction which insisted on ratifying the Constitution without amendment. Other notable Federalists were James Madison, John Marshall and George Wythe. Among the noted Anti-Federalist were Patrick Henry, George Mason, James Monroe and Benjamin Harrison V. The major concern of the Anti-Federalist was the absence of a bill of rights. Virginia finally ratified the new Constitution on June 25, 1788 by narrow vote of 89 to 79. The Convention recommended the addition of a bill of rights but its ratification was not contingent upon those changes. Following the Convention, Patrick Henry remained so hostile toward the Constitution that he refused to take part in the new government.

One month later, the State of New York ratified the Constitution but not without opposition and a long list of demands for amendments. Federalist and Anti-Federalists in the New York legislature were so deadlocked over Constitutional issues that they were unable to agree on the appointment of electors for the first Presidential Election. North Carolina did not ratify the Constitution until November 21, 1789 and Rhode Island became the last state to ratify the Constitution on May 29, 1790 thus the United States, under the new Constitution was comprised of only eleven states.

During their ratification debates, some states recommend an end to the slave trade but no state chose to address the issue of slavery in states where it existed. Native Americans, with the exception of those few who were counted for the purpose of representation in Congress, were excluded from the protections of the Constitution entirely.

The Divide Becomes Regional

On December 15, 1788, the United States of America began the process of electing its first President. The election process lasted until January 10, 1789. It was unlike any other Presidential Election in American history. The states of New York, North Carolina and Rhode Island did not participate. No popular vote was held in Connecticut, Georgia, New Jersey or Delaware. Because George Washington ran as an independent, he received the votes of both Federalist and Anti-Federalists giving him 100% of the vote. The 43,782 popular votes cast for Washington represented only 1.3% of the U. S. population. Although George Washington claimed to be independent, he clearly favored Federalist policies.

The First United States Congress met on March 4, 1789 at Federal Hall in New York City. Federalists had control in both houses. In June, James Madison proposed 39 amendments to the Constitution. 12 of the proposed amendments were approved on September 25, 1789 and distributed to the states for ratification. Ten of the twelve were ratified as amendments to the Constitution on December 15, 1791. Those ten amendments are commonly known as the "*Bill of Rights*." One of the proposals, which concerned Congressional pay raises, was not ratified until May 7, 1992 and become the 27th Amendment. The remaining proposal which referred to how members of the House of Representatives would be apportioned to the states was never ratified and is still pending.

James Madison is remembered in American history as the "*Father of the Constitution*." This title which was bestowed upon Madison was well deserved but fails to fully honor his accomplishments as a founding father. As a Federalist, Madison is credited with writing much of the Constitution and 26 of the 85 Federalist Papers supporting its ratification. Ultimately, it was Madison's willingness to compromise, in drafting the proposed amendments resulting in the

"*Bill of Rights*," which led all of the states to ratify the Constitution. In contrast, Madison soon abandoned the Federalist Party principles. More significantly, Madison and Alexander Hamilton became political enemies.

While many opposing political views developed between Hamilton and Madison, the most significant contention arose during Hamilton's term as Secretary of the Treasury. During the first session of Congress in 1790, Hamilton proposed establishing the First Bank of the United States. The plan was opposed by Thomas Jefferson, James Madison and Edmond Randolph. All three opponents were elite Virginia plantation owners. One of the major complaints by the opposition was that a National Bank would favor wealthy northern merchants at the expense of the majority of the people. Madison asserted that the federal government did not have the Constitutional authority to create such a bank. Hamilton's reply was that some powers of the Federal Government were "*implied*" in the wording of the Constitution. Hamilton states:

> "*. . every power vested in a government is in its nature sovereign, and includes, by force of the term, a right to employ all the means requisite and fairly applicable to the attainment of the ends of such power, and which are not precluded by restrictions and exceptions specified in the Constitution, or not immoral, or not contrary to the essential ends of political society.*" [25]

Hamilton based his authority on Article 1, Section 8, Clause 18. The text is often referred to as the "*Necessary and Proper Clause*" or more infamously as the "*Elastic Clause*." It had been the subject of intense debate during ratification in most states. Patrick Henry opposed the clause stating that:

> "*it would lead to limitless federal power that would inevitably menace individual liberty.*" [26]

James Madison had originally defended the clause in his article "Federalist No. 44" but this was before he authored the "*Bill of Rights*." In response to Hamilton, he offered that the 10th Amendment restricted the power of the Federal government to those expressly defined in the Constitution.

There is little doubt that at this point, Madison realized that Hamilton had never intended for the powers of the Federal government to be limited. The unfortunate outcome of this disagreement was that Hamilton won the argument. The precedent was set and from this point forward, the United States Constitution could be interpreted by the whim of public sentiment at the discretion of a handful of judges with the ability to define their own powers.

Until his death in 1804, Alexander Hamilton continued his relentless campaign of bolstering the power of the Federal Government. As Secretary of the Treasury, his financial plans were clearly biased toward the interest of Northern merchants and financiers. Hamilton's hatred toward Southern aristocracy was public knowledge and he openly displayed his resentment of agrarian society. Hamilton was a man obsessed with the influences of power and wealth. Like so many historical figures that were addicted to power, his radical attempts to manipulate the outcome of national elections were major contributors to the destruction of the Federalist Party and led to his own demise at the hands of Aaron Burr.

The Virginia Dynasty

The U. S. Presidential Election of 1796 gave a clear indication of the nation's sentiments. For the first time, an electoral map indicated a distinct division between North and South. It marked a high point for the Federalist Party and the emergence of a true 2-party system. The election winner, John Adams was the first and last Federalist to be elected President of the United States. The glory of the Federalist victory was shorted lived. Continued efforts by the Federalists to fuse the states together under one supreme government and the biased financial plans of Alexander Hamilton, gave rise to a new political party.

In the early 1790s, Thomas Jefferson and James Madison joined forces to create the Democratic-Republican Party to oppose Federalist policies. Ideologies of the new party included states' rights and a strict interpretation of the Constitution. While most of the party's strength was derived from the Southern States, they were joined by several notable leaders from Northern States who had supported the

"*Bill of Rights.*" In 1798 and 1799, Jefferson and Madison drafted resolutions which argued that it was both the right and the duty of the States to declare acts of the U. S. Congress to be unconstitutional if they were not expressly authorized within the text of the Constitution. The theory that the States have a right to refuse to enforce a law considered to be unconstitutional is commonly referred to as "*nullification.*" The theory was widely promoted by advocates of states' right and became known as the "*Principles of 98.*"

In 1800, the Democratic-Republican Party chose Thomas Jefferson as their candidate for President. Jefferson easily unseated incumbent President John Adams and in addition, the party took control of both houses of Congress. With the Democratic-Republican Party firmly in control of the executive and legislative branches of government, the Federalists scrambled to seize control of the Supreme Court prior to Jefferson's inauguration. President Adams first focused his attention on appointing a new Supreme Court Chief Justice. His first choice was former Chief Justice John Jay but Jay declined the appointment citing his poor health but also stating that the Court lacked "*energy, weight and dignity.*"[27] With time running out, Adams nominated John Marshall who was one of the last remaining Federalists from the State of Virginia. Marshall's appointment was confirmed by the Senate on January 27, 1801 but he continued to serve as Secretary of State until the Jefferson's administration took control on March 4th.

John Marshall became the longest-serving Chief Justice of the U. S. Supreme Court in American history. During his 34 year tenure, Marshall dominated the court and fully executed every principle of the failing Federalist Party. He established the principle of "*Judicial Revue*" and supported Alexander Hamilton's theory that the U. S. Constitution gave the Federal Government certain "*Implied Powers*" under Article I, Section 8. Marshall repeatedly expounded the supremacy of the Federal government over State governments and became the nemesis of every U. S. President and legislature from Thomas Jefferson through Andrew Jackson.

On January 30, 1801, the outgoing Federalist controlled 6th Congress approved the Judiciary Act of 1801. The act reduced the number of Supreme Court Justices from 6 to 5 to eliminate the possibility of a Democratic-Republican judge being appointed to the court. Taking effect on February 13, 1801, the act also significantly expanded the court's jurisdiction by creating sixteen judgeships for six judicial circuits. President Adams scrambled to appoint Federalists to each of the sixteen positions prior to the expiration of his term at midnight on March 3rd. Because Adams made appointments all the way up to the last hour of his presidency, the Judiciary Act of 1801 became known as the *"Midnight Judges Act."*

On March 4, 1801, Thomas Jefferson became the first of three consecutive Democratic-Republican Presidents from the State of Virginia. Each of the three, Thomas Jefferson, James Madison and James Monroe served two terms as President, controlling the Executive Branch of the United States Government for a period of 24 consecutive years. Mid-way through the so-called Virginia Dynasty, the Federalist Party totally dissolved.

Immediately after his inauguration, Thomas Jefferson pushed to diminish the power of the Supreme Court by rescinding the Judiciary Act of 1801 and later urged Congress to impeach the outspoken Federalist Justice Samuel Chase. It would be hard to find any political leader in the history of the United States that had more contempt for the U. S. Supreme Court than Thomas Jefferson. He once stated that:

> *"The Constitution . . . is a mere thing of wax in the hands of the judiciary, which they may twist and shape into any form they please."*[28]

Throughout his political career, Jefferson cited the U. S. Supreme Court as a source of tyranny. In his later years, he stated:

> *"The great object of my fear is the Federal Judiciary. That body, like gravity, ever acting with noiseless foot and un-alarming advance, gaining ground step by step and holding what it gains, is engulfing insidiously the special governments into the jaws of that which feeds them."* [29]

President Thomas Jefferson's policies toward low protective tariffs and restrictions on foreign trade infuriated the Northern merchants. Jefferson soon found himself embroiled in a fierce political battle with Federalists from Massachusetts. When Jefferson proposed the purchase of Louisiana from France, he was confronted by fierce opposition from the Federalists. Former Secretary of State Timothy Pickering led a contingency of Federalists from Massachusetts that

67

went so far as to entertain the idea of a separate Northern Confederacy. Another elite group from Massachusetts, known as the "*Essex Junto*," also supported the separation.

Jefferson, who had always been a proponent of strict interpretation of the Constitution, turned the tables on the Federalists by claiming since Constitution specifically granted the president the power to negotiate treaties but did not specifically restrict him from acquiring new territory, he was within his rights and powers as President. While claiming that their objections were based on Constitutional authority, the Federalists concerns were primarily economic. The Northern merchants did not want the expansion of an agrarian society that had no needs for Northern industry or Northern ports. They also feared that westward expansion of Southern culture would further diminish the power of the Federalist Party.

During his second term in 1807, Jefferson signed into law the Act Prohibiting Importation of Slaves. The law could not go into effect until January 1, 1808 because Article 1, Section 9 of the Constitution protected the slave trade for twenty years. Although Jefferson was a slave owner, he had opposed slavery since its inception. In his annual address to the U. S. Congress on December 2, 1806, he stated:

> *"I congratulate you, fellow-citizens, on the approach of the period at which you may interpose your authority constitutionally, to withdraw the citizens of the United States from all further participation in those violations of human rights which have been so long continued on the unoffending inhabitants of Africa, and which the morality, the reputation, and the best interests of our country, have long been eager to proscribe."* [30]

The unfortunate truth about the impact of the 1807 Act is that it did not have the ability to overcome greed. The African Slave Trade was still a source of great wealth to many merchants in New York and New England. While the Act influenced some merchants to venture into fields such as the lucrative opium trade, most slave traders responded by building faster ships to evade capture. Even when participating in the slave trade became punishable by death in 1820, Northern merchants continued their slave trading activities.

In all, Jefferson's two terms in office made significant contributions to sectionalism within the United States. There was little doubt that Jefferson's list of priorities put the merchants and financiers in the North much lower on the list than the agrarian interests of the Southern States. It was an issue in American history that cannot be down-played or ignored. Not only had the political fabric of the nation become bitterly partisan but was now becoming more and more divided between Northern and Southern interests. Another group on the lower end of Jefferson's priority list was the Native Americans. Throughout his life, Thomas Jefferson was fascinated by race and culture. He considered Native American's to be both uncivilized and inferior to Whites. Jefferson was determined to expand America's borders westward into Indian lands. His proffered plan of action was the assimilation of Native Tribes into White society but it was clear that he would use force if he felt it necessary to accomplish his goals.

With Jefferson's decision not to seek a third term being well known and the Federalist Party near collapse every where except New England, James Madison emerged as the most popular presidential candidate and new leader of the Democratic-Republican Party. In the election of 1808, Madison defeated his Federalist opponent Charles C. Pinkney by a very wide margin and the Democratic-Republican Party continued to dominate both houses of Congress.

During his first term, Madison continued Thomas Jefferson's efforts to dismantle all of the systems previously established by Federalist Party leaders. The twenty year charter of Hamilton's Bank of the United States expired in 1811 and was not renewed. On June 18, 1812, the United States declared war against Great Britain. Much like the American Revolution, not all Americans were in favor of a war with Great Britain. The difference this time around was that the New England States were the first to oppose the war. Opposition to the war brought a short lived revival in the Federalist Party but by the time of the Presidential election of 1812, the only real contenders were the incumbent President James Madison and his Democratic-Republican opponent DeWitt Clinton of New York. James Madison won the election by a narrow margin.

War with Great Britain waged on until February 18, 1815 during which time the Federalists of New England continued their opposition to the conflict. Madison's embargos prior to and during the war and Great Britain's blockades of American seaports had brought most of the New England states to the brink of bankruptcy.

Beginning on December 15, 1814, New England members of the Federalist Party conducted a series of meetings in Hartford, Connecticut to discuss the ongoing war and their grievances with Madison's administration. Radicals at the Hartford Convention demanded that the New England States secede from the Union and negotiate a separate peace with Great Britain. The concept of New England secession had been introduced by Josiah Quincy during the Jefferson administration. Key leaders of the convention managed to subdue radical demands.

Proposals offered by the delegates of the Hartford Convention painted a vivid picture of the sentiments of America's leaders in the early 19th century. Cries for secession illustrated that both Federalists and Democratic-Republicans held to the belief that all States had a right to secession from a government and an alliance that no longer served the needs of its citizens. Demands for the resignation of James Madison and proposing a law to outlaw the election of a president from the same state in successive terms demonstrated that resentment toward the *"Virginia Dynasty"* was a very real and dangerously divisive issue. Josiah Quincy of Massachusetts argued that slave representation in the South caused a disproportionate strength over representatives in the North. Considering that Quincy made no proposal for an end to slavery and because the New England economy was deeply dependant open the slave trade, it seems clear that the majority of the leaders of New England had no moral issue with slavery and only wanted to bring an end to what they perceived to be a political *"slave power."*

As the War of 1812 came to a close, several key figures rose to political prominence. Among the most notable of these figures were General Andrew Jackson, the Virginia born Congressman Henry Clay and John Quincy Adams, the son of former Federalist President John Adams. Within a few short years, the three men would oppose each other in one of the most dynamic presidential elections in American history.

James Madison's tenure as the 4th President of the United States ended on the same principles as it had begun. During his eight years as President, Madison fought aggressively to fulfill the policies initiated by Thomas Jefferson. Madison also managed to appoint two U. S. Supreme Court Justices, two U. S. Circuit Court Judges and nine U. S. District Court Judges; further diminishing Chief Justice

John Marshall's control of the nation's judicial system. Little attention was given to the continued slave trade or the growth of slavery during Madison's administration. Madison's policy concerning Native Americans left tribes with few choices other than to assimilate or dissipate. Like his predecessor Thomas Jefferson, Madison did not seek a third term in office.

In the 1816 U. S. Presidential election, James Monroe defeated his Federalist opponent Rufus King by an overwhelming margin. Monroe was now the third consecutive President from the State of Virginia. Unlike former President's, Jefferson and Madison, James Monroe did not aggressively seek to destroy Federalist principles.

Although Monroe openly admitted his Anti-Federalist beliefs, he cautiously sought unity among political factions. His appointment of John Quincy Adams to Secretary of State quieted much of the political hostility in New England. Because of his policies seeking national unity, Monroe's eight year term as President is often referred to as the *"Era of Good Feelings."* In addition to a lessening of partisan hostilities, the sentiments of the nation were turning from the concept of simple Jeffersonian agrarianism to that of industrialization and financial markets. These trends along with remaining debts from the War of 1812 allowed Congress to approve a 2nd National Bank. In addition, U. S. Protective Tariffs were allowed to increase from 6.5% to more than 20% during Monroe's administration.

James Monroe was one of many Virginia slave owners who sought an amicable end to the institution of slavery. Along with other political leaders in both the North and the South, Monroe also sought a way to remove free blacks from white society. He was a member of the American Colonization Society which worked to establish a colony for free blacks on the west coast of Africa. President Monroe supported the 1820 Piracy Act which provided the death penalty for participating in the slave trade. Despite the best intentions of the Act, American slave ships continued to depart New England and New York ports for another 40 years. The only American to be tried, convicted and executed for participating in the slave trade was Nathaniel Gordon who was hanged in New York on February 21, 1862.

Monroe was more aggressive than his predecessors when it came to the removal of Native Americans form their lands. While he also agreed that assimilation was the best course of action, Monroe had little patience or tolerance with the actions of tribal leaders. In 1817, he sent General Andrew Jackson to suppress the Seminole Indians in Spanish Florida.

Like A Fire Bell In The Night

Between the years 1763 and 1767, Charles Mason and Jeremiah Dixon surveyed and established a line to resolve a border dispute between the colonies of Maryland, Pennsylvania, and Delaware. Over a period of years, the survey became known as the "*Mason-Dixon line*." The line had no relevance to slavery because at that time slavery existed in all colonies, but by the turn of the 19th century, the Mason-Dixon Line had come to symbolize a division between Northern and Southern States. At the beginning of James Monroe's first term as President in 1817, there were 19 States. 11 States were north of the Mason-Dixon Line and 8 States were south of it. At that time, the imaginary dividing line still had no relevance to slavery. Slaves totaling approximately 30,000 were held in six Northern States. However, with slavery growing at an alarming rate in Southern States, the issue of disproportionate representation caused by the three-fifths clause in the Constitution was becoming a major concern within the faltering Federalist Party. Abolishing slavery would only serve to drive representative numbers higher in the South. The situation was further aggravated by the admission of Mississippi as a slave state on December 10, 1817. Thus began a pattern of alternating the admission of States to the Union based on slavery; with Illinois being admitted as a Free State on December 3, 1818 and Alabama being admitted as Slave State on December 14, 1819.

A crisis developed when Missouri submitted a request to the U. S. Congress in December, 1818, asking to be admitted to the Union as a Slave State. Federalists in Congress fiercely opposed Missouri's admission. In reality, Federalists could ill afford for Missouri to be admitted to the Union at all. Missouri had an agrarian based society and was geographically located on the west bank of the Mississippi River. There was little doubt that the new State would side with the Democratic-Republicans and the bulk of the trade would travel down the Mississippi River to New Orleans. As a stop gap measure, the

State of Massachusetts supported its District of Maine in submitting an application for Statehood as a Free State. Before a Bill could be passed by both houses of Congress, another provision was attached excluding slavery from the territories north of the 36°30' parallel except within the borders of the proposed state of Missouri. What would become known as *"The First Missouri Compromise"* was passed by the 16th United States Congress on March 6, 1820. Maine was admitted to the Union as a Free State on March 15, 1820 and Missouri was admitted as a Slave State on August 10, 1821.

It seems obvious that there were few U. S. Congressmen who realized the magnitude of the precedent that they set by approving the *"Missouri Compromise."* Founding Father and former President Thomas Jefferson responded to the passage of the Bill with shock and disbelief. He stated:

> *". . but this momentous question, like a fire bell in the night, awakened and filled me with terror. I considered it at once as the knell of the Union. It is hushed indeed for the moment but this is a reprieve only, not a final sentence. A geographical line, coinciding with a marked principle, moral and political, once conceived and held up to the angry passions of men, will never be obliterated; and every new irritation will mark it deeper and deeper. I can say with conscious truth that there is not a man on earth who would sacrifice more than I would, to relieve us from this heavy reproach, in any practicable way. the cession of that kind of property, for so it is misnamed, is a bagatelle which would not cost me in a second thought, if in that way, a general emancipation and expatriation could be effected: and, gradually, and with due sacrifices, I think it might be. But, as it is, we have the wolf by the ear, and we can neither hold him, nor safely let him go. Justice is in one scale, and self-preservation in the other."* [31]

Jefferson knew that unlike the symbolic boundary of the Mason-Dixon Line, the United States were now legally and in many ways morally divided by a line that could never be erased. Despite the fact that slavery still existed in the North, Southern States were now branded as *"Slave States"* even as American ships departed Northern ports to retrieve their human cargos. After half a century of

73

working to build a new nation, the 77 year old Jefferson watched and waited in agony knowing that disunion was inevitable. A War Between the States had started with no one firing a shot.

The End of a Dynasty

By the time of the 1820 U. S. Presidential Election, James Monroe's popularity was so great that the near defunct Federalist Party chose not to participate in the election. Other than the election of the first President, George Washington, Monroe's margin of victory was then and still is today, the largest margin of victory by any Presidential candidate in American history. Out of 232 electoral votes, one was cast for independent candidate John Quincy Adams.

In his 7th Annual Address to Congress on December 2, 1823, Monroe proclaimed that:

> *"The occasion has been judged proper for asserting, as a principle in which the rights and interests of the United States are involved, that the American continents, by the free and independent condition which they have assumed and maintain, are henceforth not to be considered as subjects for future colonization by any European powers."*

Monroe's proclamation, much of which had been written by his Secretary of State John Quincy Adams, demonstrated a clear separation of interests between the United States and other world powers. By 1850, the statement had become known as the "*Monroe Doctrine*" and would remain influential in America's foreign policies throughout the 19th and 20th centuries.

In the same manner as former Democratic-Republican Presidents Thomas Jefferson and James Madison, Monroe chose not to seek a third term as President. As Monroe's Presidency ended, so did the Federalist Party which had so bitterly opposed him.

The Rise of Sectionalism

As the 1824 Presidential Election approached, America was back to one dominant political party; the Democratic-Republican. Political ideologies were no longer divided along party lines. The divide was now a sectional one. Just as Thomas Jefferson had warned, the nation was clearly divided between Northern and Southern States.

As James Monroe prepared to leave office, it is likely that the Virginia born Speaker of the House Henry Clay had considered himself the heir apparent to the *"Virginia Dynasty."* Despite Clay's political prominence, many Southern leaders had lost confidence in Clay. Under Clay's leadership as Speaker of the House, he allowed Federalists to establish the 2nd Bank of the United States and to increase protective tariffs for the benefit of Northern merchants and industrialists. On May 22, 1824, Congress enacted the Tariff of 1824 raising the average rate to a record average of 22%. As a result of the unfavorable sentiments toward Clay, the Congressional Caucus nominated Monroe's Secretary of the Treasury, William H. Crawford of Georgia. Still Henry Clay and two other candidates received congressional endorsements. The first of those two endorsements, John Quincy Adams emerged as the most popular candidate among Northern leaders. Adams had been thrust into the national spotlight when James Monroe nominated him as Secretary of State. While his political views might have differed from those of his father, former President John Adams, he was member of one of the most prominent families in the New England States and a clear favorite in the North.

The last of the *"also-rans"* was a man whose ever-growing popularity could not be denied. Tennessee Senator and former General Andrew Jackson was undoubtedly the people's choice for President in the Deep South. He was still touted as the hero of the Battle of New Orleans and was revered as an Indian fighter during an era when fighting Native Americans was considered honorable.

As the election took place from October 26, to December 2, 1824, John Quincy Adams dominated in New York and New England. Despite facing two prominent Southerners, Andrew Jackson won more electoral and popular votes than his two Southern opponents combined. The final tally revealed Andrew Jackson the overall leader with 99 electors and 41.4 % of the popular vote, followed by John Quincy Adams with 84 electors and 30.9% of the popular vote, William H. Crawford with 41 electors and 11.2% of the popular vote and Henry Clay with 37 electors and 13% of the popular vote. No candidate held a majority of the electoral or popular vote.

Prior to 1824, the only deadlock in a Presidential election was in 1800 when Thomas Jefferson and his Vice-Presidential running mate received an equal number of votes. At that time the top vote getter would become President and the candidate with the second largest number of votes would become Vice-President. The deadlock occurred because at that time, electors were required to cast 2 votes which resulted in Jefferson and his running-mate Aaron Burr receiving an equal number of votes requiring the House of Representatives to decide the winner. The 12th Amendment to the Constitution in 1804 changed the electoral procedure but a majority of electoral votes were still required to be elected President.

The Presidency in 1824 had to be decided by the U. S. House of Representatives. They were only allowed to consider the top three candidates. Henry Clay finished fourth in the number of electoral votes and was eliminated. Outraged by the outcome of the election, House Speaker Henry Clay shifted his support to John Quincy Adams, who then was selected as President with 54% of the votes in the House of Representatives. Immediately after taking office, Adams appointed Henry Clay to his cabinet as Secretary of State. Now, Andrew Jackson was outraged, He had received the highest number of electoral votes in the general election; 15 more than nearest contender John Quincy Adams. Jackson and his supporters called the election a "*Corrupt Bargain.*" John Quincy Adams had become President of the United States having received only 30.9% of the popular vote. It was then, and still is the lowest percentage margin by a President in American history. The only election that would ever come close to that number again would be the election of Abraham Lincoln in 1860 with only 39.8% of the popular vote.

Voters in the Southern States were livid. Three of the four candidates were from Southern States yet the Presidency was awarded to the lone candidate from New England. Even more frustrating for Southerners was that John Quincy Adams was the son of a former

Federalist who had fought diligently to suppress State's Rights. While few historians focus on the impact of the 1824 election, there is little doubt that the *"Corrupt Bargain"* accelerated the nation's journey toward disunion and it only got worse from there.

Adams, like many Americans had incurred the wrath of Andrew Jackson. Andrew Jackson, as a man with only a sporadic formal education became a teacher; With only scanty legal training, he became a lawyer and a State Supreme Court justice; Having little military training, Jackson became a General and now with a very short political career, he was on the verge of becoming the President of the United States. Jackson's life history suggested that he was born to be a leader but he had one major character flaw. Andrew Jackson was a man who refused to compromise. Those acquainted with him were either his friends or his enemies and there was no in between. He was dauntless in defending his friends and vigorous in attacking his enemies. The election of 1824 left Jackson with a long list of enemies.

Soon after the 1824 election, the Tennessee legislature re-nominated Andrew Jackson for President. Ongoing hostilities between Northern and Southern interests caused the Democratic-Republican Party to splinter. Jacksons's supporters called themselves Democrats or Jacksonian-Democrats. Adversely, Adams supporters began calling themselves National Republicans. The campaign evolved into three long years of mudsling which only increased Jackson's determination to seek revenge.

Much of John Quincy Adams' four year term as President was dedicated to initiating new federal policies dealing with internal improvements. The building of new roads and canals in addition to servicing the national debt increased the demand for higher tariffs. In May of 1828, the 20th United States Congress passed a new tariff act. While additional funds were needed to pay off the national debt and fund the new internal improvements initiatives, the major goal was to protect industries in the North. The Tariff Act of 1828 was labeled by Southerners as *"The Tariff of Abominations."* Vice-President John C. Calhoun, a Southerner and Jackson supporter, attempted to have the Senate version of the bill distorted in a manner that would discourage New England legislators from supporting it. Calhoun was successful in swaying the vote of several Congressmen from New England but was unable to overcome the overwhelming support for the bill in the rapidly growing Mid-Atlantic States and the bill was passed by both Houses of Congress. It is likely that Adams was aware that signing the bill would substantially weaken him politically but signed the bill into law despite the adversity. In addition to adding fuel to the fire of sectionalism, the continual increase in protective tariffs led to the nullification crisis in the 1830s.

As if the unpopularity of protective tariffs were not enough increase support for Andrew Jackson, a more personal event occurred late in the Adams administration. Several of Jackson's opponents along with members of the elite social class in Washington, accused his wife Rachel of being a bigamist. It was no secret that Jackson had always held the City of Washington's society in complete contempt but now his sentiments had turned to deep hatred. Because of the cruel and unnecessary attack on the character of Jackson's beloved wife, many of his former opponents threw their support in favor of Jackson. The United States Presidential election of 1828 resulted in a land-slide victory for Andrew Jackson; ushering in the age of the "*Jacksonian Democracy.*" He carried 15 States and won the electoral vote by a margin of 178 to 83. He also won 56% of the popular vote as opposed to John Quincy Adams' 43.6%.

On December 22, 1828, Andrew Jackson was preparing to leave his Tennessee plantation home when his wife Rachel died of what is believed to have been a heart attack. Overcome by grief, Jackson delayed his journey to Washington. Rachel Jackson was laid to rest on Christmas Eve. Family accounts claimed that Rachel was buried in the white gown that she had planned to wear to her husband's inaugural ball. While Jackson confessed that he often prayed that he could find a way to forgive those who had so viciously slandered the love of his life, he was never able to put it behind him.

On March 4, 1829, Andrew Jackson was sworn in as the 7th President of the United States of America. For the first time, the nation had a President that had neither been born in Virginia nor Massachusetts. In his First Annual Address to Congress, Jackson proposed setting aside land west of the Mississippi River for the relocation of Native Americans. Agreeing with his proposal, Congress passed the Indian Removal Act in May of 1830. The act gave the President authority to negotiate with Native Tribes to exchange their native lands for lands in the West. It was the beginning of movement that would be remembered in American History as *"The Trail of Tears."* While Jackson was not the first and certainly would not be the last President to advocate the removal of Native Americans from their land, he was arguably the first to push the issue well beyond Presidential Authority. In the early 19th century, most Americans still held to the belief that Native Americans were inferior to the White Race. During the Jacksonian Era, sentiments toward African slaves continued to be much the same in regard to race.

Tariffs had been a major issue in Jackson's campaign for the Presidency but he made no serious attempt to address the issue until the end of his first term in office. By the summer of 1832, demands by Southern States for a reduction in tariff rates had reached an all time high. In July, Congress enacted the Tariff of 1832 which significantly lowered protective tariffs. Southerners however, still saw the tariffs as abominable. As leaders in Southern States began discussions about secession, South Carolina was developing a plan for nullification of the tariff acts. John C. Calhoun resigned as Vice-President to better defend the nullification plan. President Jackson denounced Calhoun as a traitor. It was rumored that Jackson had even threatened to have Calhoun hanged.

On November 24, 1832 the State of South Carolina adopted an Ordinance of Nullification declaring that the Tariffs of 1828 and 1832 were unconstitutional and unenforceable within the State. The Ordinance carried with it, a warning, which stated:

> *"And we, the people of South Carolina, to the end that it may be fully understood by the government of the United States, and the people of the co-States, that we are determined to maintain this our ordinance and declaration, at every hazard, do further declare that we will not submit to the application of force on the part of the federal government, to reduce this State to obedience, but that we will consider the passage, by Congress, of any act authorizing the employment of a military or naval force against the State of South Carolina, her constitutional authorities or citizens; or any act abolishing or closing the ports of this State, or any of them, or otherwise obstructing the free ingress and egress of vessels to and from the said ports, or any other act on the part of the federal government, to coerce the State, shut up her ports, destroy or harass her commerce or to enforce the acts hereby declared*

to be null and void, otherwise than through the civil tribunals of the country, as inconsistent with the longer continuance of South Carolina in the Union; and that the people of this State will henceforth hold themselves absolved from all further obligation to maintain or preserve their political connection with the people of the other States; and will forthwith proceed to organize a separate government, and do all other acts and things which sovereign and independent States may of right do." [32]

In December, Andrew Jackson easily defeated his opponent and political enemy Henry Clay in the Presidential Election and renewed his attempts to put an end to South Carolina's plan for nullification. Although Jackson was a Southerner and a proponent of State's Rights, he was still a man that rejected compromise and resented any and all challenges of his authority. Jackson deemed South Carolina's actions to be illegal and sent a proposed Force Bill to Congress asking for the authority to take military action to enforce Federal laws in South Carolina. Congress approved the Bill giving Jackson the authority to send U. S. Troops and Navy ships to Charleston.

U. S. Supreme Court Chief Justice John Marshall weighed in on the seriousness of South Carolina's threats of secession stating:

"Were an open declaration in favor of a Southern League to be made by the governments and supported by the people, I believe the terms of separation might be amicably adjust, but the course we seem inclined to take encourages South Carolina to persevere and the consequence of her perseverance must be civil war." [33]

Andrew Jackson was likely the first American President to openly declare that secession or even the threat of secession was an act of treason. In his *"Proclamation to the People of South Carolina"* on December 10, 1832, Jackson warned:

"Seduced as you have been, my fellow countrymen by the delusion theories and misrepresentation of ambitious, deluded & designing men, I call upon you in the language of truth, and with the feelings of a Father to retrace your steps. As you value liberty and the blessings of peace, blot out from

80

the page of your history a record so fatal to their security as this ordinance will become if it be obeyed. Rally again under the banners of the union whose obligations you in common with all your countrymen have, with an appeal to heaven, sworn to support, and which must be indissoluble as long as we are capable of enjoying freedom. Recollect that the first act of resistance to the laws which have been denounced as void by those who abuse your confidence and falsify your hopes is Treason, and subjects you to all the pains and penalties that are provided for the highest offence against your country. Can you...consent to become Traitors? Forbid it Heaven!"

The people of South Caroline still viewed the Ordinance as the right of a sovereign State and refused to back down and Jackson's anger continued to grow. It was reported that Jackson relayed a message to the Congressmen of South Carolina stating:

"Tell them from me that they can talk and write resolutions and print threats to their heart's content, but if one drop of blood is shed there in defiance of the laws of the United States, I will hang the first man of them I can get my hands on to the first tree I can find" [34]

Political leaders did not waiver amidst Jackson's threats and were fully prepared for war if necessary, but they soon discovered that if they seceded, they would have to go alone. Most of the other Southern States were fully convinced that Andrew Jackson was ready and capable of making good on his threats. Fortunately for the nation as a whole, the U. S. Congress was already working on a compromise bill in an attempt to settle the issue and soon passed the Compromise Tariff of 1833. On March 13, 1833, the South Carolina convention reconvened and repealed the original Ordinance of Nullification but as a symbolic gesture, nullified the Force Bill. The United States had seemingly avoided the crisis but over the next few years, most would realize that the crisis had merely been delayed. There has been a popular contingency among American historians and authors that tariffs were only a pretense and that South Carolina's true motive was the defense of slavery. In reality, there was no threat to slavery, so there could be no motivation to defend it. Considering that there were still thousands of slaves in the North and Northern merchants were still amassing large fortunes from the Atlantic Slave Trade at appears obvious that the most citizens of New

England and New York had little objection to slavery where it existed. The institution of slavery played a major economic role in both the North and the South. The U. S. Congress was so opposed to abolition that it imposed a "*Gag Rule*," preventing any legislation concerning slavery from even being introduced. Money, power and particularly the right of sovereignty were clearly the driving forces in the Nullification Crisis.

Another issue that arose shortly before the election of 1832 was the proposed renewal of the 2nd United States Bank Charter. Although the bank's charter was not due to expire until 1836, the bank's president, Nicholas Biddle, made repeated requests to Andrew Jackson for his support of an early renewal. Biddle's requests were consistently denied by Jackson. Henry Clay and other members of the newly formed National Republican Party pushed a bill through Congress to renew the bank charter but the bill was vetoed by Jackson. Later Jackson had federal funds removed from the 2nd Bank of the United States and had them deposited in state banks. Jackson's actions eventually led to the demise of the bank and a financial panic in 1837.

The End of an Era

The last days of Andrew Jackson's administration marked the end of an Era where the policies set forth by Thomas Jefferson and James Madison dominated American politics. While Jackson's original intent was to lead the entire nation in a direction set by his Democratic-Republican predecessors, his belligerent and uncompromising actions led to the splintering of the party. Andrew Jackson's presidency defined the phrase "*abuse of power*." Of the 30 executive orders which had been issued by the first seven Presidents, twelve were issued by Jackson. As a slave owner, Jackson neither defended nor opposed slavery. Being a renowned Indian fighter, Jackson gave little attention to the plight of Native Americans. It is likely that Andrew Jackson had caused more division between the States than any American since Alexander Hamilton. Even his hand-picked successor, Martin Van Buren, eventually strayed from the policies of the Jacksonian Democracy.

Another defining event which occurred during the Jackson's last term as President was triggered by the death of United States Supreme

Court Justice John Marshall in 1835. For over three decades, Marshall had swayed the decisions of the nation's highest court in favor of the principles of the former Federalist Party. Jackson appointed three U. S. Supreme Court Justices during the first six years of his presidency. At the time of Marshall's death, his only remaining ally within the Court was Justice Joseph Story from Massachusetts. After the death of Chief Justice Marshall, Jackson appointed Roger Taney to replace him. Before leaving office, he also appointed Southerners Philip Barbour of Virginia and John Catron of Tennessee to the high court. In all, President Andrew Jackson appointed six U. S. Supreme Court Justices; more than any President since George Washington.

On March 4, 1837, Andrew Jackson watched as the office of the President of the United States passed to his former Vice-President Martin Van Buren, who would continue the policies of the Jacksonian Democracy. Some say that upon leaving office, Jackson stated that he had only two regrets; in that the he did not shoot Henry Clay nor hang John C. Calhoun. It is unclear if Jackson made the statement but it exemplified Jackson's attitude.

He had consistently exercised his power as President in a manner that opposed the Constitutional definition of the office but he was never biased in the application of his abuses. In a nation that was regionally divided by the Compromise of 1820, he applied his abuses to the Southern States in the same way he abused his opponents in the North. Jackson had ascended to the highest office of a nation that was already deeply divided and only compounded the problem by creating a hostile environment on both sides.

After leaving Washington, Jackson returned to his plantation home, "*The Hermitage*" in Tennessee. He remained vocal and active in American politics until his death in 1845. His legacy as a leader could never be denied and the impact of his actions could never be erased. Despite being a Democrat and States' Rights advocate, Jackson augmented the Federalist theory that acts by the Federal government could not be challenged by the States. Because of his fiery rhetoric during the Nullification Crisis, he had forever labeled acts of resistance to Federal Law, by any State, as an act of Treason. The uncompromising Commander-in-Chief had directed his nation down an irreversible path toward a bloody conflict.

Chapter 3
The Path To War

1837 – 1859

The Period between Andrew Jackson's Presidency and the election of Abraham Lincoln was one of significant change in the United States economy, politics and public sentiment. Each change brought increased hostilities between the Northern and Southern States. By the 1850's the hostilities were so intense that physical violence was common on the floors of Congress. One Washington newspaper reporter commented: *"the only man in Congress that did not have a knife and a gun was the one who had two guns."*

As the period began with the Presidency of Martin Van Buren, the Jacksonian Democrats were in control of Congress. After more than 34 years of being lead by a Federalist Chief Justice, the nation's highest court was under the leadership of a conservative Democrat. The nation was in a major economic recession which lasted well into the 1840s. Native Americans continued to be removed from their tribal lands east of the Mississippi River and forced into the Indian Territories of present day Oklahoma; thousands died along the *"Trail of Tears."* Abolitionism became a serious issue for the first time and a wave of new political factions sprang up across the nation. Most of the new factions expressed their opposition to many issues but offered little support of anything. Factions included, Anti-Masonic, Anti-Jackson, Anti-Slavery, Ant-Immigration, Anti-Catholic, Anti-Nebraska and virtually every *"Anti-"* that you could imagine. Included in the political turmoil was the rise and fall of the Whig Party and the birth of the Republican Party.

Another major event was the admission of Texas to the Union which sparked a war with Mexico. The end result was the acquisition of vast amounts of new land. Interest in westward expansion reached an all time high during the period and the discovery of gold in California grabbed the attention of millions of people in America and abroad. Westward expansion increased the demand for railroads, resulting in a sectional struggle over the path of the proposed Trans-Continental Railroad. A number of shipping lines, funded primarily by U. S. Mail

Contracts, scheduled regular routes to and from California. America became infatuated by the concept of *"Manifest Destiny."*

Throughout the period hostile confrontations occurred between the financial interests of the North and the planters of the South. Over and over, the divisive issue of protective tariffs sparked bitter confrontations. While the abolitionist movement was on the rise, the most contested issue was the introduction of blacks into the vast territories of the west. Politicians in the North were fighting to stop the expansion of slavery in the West and politicians in the Western Territories were drafting immigration laws to prevent blacks and other non-white races from crossing their borders. In the midst of the struggles for western expansion a new concept developed which further divided the nation; the concept of *"Popular Sovereignty."*

At the end of the era, the nation was sitting on a powder keg; just waiting on a spark to ignite it. That spark came during the election of 1860. For the second time in American history a Northern candidate became President of the United States with less than 40% of the popular vote and for the second time Southerners felt that they were the victims of a *"Corrupt Bargain."* By no means was the election of Abraham Lincoln the cause of secession by the Southern States but it was the spark that caused an inevitable explosion.

The Taney Court

Following the death of long standing U. S. Supreme Court Chief Justice John Marshall, leadership of the court was transferred to Chief Justice Roger Taney. For almost 35 years, John Marshall attempted to sway the rulings of the court toward the principles of the Federalists who had placed him in office. During the last few years of his judgeship, and after the election of five consecutive Democratic-Republican Presidents, the nation's highest court had noticeably changed its political persuasions. Those persuasions shifted even further away from Federalist fundamentals under the leadership of Taney, the newly appointed Jacksonian Democrat.

Roger Brooke Taney was born into the plantation society in the Southern State of Maryland. Oddly enough, Taney was a Catholic, which was a very unpopular religion in America during his lifetime. Having been appointed Attorney General by Andrew Jackson, he was the first non-protestant Presidential Cabinet member and became the first non-protest Supreme Court Justice in American history. Taney was married to Anne Phoebe Charlton Key. Her brother Francis Scott Key wrote the lyrics to the Star Spangled Banner. Both the Taney and the Key families were pro-slavery.

The Taney Court at the beginning of 1837 consisted of two other Justices from the South and four Justices from the North. On March 3, 1837, the last day of Andrew Jackson's Presidency, Congress passed the Judiciary Act of 1837. The Act added two new Judgeships to the court bringing the total number of Justices to nine. Andrew Jackson immediately appointed John Catron of Tennessee and William Smith of South Carolina to the new positions. Both were confirmed by the Senate that same day. William Smith declined his nomination and his position was filled when incoming President Martin Van Buren appointed John McKinley of Alabama on April 22, 1837, while the Senate was in recess.

Jackson's appointments were intended to pack the Supreme Court with Justices from the South. His actions were much like those of President John Adams in 1800 when he packed the Supreme Court with Federalists. Because the Constitution did not specify the number of Justices that could be appointed, the Supreme Court was often used as a political football from the date of its creation until 1869. During that period, the total number of Supreme Court Justices varied from as few as five to as many as ten.

Unlike the Court of Chief Justice John Marshall, which favored the powers of the Federal Government, Taney's Court most often favored the rights of the States. Chief Justice Taney is best remembered for his opinion in the case of Dred Scott v. Sanford when he expressed that a Negro, whether enslaved or free, could not be an American citizen and therefore had no standing in federal court. Taney's opinions and influences were a constant irritation to leaders in the North and contributed to the increasing hostilities which would eventually lead to war. Chief Justice Taney was particularly opposed to the administration of President Abraham Lincoln. When Taney ruled that Lincoln's arrest of thousands of Americans by suspending the writ of habeas corpus was unconstitutional, it is alleged that Lincoln issued a warrant for Taney's arrest; although no warrant was ever served.

The Rise of Abolitionism

For the first sixty years of United States of America's existence, the concept of abolishing slavery had been cautiously subdued by the nation's leaders. During that period, several opportunities had arisen which could have directed the entire nation toward ending slavery but action was taken. Just as all States were complicit in the introduction of slavery, each State was guilty of supporting the growth of slavery. It was the continual failure of America's leaders to deal with the growth of slavery which led to the birth of the abolitionist movement.

Depending on their motivation, American abolitionists could easily be separated into three distinct groups. The first group is made up of those individuals who opposed slavery for religious or moral reasons. Others were motivated by their perception of social injustice. Still another group of prominent abolitions were those individuals who promoted the abolition of slavery for the sole purpose of political gain. It is important to note that while members of all three groups were opposed to slavery; it was rare that any of them believed in racial equality between blacks and whites. Only a handful of abolitionists were truly concerned about the black race as a whole.

Some religious groups such as the Quakers had openly opposed slavery since the colonial days of America but the religious aspects of abolitionism did not gain substantial momentum until the later days of the Protestant religious revival movement known as the "*Second Great Awakening.*"

Presbyterian minister Lyman Beecher, best known for his religious views of slavery, was also among the earliest Americans to promote the theory that the Western Territories held the key to America's future and success. Notorious for his anti-Catholic views, it is believed that his preaching on the subject while in Boston, contributed to the burning of the Catholic Ursuline sisters' convent in 1834. In his nativist tract, "*A Plea for the West,*" Beecher expressed that God had prepared the West to be mighty; reinforcing his contention that the new frontier should be void of both slavery and Catholicism.

Harriet, Lyman & Henry Beecher by Mathew Brady
New York Public Library Digital Collections

Two of Beecher's children were also well-known abolitionists. His son, Henry Ward Beecher raised money to supply rifles, known as "*Beecher's Bibles*" to anti-slavery radicals in Kansas. Lyman Beecher's daughter, Harriet Beecher Stowe married the religious theologian and social activist, Calvin Ellis Stowe. Harriet fueled the flames of abolitionism with her novel "*Uncle Tom's Cabin,*" depicting the cruelty of slavery. Her popular novel outraged many American's and promoted a general hatred toward Southern culture and society.

Unitarian ministers Thomas Wentworth Higginson and Theodore Parker shared religious views in opposition to slavery. Both men were members of a group known as the "*Secret Six,*" after secretly funding John Brown's raid at Harper's Ferry, Virginia. Thomas Wentworth Higginson was the more radical of the two with regard to abolitionist views. During the War Between the States, Higginson commanded a black regiment in the Union Army. In addition to being an abolitionist, Higginson was an early women's rights advocate. In the late 19th century, he became heavily involved in America's socialist movement. In the early 1900s Higginson helped to establish the Intercollegiate Socialist Society, which was a wing of the Socialist Party of America.

Theodore Parker was a Transcendentalist and reforming minister of the Unitarian Church. As a radical theologian, he broke with orthodox Unitarian beliefs in the 1840s. While serving as minister to the 28th Congregational Society of Boston, Parker's immense congregation included abolitionists Louisa May Alcott, William Lloyd Garrison, Julia Ward Howe, Samuel Gridley Howe and Elizabeth Cady Stanton. Parker exemplifies the view of most religious abolitionists; that despite a slaves' God-given right to be free, the black race was still inferior to the white race. He has been quoted as saying:

> *"the superior race has nothing to fear from them if they are set free. They are childlike, docile, and unintelligent."*

Parker consistently expressed his belief that Whites were superior to other races. He described Mexicans as:

> *"A wretched people; wretched in their origin, history, character, who must eventually give way as the Indians did."* [35]

Abolitionists who opposed slavery because of their religious views were likely the least effective in influencing the sentiments of the nation as a whole. Their followers were general members of their own congregation or small social circles. Their efforts could easily be ignored by the members of Congress by expressing that religious issues were not subject to action by the Federal government.

Perhaps the loudest voices in the abolitionist movement were those who contended that slavery was a moral issue. These individuals were generally well known authors, successful publishers or the wealthy elite. Ironically, some of these abolitionists were from affluent families who had made their fortunes in the slave trade.

Among the earliest and perhaps the most prominent of all abolitionist newspaper publishers was William Lloyd Garrison. He and his partner Isaac Knapp co-founded the *"Liberator"* newspaper in 1831. The newspaper later became the official publication of the New England Anti-Slavery Society which was also co-founded by Garrison. Published weekly in Boston, the *"Liberator"* operated continuously for thirty-five years. Demanding an immediate end to slavery, the harsh inflammatory rhetoric in the *"Liberator"* incited violent reactions in Southern states where it was sometimes distributed. Hostilities toward the newspaper in the South increased to the point that the South Carolina Vigilance Committee offered a $1,500 reward for the identity of anyone circulating the publication, the State of North Carolina indicted Garrison for felonious acts and the State of Georgia offered a $5,000 reward for information leading to his conviction for violating state laws.[36] Resistance to Garrison's publication was not restricted to the South. His radical demand for emancipation at any cost, brought fiery protests from many in the North. He often faced angry mobs in New England. During an anti-abolitionist riot in 1835, Garrison was dragged through the streets of Boston by an angry mob.

Garrison's views toward the government and the Constitution of the United States were also radical. He was among the few abolitionists who supported dissolution of the Union. Along with others such as Wendell Phillips, he contended that continuation of slavery in a union of Free States caused the entire nation to be complicit in the act. Garrison blamed the founding fathers for failing to deal with slavery during the Constitutional Convention and called the Constitution a *"covenant with death"* and *"an agreement with Hell."*[37] His slogan became *"No Union with Slaveholders."* Nothing would have pleased him more than for the slave-holding states to secede and go their separate ways. Because he viewed the United States government as corrupt, Garrison refused to become involved with politics. Despite the unpopularity of the *"Liberator,"* Garrison continued to publish the newspaper until the ratification of the 13th Amendment to the Constitution in December, 1865.

Abolitionist Horace Greeley was the founder and editor of the New-York Tribune. Unlike William Lloyd Garrison, Greely was deeply involved in American politics. He was a co-founder of the Republican Party in 1854 and served for a short time as a U. S. Representative from the State of New York. As an abolitionist, Greely denounced slavery as immoral but also used the issue as a tool to bring himself into prominence in national politics. In addition to his radical abolitionist views, Greely was influenced by the political and economic theory of socialism. These views were likely impacted by his association with Karl Marx, co-author of the *"Communist Manifesto."* Marx was hired by the New-York Tribune as a London-based European correspondent. During his ten years of employment, Marx wrote numerous articles concerning the political and economic conditions in Europe but also wrote opinions of the War Between the States. Marx considered the war to be a struggle over economic issues. In the 1860s, he became an admirer of Abraham Lincoln and applauded him for his stand against the introduction of slavery into the Western Territories of the United States. Horace Greeley agreed with Marx on the unfair economic advantage of slave labor over wage based labor.

From its inception, Greeley's New-York Tribune served as a voice for the dominant Whig Party. At the Whig Party's convention in 1852, Greeley met Alvan E. Bovay of Wisconsin. The meeting sparked a dialogue between the two men would led to the establishment of the Republican Party in 1854. During the 1850s, the New-York Tribune reached a circulation of about 200,000; one of the largest circulations of any newspaper in the nation at that time. With the ability to influence a vast number of voters, the New-York Tribune became the corner-stone of the Republican Party movement. While the newspaper often expressed radical abolitionist views, the Republican Party as whole did not.

Antebellum women had no lawful political power but some of their abolitionist cries were heard louder than those of their male counter-parts. Three daughters of Presbyterian minister Lyman Beecher's daughters, Catharine, Isabella and Harriett were political activists. Catharine Beecher was not only opposed to slavery but fought against social injustices toward Native Americans. Isabella Beecher married abolitionist John Hooker in 1841. After years of supporting the abolitionist movement, Isabella Beecher Hooker became a well known activist in the Women's Rights movement.

Above all the other children of Lyman Beecher, the best know and most influential was his daughter Harriett. The seventh of thirteen

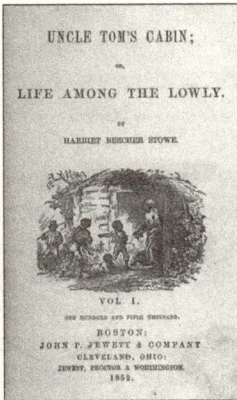

"Uncle Tom's Cabin"
by Harriett Beecher Stowe
John P. Jewett & Co., 1852

children, Harriet Elisabeth Beecher married biblical scholar Calvin Ellis Stowe in 1836. Both Harriett and Calvin were vocal critics of slavery. Together they supported the efforts of the Underground Railroad and temporarily housed several fugitive slaves in their home. Harriett Beecher Stowe's greatest contribution to the abolitionist movement came with the publishing of her epic novel "*Uncle Tom's Cabin*." The story was first published as a serial in the anti-slavery newspaper "*National Era*." It was first published in book form in 1852. Within one year, the two volume book sold more than 300,000 copies in the United States. The heart-wrenching story which depicted the cruelty of slavery, ended with the leading character "*Uncle Tom*" being beaten to death. Although the story was fictional, Americans became outraged. Considering that the abolitionists' only power was their ability to influence public sentiment, it is likely that Harriet Beecher Stowe was among the greatest abolitionists of all.

Julia Ward Howe was another influential contributor to the Abolitionist movement. Her husband Dr. Samuel Gridley Howe was a well known anti-slavery activist and member of the group known as the "*Secret Six*." In comparison, Samuel Howe's influences from his activities as an abolitionist, paled in comparison to those of his wife Julia. In 1858 and 1859, members of the "Secret Six," Samuel Howe, Thomas Higginson, Theodore Parker, Franklin Sanborn, Gerrit Smith, and George Stearns conspired with John Brown to organize an armed slave revolt. The result of the conspiracy was John Brown's failed attempt to capture a Federal arsenal at Harper's Ferry, Virginia. After Brown's capture, Samuel Howe fled to Canada for short time to avoid arrest. John Brown was tried, convicted and sentenced to be hanged on December 2, 1859. After Brown was convicted, famed poet Ralph Waldo Emerson commented:

> "*that new saint, than whom none purer or more brave was ever led by love of men into conflict and death,--the new saint awaiting his martyrdom, and who, if he shall suffer, will make the gallows glorious like the cross.*" [38]

The execution of John Brown made him a martyr in the hearts and minds of many anti-slavery advocates but his violent and radical actions struck fear in the hearts of others. No one was more devastated by John Brown's execution than Julia Ward Howe. She became infatuated by both the life and the death of the ruthless killer. In the early years of the War Between the States, the song *"John Brown's Body"* became a popular marching tune among Union soldiers. They often created their own lyrics that were sometimes coarse or even irreverent. On an occasion of hearing the song sung by marching troops and knowing Julia Ward Howe's passion for the late John Brown, the Reverend James Freeman Clarke suggested to Julia that she should write proper lyrics to the song which would boost the morale of the troops. Because of Reverend Clarkes' suggestion, Julia Ward Howe wrote *"The Battle Hymn of the Republic."* Although it has become one of most famous patriotic songs of all time, the lyrics demonstrated a very dark side of Julia Ward Howe. It is possible that she was prophesying that God would avenge the death of John Brown. Despite the damning nature of the fiery lyrics, *"The Battle Hymn of the Republic"* vaulted Julia Ward Howe into the national spotlight. The downside of the popular song is that it would later be used by President Abraham Lincoln and Radical Republicans to support the continuation of America's bloodiest war.

Like many abolitionists, Julia Ward Howe's Anti-slavery views did not translate to racial equality. In her 1860 book, *"A Trip to Cuba,"* she expressed her belief in the inferiority of the Black Race stating:

> *"The negro of the North is an ideal negro; it is the negro refined by white culture, elevated by white blood, instructed even by white iniquity; - the negro among negroes is a coarse, grinning, flat-footed, thick-skulled creature, ugly as Caliban, lazy as the laziest of brutes, chiefly ambitious to be of no use to any in the world."* [39]

Howe's statements reflect views shared by many white Americans in the 19th Century; even those who were bitterly opposed to slavery.

Unique among abolitionists with moral objections to slavery was Lysander Spooner. He was also an individualist anarchist; believing an individual has the right to govern himself. Unlike William Lloyd Garrison, Spooner insisted that there was no protection of slavery in the Constitution. In his 1845 pamphlet *"The Unconstitutionality of Slavery,"* Spooner expressed that none of the State governments specifically authorized slavery and that the United States Constitution contained clauses contradictory to slavery. Spooner also believed slavery was a violation of natural law. Spooner opposed the Federal government just as much as he opposed slavery. Challenging the United States as a corrupt monopoly, Spooner opened his own American Letter Mail Company in 1844 with hub offices in Baltimore, Philadelphia, and New York. Offering significantly lower rates than the United States Post Office, the Federal government considered the company's acts to be criminal and went after the American Letter Mail Company with a vengeance. At one point, U. S. Marshalls arrested Philadelphia office manager Calvin Case, for conveying letters contrary to the laws of Congress. By 1851, the American Letter Mail Company was forced out of business.

Lysander Spooner was particularly hostile towards U. S. President Abraham Lincoln. He believed in the Union but defended the secession of Southern States as "*a right that was embodied in the American Revolution.*" He expressed that Lincoln's war of Northern aggression was *"purely pecuniary"* and had no legal or moral basis. As Abraham Lincoln and Radical Republicans began their attempt to portray the War Between the States as a war to end slavery, Spooner became infuriated by what he considered to be contemptuous lies by the Republican Party. After the war, Spooner wrote a series of essays titled *"No Treason."* In these essays, Spooner continued to attack the motives and actions of the Republican Party and the martyred President Abraham Lincoln.

Reflecting on the Republican Party's contention that United States government was one of consent by the governed, Spooner proclaimed that:

> *"The only idea they have ever manifested as to what is a government of consent, is this - - that it is one to which everybody must consent, or be shot . . . All of these cries of having abolished slavery, of having saved the country, of having preserved the union, of establishing a government of consent, and of maintaining the national honor are all gross, shameless, transparent cheats."* [40]

95

Lashing out at President Ulysses S. Grant, Spooner stated that the Republican Party had *"put their sword into the hands of the chief murderer of the war."* Much of Spooner's frustration and anger with the Republican controlled government was the knowledge that both before and during the war, the cries of the abolitionists had fallen on deaf ears. Lysander Spooner's moral objections to slavery were much the same as other abolitionists. What made Spooner unique is in addition to his belief that blacks had the right to be free but had the same rights as whites according to the laws of nature. His belief in racial equality was rare in the mid-nineteenth century.

The efforts of abolitionists who had religious or moral objections to slavery had little impact, other than to increase anger in a nation already gripped by hostility. The only abolitionists with the power to end slavery were the congressional leaders. In Congress, the group was clearly a minority even within the Republican Party where they were considered radicals.

"Hon. Thaddeus Stevens of Penn."
Brady-Handy Collection
U. S. Library of Congress

Thaddeus Stevens was a radical among radicals in the abolitionist movement. As Chairman of the House Ways and Means committee during the War Between the States, he was considered to be the most powerful man in Congress. He was often one of the most vocal critics of the Lincoln administration. Stevens expressed an uncommon concern for the rights of Blacks. His support for racial equality might have been influenced by his twenty-year relationship with his mulatto housekeeper, Lydia Hamilton Smith. The exact nature of that relationship is uncertain but Smith was at Stevens' bedside when he died and received a sizeable inheritance from Stevens' will.

Stevens began his conflicted political career as a member of the Anti-Masonic Party. Although Stevens later became a member of the Whig, Know-Nothing and Republican parties he remained opposed to

Masonry for the rest of his life. Many historians contend that Stevens originally joined the abolitionist movement for political gain. While this may be true, it seems clear that at some point in his life, Stevens developed a passion not only for abolishing slavery but also for promoting racial equality.

When Stevens joined the Whig Party, he associated himself with a minority faction of the party known as "*Conscience Whigs*." The group received the nick-name because of its moral objections to slavery. The majority faction in the Whig Party, known as "*Cotton Whigs*" was led by prominent New England members associated with the textile industry who downplayed the slavery issue. Stevens and his fellow "*Conscience Whigs*" bitterly opposed the "*Compromise of 1850.*" The Compromise, which was intended to avoid a confrontation between Free and Slave States, caused dissention within the Party. This dissention combined with the election of "*Cotton Whig*" President Zachary Taylor, caused Stevens and several of his associates to join the Know-Nothing Party.

The Native American Party, nick-named the Know-Nothing Party, was founded in the mid to late 1840s in response to a sudden influx of immigrants. Because many of the new immigrants were German and Irish Catholics, the party was opposed to both immigration and Catholicism. Because of its strong nativist view, the Party quickly became popular and changed its name to the American Party. With the collapse of the Whig Party in 1854, the American Party was able to fill more than fifty seats in the House of Representatives and elevate their leader, Nathaniel Banks, to Speaker of the House. Like most political parties of the time, slavery was not a primary issue to most of its members. Those with radical abolitionist views such as Thaddeous Stevens and party leader Nathanial Banks, soon joined the newly formed Republican Party.

In October of 1858, Stevens was elected to the U. S. House of Representatives as a Republican. As the Republicans gained a plurality in the House, tempers began to flare and Thaddeous Stevens was among the chief agitators. He supported Justice John McLean as a Republican candidate for President in 1860. Stevens and his fellow abolitionists were clearly a minority faction of the Republican Party in 1860. After Abraham Lincoln won the 1860 election, Stevens was often opposed to the President's policies.

97

Much has been written about a suggested mutual respect between Stevens and Lincoln but history does not support that theory. Precious few men gained the respect of Thaddeous Stevens during his lifetime and it is unlikely that Abraham Lincoln was one of them. Abraham Lincoln was a moderate among Republicans; primarily concerned with preserving the Union. Stevens was a radical; determined to punish Southerners that he viewed as traitors.

Stevens suffered one of his greatest disappointments in the summer of 1864. After three years of unbelievable carnage, Americans were growing tired of the war. Stevens and others managed to convince the radical faction of the Republican Party to abandon Lincoln's policies and promote the continuation of the war as a heroic effort to end slavery. The tactic was successful in swaying the sentiments of other members of Congress. With the pro-slavery advocates from the Southern States absent, it seemed that Stevens had things going his way. On January 11, 1864, Senator John Brooks Henderson of Missouri submitted a joint resolution for a Constitutional Amendment to abolish slavery. On April 8, the resolution was approved in the Senate by a vote of 38 in favor and 6 opposed. Thaddeous Stevens, leading the radical Republicans in the House of Representatives, was confident that the result would be the same when brought to a vote in the House but he was wrong. When brought to a vote on June 15, 1864, the House of Representatives was a full thirteen votes short of passing the resolution; with 93 votes in favor and 65 votes opposed. Angered and frustrated, Stevens reluctantly joined with President Lincoln and his cabinet, in a scheme to bribe House members who had opposed the resolution. On January 31, 1865, the resolution was finally approved by the House of Representatives.

Stevens has been quoted as saying, "*the greatest measure of the nineteenth century was passed by corruption.*" Whether or not the quote is accurate, Stevens was clearly disappointed in the House members' reluctance to support an end to slavery. His continued efforts to bring about racial equality led to citizenship for blacks with the ratification of the 14th Amendment in 1868. Years of struggles in accomplishing his goals left Stevens a bitter man. After the war, he led a vindictive campaign to punish the Southern states and insisted that they remain as conquered territories and not be allowed to return to the Union. Stevens also remained bitter about ongoing racism in both the North and the South. In one of his last speeches, Stevens stated:

> *"While nature has given us every advantage of soil, climate and geographical position, man still is vile. But such large steps have lately been taken in the true direction that the patriot has a right to take courage."* [41]

Steven's died on August 11, 1868. Like Lincoln, his casket was allowed to lie in state in the rotunda of the U. S. Capital building. African-American soldiers served as the guard of honor. As per his wishes, Steven's was buried in a cemetery which allowed burials from all races.

John C. Frémont was another prominent figure among radical Abolitionists. During his controversial life, Frémont was a Military Governor of California, United States Senator, U. S. Army General, early explorer of the Western Territories and two-time Republican candidate for President of the United States. He was also the not so admired son-in-law of fiery Democratic Senator Thomas Hart Benton.

John C. Frémont by Fabronius
Boston : L. Prang & Co., 1861.
U. S. Library of Congress

Frémont's controversial character was described as impetuous, contradictory. self-justifying and self-defeating. One factor that may have contributed to John Frémont's unusual character was his illegitimate birth. John's mother, Anne, was the daughter of a prominent Virginia planter. At age seventeen, she married the wealthy Major John Pryor of Richmond. Upon discovering that his wife was having an affair with a French immigrant employee, John Pryor published a divorce petition, charging his wife with criminal intercourse. His wife, Anne Whiting Pryor fled Richmond with her lover, a man named Frémon or Frémont, in July of 1811. The result of their departure caused a well publicized scandal. Their son John Charles Frémont was born out of wedlock in Savannah, Georgia on January 21, 1813. The true identity of his father, who died in 1818, is still disputed. It is likely that the scandal surrounding John Frémont's birth led to his resentment of Southern culture.

Although John C. Frémont was a prominent and active member of the abolitionist movement, most of his endeavors ended in failure. Ironically, it was some of Frémont's failures that paved the way for an eventual end to slavery. After California became a State in 1850, Frémont won a U. S. Senate seat running as a Democrat. He was aided by the political influence of his father-in-law, Missouri Senator Thomas Hart Benton. After serving less than six months, he was defeated in a re-election bid as a Free Soil Democrat in 1851. His defeat was due largely to his radical opposition to slavery. Failing to win re-election persuaded him to abandon the Free Soil Democrats in favor of the newly formed Republican Party in 1854. He advanced quickly within the Republican ranks and became the Party's Presidential nominee during the election of 1856. The result was yet another failure as he was soundly defeated by Democratic candidate James Buchanan. Not only did Frémont lose the election but failed to carry his home State of California. His father-in-law, Thomas Hart Benton applauded his efforts but supported James Buchanan for President.

Frémont's disastrous defeat in the 1856 election effectively removed him from any political consideration by the Republican Party but like so many other times in his life, failure led to opportunity. The new Republican Party favorite, Abraham Lincoln, narrowly won the Presidential election in 1860. After war broke out in 1861, Lincoln began to extend favors to members of the Republican Party. Lincoln wanted to appoint John Frémont as the American minister to France because of Frémont's French ancestry and his stance on slavery. Lincoln's Secretary of State William Seward objected and no appointment was made. Lincoln instead, commissioned Frémont as a Major General in the Union army and made him Commander of the Department of the West on July 1, 1861.

On August 30, 1861, General Frémont issued a proclamation putting the State of Missouri under martial law and decreed that the property of all rebels, including slaves would be confiscated and that confiscated slaves would subsequently be emancipated. President Lincoln had not been notified and only learned of the proclamation by reading about it in the newspaper. Lincoln immediately asked Frémont to remove the paragraph pertaining to slaves from the proclamation. Frémont wrote a reply to Lincoln refusing the request and sent his wife, Jesse Benton Frémont, to Washington to further express his views. President Lincoln's reception of the General's wife was far less than cordial as he scolded her for her husband's actions. The angered President publicly denounced Frémont's proclamation and ordered the General to immediately modify it to conform to current federal law. Knowing that he could ill afford to continue with Frémont's insubordination, Lincoln sent Postmaster General Montgomery Blair, Quartermaster General Montgomery Meigs and Adjutant General Lorenzo Thomas to Missouri to asses the condition of the Department of the West. Montgomery Blair issued a particularly damning report, stating that the Department was in a state of complete disorganization and that Frémont seemed stupefied. Blair's report, along with concurring reports from Meigs and Thomas led to the removal of General Frémont as Commander. Frémont was left with a bitter hatred for both Abraham Lincoln and Montgomery Blair. A division in the Republican Party in 1864 allowed Frémont an opportunity for revenge. Radical Republicans, who were unhappy with Abraham Lincoln, nominated Frémont for President. After allowing Lincoln to stress for several months, he struck a deal with the President. Frémont agreed to withdraw from the Presidential race if Lincoln agreed to fire Montgomery Blair. To Frémont's delight, Lincoln was in an embarrassing and desperate situation and accepted the terms of the agreement. After President Lincoln fired Blair, Frémont rescinded his nomination leaving Republicans with the option of voting for a Democrat or supporting Abraham Lincoln for President. The devious bargain reunited the Republican Party, giving them the strength and direction to forge a proposal for a Constitutional Amendment which would end slavery. The incident was clearly John C. Frémont's greatest contribution to the cause.

Within the ranks of political leaders in the abolitionist movement, Charles Sumner could be considered the "*Chief Antagonist*." Being a powerful orator, Sumner was capable of turning the Senate floor into a battle ground with his fiery rhetoric. It was the exercise of this exceptional talent which almost led to his death in 1856. His role as a radical leader in the United States Senate mirrored that of radical leader Thaddeous Stevens in the U. S. House of Representatives.

Charles Sumner was born in Boston, Massachusetts on January 6, 1811. Like most leaders from New England, Sumner was a Harvard graduate. Being born into a lower middle-class family, Sumner was never a part of Boston's elite "*Brahmin Society*." His radical behavior

Senator Charles Sumner
U. S. Library of Congress

caused as much hostility in New England as it did in the rest of the nation. Unlike his fellow abolitionist William Lloyd Garrison, Sumner was able to avoid being dragged through the streets of Boston by angry mobs, opposed to his radical views. Sumner was clearly a man with total contempt for compromise and a passion for vengeance. His unyielding convictions and abhorrent rhetoric contributed as much as anything, to the War Between the States. His radical opposition to the "*Compromise of 1850*," led to the political downfall of one of New England's most inspiring leaders; Daniel Webster.

Charles Sumner's opposition to slavery was motivated more by the legality of the institution than any moral objection to it. During the western frontier violence often referred to as "*Bleeding Kansas*," Sumner fanned the flames of war. On May 19 and 20, 1856, he gave a lengthy speech on the floor of the Senate which he called a "*Crime against Kansas*." During the two-day speech he alleged that the goal of the slave owners was to rape a virgin territory. Senators Stephen A. Douglas of Illinois and Andrew Butler of South Carolina were the main targets of his allegations. Sumner singled out Andrew Butler stating:

> "*The senator from South Carolina has read many books of chivalry, and believes himself a chivalrous knight with sentiments of honor and courage. Of course he has chosen a mistress to whom he has made his vows, and who, though ugly to others, is always lovely to him; though polluted in the sight of the world, is chaste in his sight -- I mean the harlot, slavery. For her his tongue is always profuse in words. Let her be impeached in character, or any proposition made to shut her out from the extension of her wantonness, and no extravagance of manner or hardihood of assertion is then too great for this senator.*" [42]

In his attack on Senator Butler, Sumner was asserting a claim that had become popular among Northern Congressmen who desired to insult and intimidate their Southern colleagues. Throughout his oration, Sumner wittingly accused Butler of defending slavery for the

102

purpose of forcing his female slaves to engage in unwanted sex. While often unsubstantiated, similar allegations were frequent in Congress at that time. The allegations did nothing to resolve issues in Congress but they were highly successful in producing a violent response from the Southern legislators at which they were aimed. As Sumner continued his personal attack on Butler, Senator Douglas commented that the foolish "*Sumner was going to get himself killed.*" Senator Douglas' prediction was almost proven to be true.

Two days after the speech, a cousin of Senator Andrew Butler, South Carolina Representative Preston Brooks, confronted Sumner as he sat at his desk in the near empty Senate Chamber. Brooks told Sumner that he had read his speech and contended that Sumner had unjustly libeled both the State of South Carolina and his cousin Andrew Butler. As Sumner attempted to rise, Brooks began beating

Title: "*Southern Chivalry - Argument versus Club's*" by John L. Magee

him with his cane. Sumner fell to the floor beneath his desk but Brooks continued his attack. Blinded by has own blood, Sumner managed to stagger down the isle of the Senate floor where he collapsed. While the injured Senator was unconscious, Brooks continued to beat him unmercifully. Several Senators attempted to rescue Sumner but South Caroline Representative Laurence M. Keitt pulled a pistol and prevented them from interrupting the beating. Sumner suffered severe head trauma and very nearly died. The brutal beating caused Sumner to be absent from the U. S. Senate for three years.

Sumner's beating was representative of the intense hatred that had developed between Congressmen from the North and those from the South. While numerous sectional differences may have influenced the sentiments of many American citizens, members of the United States Congress had abandoned all causes in favor of perpetuating their violent aggressions. It could easily be contended that stubborn pride and childish insults were as much a cause of the War Between the States as any other issue.

103

A summary of the efforts of abolitionists prior to and during the early years of the War Between the States reveals that their actions did very little to bring about an end to slavery. It is true that many prominent religious leaders of the time had persuaded thousands of their followers that slavery was adverse to the laws of God but had no legal authority to take action. Brilliant authors and songwriters had both inspired and outraged their fans concerning the brutality of slavery. Leading journalists and renowned social activists persuaded many more Americans with their moral objections. Political parties had risen and fallen while arguing the legal issues of slavery but with all abolitionist factions combined, they were clearly a minority. Republican abolitionists were even a minority within their own party.

The many opponents of the abolitionist movement were far more than just the slave owners of the South. Perhaps the greatest of all enemies regarding the abolitionist movement in America was apathy. While there were Americans in both the North and the South that were opposed to slavery, little thought was given to the issue. Two-hundred and fifty years of slavery in North America had created a culture of complacency. In addition, few Americans were willing to think about the price that might be paid in an effort to end slavery. A strong pro-slavery sentiment existed in the Mid-Atlantic and New England States. New York's growing merchant trade was heavily influenced by the raw products produced by the plantations of the South. More heavily influenced were the textile mills of New England. Still clinging to deep-rooted Puritan beliefs, many citizens of New England still believed that the role of the black race as slaves had been ordained by God; others simply believed that blacks were inferior beings.

With slavery being embedded in the Constitution and the laws of the United States, the abolitionist movement was helpless in bringing an end to the human bondage. What they needed was a majority in Congress. At the time of Abraham Lincoln's election in 1860, slavery existed in 16 of the 33 States and in Washington D. C. That same year, the Republican Party gain a plurality in the U. S. House of Representatives but the majority of the party still supported slavery in the states where it existed. It is easily concluded that the cries of the abolitionists had been heard by hundreds of thousands of Americans but the population of the United States had surpassed thirty-one million by 1860. Many Americans and their elected officials remained unwilling to put an end to an institution that existed since the days of the first colony.

104

Manifest Destiny

As a result of the Louisiana Purchase in 1803, the United States acquired approximately 827,000 square miles of land west of the Mississippi River. In the early 19th century, there were still substantial opportunities for westward expansion along the Ohio River and in the regions east of the Mississippi River stretching to the Appalachian Mountains so there was little interest in the Louisiana Territory. It was a wild untamed wilderness inhabited by Native American tribes.

In 1845, Texas was admitted to the Union by a joint resolution of Congress. The United States was increasingly divided by sectional interests and the proposal to admit Texas into the Union as a slave state only added to the hostilities already existing between political parties. Supporting the annexation of Texas and weighing in Oregon boundary dispute, popular columnist, John O'Sullivan wrote an editorial in the Democratic Review and later in the New York Morning News, titled *"Manifest Destiny."* In his editorial, O'Sullivan claimed that it is:

> *". . . by the right of our manifest destiny to overspread and to possess the whole of the continent which Providence has given us for the development of the great experiment of liberty and federated self-government entrusted to us."* [43]

As a result of O'Sullivan's editorial, America now had a new motto for westward expansion. He had created a vivid image of America's glorious destiny in the minds of many Americans; an image that would continue to grow and flourish.

American progress - Westward the course of destiny - Westward ho! - Manifest destiny
by John Gast, 1872 - Published George A. Crofutt - Source: U. S. Library of Congress

As many people had predicted, the annexation of Texas lead to a war between the United States and Mexico. Ending in victory for the United States, the Mexican-American war lasted less than two years. The war officially ended with the signing of the Treaty of Guadalupe Hidalgo on February 2, 1848. By the terms of the treaty, the border of Texas was established along the Rio Grand River and Mexico ceded lands between the Rio Grand River and the Pacific Ocean which comprised most of what is now California, New Mexico, Arizona, Nevada, Utah, Wyoming and Colorado. In exchange, the United States paid 15 million dollars to Mexico and paid off the claims of American citizens against Mexico up to 3.25 million dollars. America's vision of *"Manifest Destiny"* had now become a reality.

Brigham Young
By Charles Carter

During the period of time that the United States had been busying itself with the prosecution of a war with Mexico, another chapter in the story of *"Manifest Destiny"* was quietly unfolding. In 1847, a religious group, commonly known as *"Mormons"* entered the Salt Lake Valley of present day Utah. The Mormons, under the leadership of pioneer Brigham Young, brought with them their own hierarchical government and a unique cooperative ethic. After being driven out

106

of Illinois and other parts of the Mid-West by violence and hatred, the Mormons developed a society of isolationism and expanded its settlements over a vast desert region which became known as the *"Mormon Corridor."* With settlements stretching from the Gila River in the south to an area near what is present day Montana, it was virtually impossible to travel by land from the United States to the Pacific Coast without passing through Mormon territory. Mormons quickly developed a commonwealth among settlements. They created and maintained a co-operative irrigation system allowing them to turn desert lands into farming communities. Mormons under the leadership of Brigham Young were proponents of slavery. They believed that the Black Race had been cursed by God. Mormons also believed in plural marriage or *"Polygamy."* Most 19th Century Americans believed that the practice of polygamy was an immoral act. They also believed that the Mormon religion was bogus and did not represent true Christianity. In 1849 Mormon leaders petitioned the United States government for admission to the Union as the State

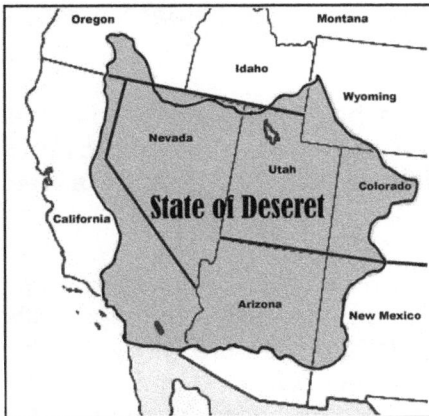

of Deseret. The proposed State would encompassed nearly all of present-day Utah and Nevada and portions of California, Arizona, Colorado, New Mexico, Wyoming, Idaho, and Oregon. The ensuing controversy over the proposal was not settled until the creation of the Utah territory in the *"Compromise of 1850."* During the first decade of Mormon settlements in the western regions, their control of the area became a menacing presence to the interests of both the Northern and Southern States. It was so menacing in fact that the Mormon settlers were involved in an armed confrontation with the United States government that lasted from May of 1857 to July of 1858.

Another fiery dispute arose between Northern and Southern interests when U. S. Representative David Wilmot of Pennsylvania proposed that a proviso be attached to the Treaty of Guadalupe Hidalgo which would ban slavery in the territories acquired from Mexico. Wilmot's arguments for passage of his proviso were not aimed at slavery where it existed. He offered no religious, moral or legal objections to slavery. Wilmot could clearly be identified as a *"Free Soiler."* He believed, that kept within its given limits, slavery would eventually bring about its own demise. In a speech before the U. S. House of Representatives, Wilmot stated:

> *"I plead the cause and the rights of white freemen. I would preserve to free white labor a fair country, a rich inheritance, where the sons of toil, of my own race and own color, can live without the disgrace which association with negro slavery brings upon free labor."* [44]

Wilmot's views asserting the superiority of the white race were common in all political parties during the antebellum period. Wilmot became an influential member of the Republican Party and was instrumental in drafting party platform resolutions which would define the party's plans for the new territories; a plan that would not only exclude slavery but free blacks as well. Another cleverly crafted plan of the Republican Party was the removal of Mormons from the western territories under the guise of removing the barbaric practice of polygamy.

The proposed bill which would have attached Wilmot's proviso to the Treaty of Guadalupe Hidalgo, died in Congress but the controversy continued. A proposal to accept California into the Union as a free state resulted in further hostilities.

As the borders of the United States reached the California shores, millions of Americans set their sites on the new territories with everyone having their own agenda. While most were motivated by the hope for new opportunities, owning their own land and even the romance of adventure in the west, others were motivated by contemptuous greed and an incredible lust for power. Like everything else in the country at that time, there were bitter disagreements between citizens of the Northern and Southern States over the future of the new territories. It cannot be denied that while the concept of *"Manifest Destiny"* should have been a giant step in the growth and prosperity of the United States, it was in reality, another step toward a bloody divide. As the fires of sectional differences smoldered over westward expansion, a single event which occurred in 1848 would turn those fires into a blazing inferno.

Gold

In 1847, a German born pioneer named John Sutter (Johann August Suter) contracted James W. Marshall to build a sawmill on his property along the South fork of the American River in Central California. Marshall is credited with discovering gold at the mill site on January 24, 1848; even though some historians contend that the gold was actually found by children who enjoyed playing along the river. The event triggered frenzy of immigration to the region. There were very few individuals who directly profited from California gold rush but many, who supplied transportation and supplies to the thousands of people seeking their fortune, became millionaires.

James Marshall at Sutter's Mill
daguerreotype by R. H. Vance
U. S. Library of Congress

News of the discovery was slow to reach the Eastern United States. The New York Herald reported the discovery in August of 1848 and President James K. Polk announced the discovery in his address to Congress on December 5, 1848. At the time of the discovery, California was part of Mexico and isolated from most of the world. There were very few established overland routes and no trans-continental railroad, telegraph lines or pony express. It was the lack of communication that encouraged the United States to issue contracts for the transfer of mail to and from California. These lucrative contracts provided a financial base for the expansion and growth of prominent shipping firms in New York. Early contracts were awarded to George Law's U.S. Mail Steamship Company and William H. Aspinwall's Pacific Mail Steamship Company. The New York firm of Howland & Aspinwall was already a well established mercantile firm with a substantial fleet of ships built with funds derived from the Atlantic slave trade and the China opium trade. The demand for a faster route to California led to the establishment of a railroad across the Isthmus of Panama. Another American who profited from the California trade route was

Cornelius Vanderbilt. During and after the War Between the States, Vanderbilt turned his attention to railroads. His dominance of the United States transportation industry during the 19th Century assisted him in becoming one of the richest Americans of all time.

It is estimated that more than 300,000 people from the United States and other countries, hurried to California during the gold rush. Much of the easily accessible gold was extracted during the first year. As gold became more difficult to find, hostilities arose between Americans and foreigners. As the mass of newcomers drove Native Americans from their hunting grounds, some local natives responded be attacking miners. These actions led to counter-attacks where natives were sometimes slaughtered. Those who were able to survive attacks by miners were separated from their food gathering areas and many starved. The discovery of gold also added new concerns over slavery. As miners worked harder to extract gold, there was a fear that slave owners might have the unfair advantage of free labor if they moved into the gold fields.

For many, the California gold rush fueled a dream of instant wealth but others had a different dream in mind. In the North there was a growing sentiment that America had grown corrupt and the new frontier offered a chance for redemption by creating a pure society; a society created and controlled by the Federal government. In the South there was a growing sentiment that the settlers in the new frontier had the right to determine their own destiny. More than ever, the social and political views of the nation were split North and South. The intense and hostile struggle for control of the western frontier led to one of the nation's greatest compromises. The compromise that was intended to defuse the bitter conflict between the two factions brought even greater hostilities. The focus of those hostilities could be expressed in a single word; the dreaded word "*Sovereignty*."

The Compromise of 1850

The acquisition of vast new territories and the ensuing gold rush shifted the county's attention westward. In 1849, California asked for admission to the Union as a free state. A problem that existed was that California was divided by the permanent legal boundary between free and slave states which had been established by the Missouri Compromise of 1820. In addition, the newly established boundaries of the State of Texas were also divided by the line. Ironically, it was the Texas border dispute that nearly led to a military confrontation.

In 1850, Texas had been a State for only five years. Many Texans felt that the United States government had failed to fulfill the promises made in exchange for annexation. The Republic of Texas had been in deep debt, was plagued with border incursions by Mexico and was threatened by hostile Indian tribes. The newly formed State of Texas was still suffering from those issues in 1850. A proposal to seize a large portion of Texas lands brought Texas to the brink of secession and war.

A compromise drafted by Whig Senator Henry Clay of Kentucky and supported by Democratic Senator Stephen Douglas of Illinois, focused on reducing many of the sectional conflicts in 1850. It was during the debates over the compromise that Douglas perpetuated the concept of *"Popular Sovereignty."* The final compromise consisted of several bills. Texas was paid $10 million in exchange for ceding their property in present day New Mexico and all property north of 36°30' parallel. California was admitted to the Union as a free state, the territories of Utah and New Mexico were organized. The slave trade was abolished in Washington D. C. but slavery was not. A stronger Fugitive Slave Act was passed providing punishment and fines for officials who did not enforce the law. While the Compromise satisfied the interests of most Congressmen, it proved to be a temporary solution.

The debates and the final resolves of the Compromise of 1850 were clear indications that no political party at that time was willing to oppose slavery in the areas where it already existed. Their motives for opposing the expansion of slavery into the new territories were varied and seldom reflected a view in support of racial equality. In most cases, their plans and dreams for the western frontier were exclusive to the white race as they continued their efforts to exclude other races from the new territories.

The Kansas-Nebraska Act

The Kansas-Nebraska Act which was passed by Congress in 1854, had the effect of repealing provisions of the Compromise of 1820 and the Compromise of 1850. The Act has been credited with causing the fierce hostilities which led the United States into its deadliest war. Drafted by Democratic Senator Stephen Douglas of Illinois, the Act created the separate territories of Kansas and Nebraska which opened up thousands of square miles of land for new settlement. By organizing the new territories under the principles of *"Popular Sovereignty,"* Douglas and other Democrats believed that removing the issue of slavery from the authority of the Federal government and placing it in the hands of the people would quiet hostile sectional differences but passage of the Act had quite the opposite effect. During the debates, it became evident that creation of the Kansas and Nebraska territories were the first step in establishing a northern route for the Trans-Continental Railroad; a path bitterly opposed by Southerners. The most contentious issue among Northerners was *"Popular Sovereignty."* Northern Democrats wanted the citizens of territories to decide the issue of slavery but those Northerners who held liberal Federalist views wanted the Federal government to decide. The division of Northern interests resulted in the birth of new political parties and the collapse of the Whig Party. Many of the former Whigs joined the anti-immigrant *"Know-Nothing Party."* Others joined the newly formed Republican Party.

The numerous violent and sometimes deadly confrontations which occurred in the Kansas Territory following passage of the Act are often described by the phrase *"Bleeding Kansas."* Many historians theorize that the one and only issue which instigated the violence was the expansion of slavery. A contradiction to that theory could be demonstrated by the fact that during the first fifty years of the 19th Century, many laws had been passed concerning the expansion of slavery without resulting in deadly violence.

Unlike previous acts and compromises, the Kansas-Nebraska Act was the first to place the decision making authority in the hands of the people, thus over-riding the authority of Federal government. This authority, which was labeled *"Popular Sovereignty,"* was a much greater issue than expansion of slavery. Sovereignty was the same issue which led to the desperate struggle to ratify the United States Constitution. The issue was just as continuous in the 19th Century.

"Bleeding Kansas" was less a result of the differences concerning the expansion of slavery than it was a disagreement over who had the authority to make the decision. Although popular sovereignty was included in a portion of the Compromise of 1850, it had little impact on the slavery issue at that time. Suddenly in 1854, there was a real possibility that popular sovereignty might allow Kansas to be admitted to the Union as a slave state. The social injustice or moral evils of human bondage was not the primary issue. As David Wilmot had expressed in his proviso during the Mexican-American War, slavery was both a disgrace and a threat to the interests of free white labor. In addition, slavery could bring about the condition of blacks living in the confines of a white society. Another troubling issue was that of miscegenation or the amalgamation of races. It was an issue particularly troubling to both Stephen Douglas and his political opponent Abraham Lincoln. In speech concerning the U. S. Supreme Courts' Dred Scott decision, Lincoln supported the views of Stephen Douglas on amalgamation while pointing out the weaknesses of Douglas' plan to prevent it. Like many of Lincoln's speeches, he tends to challenge the legitimacy of Douglas as a legislator by referring to the former Supreme Court Justice as *"Judge Douglas."* During his 1857 speech, Lincoln responded to the Douglas' views on amalgamation by saying:

> *"But Judge Douglas is especially horrified at the thought of the mixing blood by the white and black races: agreed for once—a thousand times agreed. There are white men enough to marry all the white women, and black men enough to marry all the black women; and so let them be married. On this point we fully agree with the Judge; and when he shall show that his policy is better adapted to prevent amalgamation than ours we shall drop ours, and adopt his."*

Lincoln goes on to express that:

> *"A separation of the races is the only perfect preventive of amalgamation but as all immediate separation is impossible the next best thing is to keep them apart where they are not already together. If white and black people never get together in Kansas, they will never mix blood in Kansas."* [45]

Lincoln's words clearly express that it was not just slavery that he hoped to exclude from the territories but the entire black race as well. Lincoln became a rising star during the on going controversies concerning the Kansas Nebraska Act. Passage of the Act provided the motivation for formation of the Republican Party. It was also instrumental in promoting the development of a new political tactic which would play a major role in the Republican plan to shape the future of the western territories. The new tactic relied on the use of mass immigration as a tool to gain political control. The tactic was successful in controlling the adoption of the Constitution in Kansas and remains a common tactic in American politics today.

Kansas drafted four Constitutions before one was finally accepted which allowed admission into the Union. The only common element among the four was that they were all clearly dedicated to the rights of white males. Delegates on both sides of the slavery issue drafted proposals for a new Constitution which would exclude free Negroes and Mulattoes from residence in Kansas. Only one out of the four proposals excluded the word *"White"* when defining the rights of citizens but that proposal was rejected.

In 1854, a Massachusetts group led by Eli Thayer established the New England Emigrant Aid Company for the purpose of transporting and supporting anti-slavery immigrants to Kansas. The intent of the company was to create an unbalanced voting population which would favor the admission of Kansas to the Union as a free state. Combined with the aid of smaller immigration aid groups and the influx of *"Free-Staters,"* the group was eventually successful in gaining control of Kansas Politics.

In October of 1855, "Free-Staters" gathered in the town of Topeka, to draft a Constitution. Free Soil militant James Henry Lane served as President of the convention. The pro-slavery *"Law and Order Party"* protested the convention and did not participate. As a result of their absence, the proposed *"Topeka Constitution"* was overwhelmingly approved. The document banned any form of slavery in Kansas. One portion of the document limited voter rights to *"Every white male person, and every civilized male Indian who has adopted the habits of the white man, of the age of twenty-one years and upward."* When submitted for a vote of the people, a clause for the *"Exclusion of Negroes and Mulattoes"* was listed separately on the ballot. After voters approved the Topeka Constitution, it was submitted to the United States Congress with a request for Kansas to be admitted into the Union as a free state. Most U. S. Congressmen viewed the whole Topeka movement as corrupt and the proposed Constitution was rejected. In a special address to Congress, President Franklin Pierce stated:

> *"No principle of public law, no practice or precedent under the Constitution of the United States, no rule of reason, right, or common sense, confers any such power as that now claimed by a mere party in the territory. In fact, what has been done is of a revolutionary character. It will become treasonable insurrection if it reaches the length of organized resistance by force to the fundamental or any other federal law. "* [46]

A second attempt to draft a Kansas Constitution was made in 1857. Pro-slavery advocates organized a new convention in the town of Lecompton. The proposal adopted by the delegates of the convention was submitted for a vote of the people with a two options. The first option was to approve the Constitution with slavery. The second option was to approve the Constitution without slavery. A Constitution without slavery would ban the importation of new slaves but allowed residents to keep the slaves that they already owned. This time the anti-slavery faction protested and the Constitution with slavery was overwhelmingly accepted. Unlike the *"Topeka Constitution,"* the new *"Lecompton Constitution"* gained national attention. The Lecompton Constitution was bitterly opposed by the newly formed Republican Party and was a major issue in the Party's platform.

Even as the pro-slavery advocates were drafting the Lecompton Constitution, the Free-Staters were electing a new Governor and members of a new Free-State legislature. The new legislature was quickly called into special session and scheduled a new election on the Lecompton Constitutions. During the new election, voters rejected the pro-slavery document and authorized yet another Constitutional Convention. Despite the results of the new election, President James Buchanan submitted the Lecompton Constitution to Congress with the recommendation that Kansas be admitted to the Union as a slave state. In his second annual address to Congress, President Buchanan stated:

> *"The Supreme Court of the United States had previously decided that all American citizens have an equal right to take into the Territories whatever is held as property under the laws of any of the States, and to hold such property there under the guardianship of the Federal Constitution so long as the Territorial condition shall remain. This is now a well-established position, and the proceedings of the last session were alone wanting to give it practical effect. The principle has been recognized in some form or other by an almost unanimous vote of both Houses of Congress that a Territory has a right to come into the Union either as a free or a slave State, according to the will of a majority of its people. The just equality of all the States has thus been vindicated and a fruitful source of dangerous dissension among them has been removed."* [47]

Unfortunately, the dangerous dissension among the States, referred to by President Buchanan, had not been removed. The entire nation was in an uproar. The Free-Staters convention held at Leavenworth, Kansas, in 1858, produced yet a third proposed Constitution. It was the first and only proposal which did not include the word "White." In addition, it was the first proposal which did not exclude "Negroes and Mulattoes," from Kansas but like previous proposals, it was clearly a partisan document. Because of the heated controversy both the Lecompton Constitution and the Leavenworth Constitution were soundly rejected by the U. S. Congress on August 2, 1858.

In 1859, the Free State factions were firmly in control of Kansas politics. A fourth and final Constitutional Convention was held in the town of Wyandotte, Kansas in July. While the Wyandotte Constitution did not exclude *"Negroes and Mulattoes,"* the word *"White"* was a significant part of the document. The document was easily approved by voters in October and was presented to the President and

Congress of the United States with a request for the admission of Kansas to the Union as a "*Free State.*" A bill for the admission of Kansas to the Union stalled in the Senate. It was not until the resignation of Senators from seven seceding States that Kansas became a State on January 29, 1861.

The contention that "*Bleeding Kansas*" was a struggle between the forces of good and evil is yet another incredible myth in American history. The seven years of violent conflict was pure evil on all sides. There was no struggle for the rights and equality of men as expressed in the Declaration of Independence. Interests were focused on the rights and the superiority of the white race. Even those who rejected the expansion of slavery into the Kansas Territory sought to exclude the black race entirely. They only acknowledged the rights of those Native Americans who conducted themselves in the same manner as white men. Hatred, greed, and the lust for power set the stage for violent fanatics and murderers such John Brown to be viewed as heroes.

"The Tragic Prelude" Painting by John Steuart Curry

While the leaders of all factions proclaimed the righteousness of their cause amidst a narcissistic delusion of grandeur, nothing about "*Bleeding Kansas*" demonstrated heroism, the perpetuation of American principles or even human compassion. Nothing about the tragic events which occurred in the 1850s can be justified by any persuasion of history. It was nothing more than a senseless bloody battle leading the nation into an even bloodier war.

117

Rise of the Republican Party

The government, the social structure and the very character of the United States of America has been established and defined by many political ideologies. Amidst the rise and fall of numerous political parties, the Republican Party of 1854, was unique in almost all respects. It is important to note that the Republican Party of the 19th Century is not same as today's Republican Party. The "*Grand Old Party*" or the "*Party of Lincoln*," as it has been called was the liberal party of the 19th Century. Its "*tax and spend*" policies better resembled the modern day Democratic Party. It was also a party that promoted the re-distribution of wealth. That wealth was often re-distributed into the pockets of America's most affluent financiers and businessmen.

Much of what has been written about the Republican Party is associated with bringing an end to slavery. While it easily contended that the passage of the 13th Amendment was due to the efforts of Radical Republicans, it is important to realize that bringing an end to slavery was not the original goal of the Party. The Republican Party platform of 1860 defended slavery in those States where it existed by stating:

> "*The rights of the states, and especially the right of each state to order and control its own domestic institutions according to its own judgment exclusively, is essential to that balance of powers on which the perfection and endurance of our political fabric depend.*" [48]

Incoming President Abraham Lincoln repeated those words during his inaugural address on March 4, 1861. He confirmed his personal commitment to the protection of slavery by stating:

> "*I now reiterate these sentiments, and in doing so I only press upon the public attention the most conclusive evidence of which the case is susceptible that the property, peace, and security of no section are to be in any wise endangered by the now incoming Administration.*"

Sparked by the passage of the Kansas-Nebraska act, the Republican Party was founded during the administration of Democratic President Franklin Pierce. It was Pierce who polarized the nation by promoting the Kansas-Nebraska Act and signing it into law on May 30, 1854.

Much like the first term of former President Andrew Jackson, Pierce entered the Presidency engulfed by a shroud of grief. Just weeks after his election, Pierce, his wife Jane and their 11-year old son, Benjamin, were involved in a train derailment near Andover, Massachusetts. The couple's young son *"Benny"* was crushed to death during the crash. The discovery of the mangled body of their son drove both Franklin and his wife Jane into years of deep depression. It is likely Franklin Pierce's calloused views toward sectional differences were a result of his depression. Pierce made it clear that he had neither the inclination nor the patience to address the issues surrounding the Kansas-Nebraska Act. In his inaugural address, Pierce unsympathetically proclaimed that:

> *"The policy of my Administration will not be controlled by any timid forebodings of evil from expansion."* [49]

Pierce also warned of the dangers of the Federalist views promoting the increase of a strong central government and proclaimed that his administration would restrict those powers whenever and wherever possible, stating:

> *"The dangers of a concentration of all power in the general government of a confederacy so vast as ours are too obvious to be disregarded. You have a right, therefore, to expect your agents in every department to regard strictly the limits imposed upon them by the Constitution of the United States."*

The Pierce administration bore witness to sweeping changes in American politics. Those changes included the collapse of the Whig Party, the rise of the anti-immigrant Know-Nothing Party and a North-South sectional divide in the Democratic Party. The period also included the birth of the Republican Party.

Founding members of the Republican Party came from many political persuasions but most were former members of the anti-slavery factions of the Whig Party, known as *"Conscience Whigs."* Other

Republicans came from the Democratic Party faction known as *"Free Soilers."* An even smaller number came from the *"Know-Nothing Party."*

Use of the term *"anti-slavery"* in reference to America's political parties in the 1850s is ambiguous and extremely misleading. While virtually all parties during that period had members with abolitionist views, no party prior to the War Between the States adopted abolitionism as a part of their political platforms. Most Republicans restricted their slavery objections to the expansion of slavery into the western territories. Motives for those objections extended far beyond the rationale of morality or social justice. The words of Republican leaders clearly indicated that in addition to excluding slavery from the territories; they would exclude free blacks as well. David Wilmot, chairman of the committee which drafted the first Republican Party platform promised to defend the rights of white men and reserve the new territories to the inherent rights of white laborers. Abraham Lincoln expressed his desire to keep blacks separated from areas where blacks and whites were not already together. His desire for racial purity in the territories is demonstrated by the statement:

> *"I am still in favor of our new Territories being in such a condition that white men may find a home-may find some spot where they can better their condition-where they can settle upon new soil and better their condition in life. I am in favor of this not merely for our own people who are born amongst us, but as an outlet for free white people every where."* [50]

As the Presidential Election of 1856 approached, the Democratic Party was still the dominant party in both the North and the South. Democrats easily controlled the Senate and could only be blocked in the House of Representatives by a coalition of the Know-Nothing Party and the Opposition Party. Rather than the Republican Party, it was the Know-Nothing Party which was gaining the most momentum in 1856. The Know-Nothing Party, which later became the American Party, was attracting many of the former Whigs by campaigning against Immigration.

The Republican's first national platform suggests that the Party had not fully developed its long range plans. The first two of its nine resolutions in the 1856 platform addressed the basic principles of the Party. A third resolution suggests that sovereignty in regard to the territories was vested in the powers of the U. S. Congress. This resolution also opened the door for resolving the issue of Mormon control in the Utah territory by stating:

> *"It is both the right and the imperative duty of Congress to prohibit in the Territories those twin relics of barbarism-- Polygamy, and Slavery."*

Both the fourth and fifth resolutions were dedicated to issues directly related to the Kansas Territory. Resolution six condemned the controversial Ostend Manifesto; a document which suggested that it would be in the best interest of the nation and the world, for the United States to take Cuba by military force if Spain refused to sell the island.

Resolutions seven and eight revealed two key elements to the Republican plan. Both would be repeated in the Republican Party platform of 1860 and were essential in achieving the Party's ultimate goals. Resolution seven stated that:

> *"A railroad to the Pacific Ocean by the most central and practicable route is imperatively demanded by the interests of the whole country, and that the Federal Government ought to render immediate and efficient aid in its construction, and as an auxiliary thereto, to the immediate construction of an emigrant road on the line of the railroad."*

The sentence was carefully crafted to include the word *"central."* All political factions at that time favored the construction of a trans-continental railroad but Southerners demanded that the railroad be built along an established route which traversed several Southern States. The Republican plan required that the railroad be routed across the thousands of square miles of government owned lands in the new territories. In reality, the route was more northern than central and because Chicago would be a major hub, Northern Democrats favored the plan as well.

121

Resolution eight, which demanded improvements of rivers and harbors, also supported Northern interests. Northern States had established railroads, steamship lines and ocean going fleets which would provide transportation and supplies from the East to the West Coast. The ninth resolution was an invitation to members of other parties to join in the Republican cause.

Republican Party members contended that "*Popular Sovereignty,*" as included in the Kansas-Nebraska Act was a blatant violation of the terms that were established by the Missouri Compromise. Ironically, the Missouri Compromise allowed the extension of slavery into the western territories south of the 36°30' parallel. This contradiction is indicative of the sometimes irrational views of the Party.

Republicans held their first national convention at Musical Fund Hall in Philadelphia, Pennsylvania in June of 1856. They chose former California Senator John C. Frémont over U. S. Supreme Court Associate Justice John McLean as their nominee for President. The choice proved to be a disaster for the Party. During the election, Frémont won less than one-third of the popular vote and received only 114 of the 296 electoral votes.

In the six year period preceding the War Between the States the Republican Party continued to grow in size and political influence. The strength of the Party was vested in three very influential groups. They could best be described as "communicators," "legislators," and "financiers." The first group, the "communicators," was composed of many of America's leading editors, publishers and authors. This group was the voice of the Party. With their popular and widely distributed publications, they were able to support the election of Republican candidates and influence the sentiments of the nation. Republican Horace Greeley's "*New-York Tribune*" reached more than 200,000 readers. Gamaliel Bailey's publication, "*The National Era*" included the patriotic and abolitionist works of John Greenleaf Whittier and was the first to publish Harriet Beecher Stowe's popular novel, "*Uncle Tom's Cabin.*" Some of the articles which were published in the National Era were so biased and inflammatory that an angry mob held Bailey and his staff hostage for three days inside their Washington D. C. office. Regardless of the validity of the articles and writings circulated by this group, they had the power to sway the sentiments of thousands of Americans in a direction that contributed to the growth and further success of the Republican Party. No one was more aware of, or more capable of using the powers of public sentiments than a Republican hopeful named Abraham Lincoln. In his first public debate with Senator Stephen Douglas, Lincoln stated:

> *"Public sentiment is everything. With public sentiment, nothing can fail; without it nothing can succeed. Consequently he who moulds public sentiment, goes deeper than he who enacts statutes or pronounces decisions. He makes statutes and decisions possible or impossible to be executed."* [51]

The second group, the "legislators," was made up of both current and former Congressmen who demonstrated the ability to influence the actions of Congress. Members of the group were divided between moderate and liberal views. Moderates tended to focus on the goals of the Party; particularly those goals which related to the western territories. Liberals tended to focus on conflicts relating to section interests. An even smaller faction focused their attention on issues relating to slavery. Because the abolitionist views of these men were so different from the rest of the party, they were given the label *"Radical Republicans."*

The third and most powerful of the three groups, the "financiers," was comprised of the wealthy merchants and industrialists of the North who provided funding for the Republican Party. Some of these men were heirs to family fortunes which were often times derived from the African Slave Trade or the opium trade. Others, such as Cornelius Vanderbilt had generated tremendous wealth from providing transportation and supplies to the west. Many more established or expanded their financial empires by profiteering during the War Between the States. Often known for their philanthropy, they seldom expressed their political views publicly. Much like wealthy American's today, they were aware that the political arena was often a financial liability and held to the popular philosophy that it was much more profitable to buy a politician than to become one. Even though they operated behind the scenes, this elite group of wealthy Republicans dictated many of the Party's policies and controlled virtually ever Republican political candidate. Like members of the other groups, some of the financiers were opposed to slavery but they were more focused on the wealth potential in the West. Many members of this elite group were truly concerned with preserving the Union but regardless of their motives each of these men had their own designs for the future of the Western Territories. During the War Between the States, they were responsible for founding the powerful secret society known as the "*Union League*." It was the power and wealth of the League that rescued the Republican Party and the political career of Abraham Lincoln during the election of 1864.

With all three of these groups combined, the Republican Party had the loudest public voice, a tremendous influence on the acts of Congress and was backed by incredible wealth. By 1860, it could easily be contended that they had created the "*Perfect Storm*." By the end of the War Between the States, the Republican Party could better be described as a "*Three-Headed Monster*."

Chapter 4
War and Deceit

1860 – 1865

The five year period between the election of President Abraham Lincoln in November of 1860 and the ratification of the Thirteenth Amendment to the U. S. Constitution in December of 1865, is the most researched and most written about period in American history. Countless books have been published about the so called "*Lost Cause*" of the Confederacy but only a relatively small number of these books have addressed the "*Northern Cause*," particularly the motives of the Republican Party.

A popular consensus among Americans today is that in 1861, the United States military forces engaged in a noble war to abolish slavery. Even though this theory is taught in our public schools and major universities, there are many flaws in that theory. One flaw which is often overlooked is that if the war was truly waged to abolish slavery, the act would amount to changing the Constitution and the laws of the United States at the point of a gun. In essence, the act would be a "*coup d'état*" or military overthrow of the government. As proven by the events of 1865, the only act that could or ever did end slavery was an amendment to the United States Constitution. Another imperfection of the theory is demonstrated by the struggles in Congress to pass such an amendment, even with the absence of most Southern members of Congress. Even more sorrowful is that with few exceptions, the words and deeds of America's leaders clearly indicated that their primary interests were focused on the rights and prosperity of the white race. Undoubtedly, there were some leaders who expressed concerns about racial injustice but they were clearly a minority within all political parties. Despite the insistence of contemporary scholars that the primary cause of the War Between the States was slavery, there is overwhelming evidence to the contrary. On April 15, 1861, President Abraham Lincoln issued a proclamation calling forth "*the militia of the several States of the Union, to the aggregate number of seventy-five thousand.*" While represented as an act to put down a rebellion, it was essentially a declaration of war. It is important to realize the position of the Federal government and the condition of the nation at that time.

The Republican Party controlled both the executive and legislative branches of government. Both the Republican Party and the President defended slavery as *"the right of each state to order and control its own domestic institutions according to its own judgment exclusively, is essential to that balance of powers on which the perfection and endurance of our political fabric depends."* The only law concerning slavery which had been passed by Congress was one that would make slavery perpetual and irrevocable in the States where it existed. Just six weeks earlier, the President proclaimed to the nation that he had no purpose or inclination to interfere with slavery in the States where it existed.

There are no historical facts that can conclude that the United States government allowed for military action to be taken against the Southern States for the purpose of ending slavery. Before, during and long after the War Between the States, efforts were made to exclude blacks, eradicate Native American tribes and diminish Mormon control of the Utah Territory. Throughout the 19th Century, the Republican Party was at the forefront of these efforts.

It is important to remember that the Republican Party did not represent the interests of the entire nation. It was a sectional party which only concerned itself with the interests of a select group in the North. Even in the North, they were opposed prominent Democratic leaders such as Stephen Douglas. The Republican Party completely dominated the United States Congress from 1861 to 1875. During this period, it was able to pass new laws without significant resistance. In addition to writing laws which forever changed the nation, they were able to perpetuate their version of the causes and the necessity of the War Between the States.

An examination of the Republican Party platform of 1860 reveals that they had a solid plan for the future of the nation. Their plan was clearly focused on the expansion and control of the Western Territories. The platform also indicated that although the party was bitterly opposed to the expansion of slavery into the western territories, it was willing to support and able to contend with slavery in the States where it existed. In an obvious attempt to re-assure the

Southern States that the Party supported their rights to control their own domestic institutions, the 1860 platform denounced the invasion of any State by a military force. Few Republicans believed that the Southern States would make good on their threat of secession; that proved to be a serious error in judgment.

As the Southern States began to secede, the Republican Party was forced to reverse its position on the use of military force. They defended their new position by contending that the use of force was for the sole purpose of preserving the Union. Nothing within the 1860 Republican Party platform suggested that they would attempt to interfere with slavery in the States where it existed.

In contrast, a comparison of the 1864 Republican Party platform to the platform of 1860 reveals a radical difference in sentiment. There is little doubt that a fear of losing in the 1864 election influenced those sentiments. During that four year period, the master plan of the Party never changed. By the end of 1863, virtually every goal of the Party had been achieved. The only task that they had failed to complete was to "*forever silence*" those who opposed them. Although the goals of the party did not change, it is obvious that their mission statement did. The question that arises is: when and why did the story change?

The Republican Plan

In order to fully understand the overall plan developed by the leaders of the Republican Party, you have to understand their history and the deep rooted passions which motivated them. It began with their ancestor's strong Puritan beliefs; a belief in both racial and religious purity. After the new nation was born, they were driven by the desire for a powerful central government that would perpetuate their views. As the Party evolved from Federalist, to Whig and finally to Republican ideologies, they held firm to those desires. They rejected any and all opposing views of government. Demanding that the former "*league of friendship*" among States, be replaced with a more perfect form of Union, they attempted to deny a bill of rights to the American people. Being over-shadowed by almost fifty years of Democratic rule, especially the reign of the "*Virginia Dynasty*," their passions turned to hatred; a hatred which was always facing southward. Like their non-reformist forefathers, they believed that the nation as it existed had become corrupt and the only salvation would be to preserve the purity of Western Territories.

The plan developed by the Republican Party during the years leading up to the 1860 Presidential Election had some very simple goals but actions required to accomplish those goals were numerous and complex. Republican motives could easily be described as *"Manifest Destiny"* on steroids. Everything was focused on the Western Territories of the United States.

Believing that the vast lands in the West could be kept racially and religiously pure, they planned to establish a *"White Christian Dynasty."* Their views of the West also included visions of great wealth. The plan was driven by unbounded greed and a lust for power. It required complete control of all land and government in the territories. Execution of the plan depended on the completion of a trans-continental railroad supported by major improvements to existing harbors and along navigable rivers. They needed complete Republican control of the U. S. Congress. A key element in gaining that control involved a system of providing public lands to promote immigration which would establish a dedicated constituency for the Party. Control of the land would insure that the Party could filter out unwanted races and religions. Most importantly, a full execution of the Republican plan would require increased taxes and control of the nations banking system. Following the 1860 election, all of the Republican goals seemed to be well within their reach. They had a strong public voice, their President in office, a plurality in the House of Representatives and incredible wealth among their members. The greatest obstacle to their plan was the power of the Southern States. If they stayed in the Union, the Southern States would be formidable opponents in Congress. If they seceded, they would take with them the majority of the Federal Government's income which at the time was derived from protective tariffs. Either way, it was imperative that the Republicans not only *"Rebuke"* them but *"Forever Silence"* them.

Evidence of the Republican Party's plan for a *"White Christian Dynasty"* can be found in the words of Republican leaders, laws introduced and passed by a Republican controlled Congress and within the Party's platform.

Like most political parties of the mid-nineteenth century, many Republican leaders touted the superiority of the *"White Race."* This sentiment was frequently expressed by Abraham Lincoln. While he most often directed his comments toward the inferiority of Blacks, he sometimes included demeaning remarks about Native Americans and even Mexicans. In several lectures concerning discoveries and inventions, Lincoln asked:

> *"Why did Yankees, almost instantly, discover gold in California, which had been trodden upon, and over-looked by Indians and Mexican greasers, for centuries?"* [52]

Since it is known that a Mexican cattleman named Francisco Lopez found gold in California is 1842, Lincoln's comment was lacking in accuracy but it is clear that his use of the term *"greaser"* was meant to place the Mexican race in a lower class than whites.

In his debates with Stephen Douglas, Lincoln made numerous comments concerning the superiority of the white race. During his fourth debate Lincoln stated:

> *"I am not, nor ever have been, in favor of bringing about in any way the social and political equality of the white and black races, that I am not nor ever have been in favor of making voters or jurors of negroes, nor of qualifying them to hold office, nor to intermarry with white people; and I will say in addition to this that there is a physical difference between the white and black races which I believe will forever forbid the two races living together on terms of social and political equality. And inasmuch as they cannot so live, while they do remain together there must be the position of superior and inferior and I as much as any other man am in favor of having the superior position assigned to the white race."* [53]

There is little doubt that for most, if not all of Abraham Lincolns' life, he was opposed to slavery but never saw blacks as his equal. He dedicated much of his political career to the separation of the white and black races. As President, he appointed Methodist minister James Mitchell as the first and only U. S. Commissioner on Negro Colonization. In August of 1862, Mitchell arranged for five free black ministers to meet with Lincoln. During the meeting Lincoln stated:

"You and we are different races. We have between us a broader difference than exists between almost any other two races. Whether it is right or wrong I need not discuss, but this physical difference is a great disadvantage to us both, as I think your race suffers very greatly, many of them, by living among us, while ours suffers from your presence." [54]

Lincoln's continued efforts to remove Blacks by colonization in other parts of the world, suggests that he truly believed this goal could be accomplished. In a debate with Senator Stephen Douglas, he stated:

"I have said that the separation of the races is the only perfect preventive of amalgamation. I have no right to say all the members of the Republican Party are in favor of this nor to say that as a party they favor it. There is nothing in their platform directly on the subject. But I can say, a very large portion of its members are for it, and that the chief plank in their platform - opposition to the spread of slavery - is most favorable to that separation. Such separation, if ever effect at all, must be effected by colonization; and no political party, as such, is now doing anything directly for colonization. Party operations, at present, only favor or retard colonization incidentally. The enterprise is a difficult one; but where there is a will there is a way; and what colonization needs most is a hearty will. Will springs from the two elements of moral sense and self-interest. Let us be brought to believe it is morally right, and, at the same time, favorable to, or, at least, not against, our interest, to transfer the African to his native clime, and we shall find a way to do it, however great the task may be."

His statement clearly indicates that he was opposed to Blacks living in a White society. It also indicates that Lincoln believed that his party's platform only opposed the expansion of slavery and not the existence of it.

When it came to Lincoln's personal view of Blacks in the Western Territories, he was even less subtle. In one of his earliest speeches condemning the Kansas-Nebraska Act, Lincoln contended that Thomas Jefferson had intended that the Western Territories be reserved for the benefit of Whites only. Lincoln stated:

"It is now what Jefferson foresaw and intended – the happy home of teeming millions of free, white, prosperous people and no slave amongst them." [(55)]

Further evidence of the opposition to Blacks in the Territories was revealed during Lincoln's last debate with Stephen Douglas during which he stated:

"I am still in favor of our new Territories being in such a condition that white men may find a home; may find some spot where they can better their condition; where they can settle upon new soil and better their condition in life. I am in favor of this not merely for our own people who are born amongst us, but as an outlet for free white people every where." [(56)]

Lincoln was only one of many Republicans who spoke of a *"White"* territory. David Wilmot, prominent leader of the Free-Soil faction, clearly expressed that he and his Free-Soil followers believed that the territories should be reserved for people of their own race. In regard to slavery, the very existence of the black race in the territories was more of a concern than the evils or the injustice of slavery.

The greatest threat to racial purity in the territories was the expansion of slavery. As the Republican Party came to power in 1860, every Free State west of the Appalachian Mountains had laws which either discouraged or prevented free blacks from immigrating to their State. The State of Indiana and President Lincoln's State of Illinois had some of the strictest immigration laws. Black laws in Michigan, Minnesota and Wisconsin were less prevalent and less restrictive than those of other Free States. In States where blacks were not totally excluded, it was common for State Law to require blacks to post a bond to guarantee their good behavior. Black exclusion laws were passed in the Oregon Territory long before the Republicans arrived on the scene. Because of the 1849 gold rush, California was the prize of the west but it was very nearly admitted into the Union, at least in part, as a Slave State. California legislators attempted to include a clause in their State Constitution which would prevent Free Blacks from immigrating to the State. Although the clause was stricken from the final draft of the Constitution, the State was able to draft laws which would discourage blacks from entering California. Lawmakers were equally hostile toward most other non-white races.

Alexis de Tocqueville was a French diplomat, political scientist, and historian. He was best known for his publication; "Democracy in America." His writings were based on his travels in America during the 1830s and are considered to be classic works of sociology and political science. Tocqueville noted that:

> "race prejudice seems stronger in those states that have abolished slavery than in those where it still exists, and nowhere is it more intolerant than in those states where slavery was never known."

Another of Tocqueville's observations reflects on the principles which motivated members of the Republican Party. Many of them held tight to the Puritan beliefs of their ancestors. Puritans traveled to the new world because they believed that the governments and religions of Europe were corrupt and they saw a chance to start over in a land that could be religiously and even racially pure. In his writings Tocqueville states:

> "I think I can see the whole destiny of America contained in the first Puritan who landed on those shores."

All of America's original thirteen colonies were established on the principles of Christianity. Colonial laws and governances were strictly tied to Christian beliefs. In most Colonies a person could be put to death for denying that Jesus Christ was the son of God. Westward expansion into the new territories brought with it a dream of religious cleansing. Many Republicans, along with other Americans believed that John Winthrop's dream of "A City upon a Hill" had been tainted and envisioned that the American West could become a "Model of Christian Charity."

Republicans were very serious about racial purity in the West. Excluding Jews from the West, presented few problems. Anti-Semitism in America had been present since the days of the earliest settlements. With the exception of a handful of small Jewish Congregations in California, the Jewish faith was non-existent in the Western Territories for most of the 19th Century.

The issue of whether or not to allow Catholics to immigrate to the Western Territories was more contentious. Presbyterian minister Lyman Beecher and several of his well known children were prominent members of the Republican Party. In addition to being a vocal opponent to the expansion of slavery, Beecher believed that the shinning promise of America's future would be fulfilled in the West. In his book "*A Plea for the West*," Beecher expounded on the importance of westward expansion but warned that foreign immigration and Catholicism was a threat to society. Many of the Republican Party members shared the same sentiments as Lyman Beecher but foreign immigration was a big part of the Republican plan. A large number of foreign immigrants were German or Irish Catholics. There was an obvious concern that excluding Catholics from the Territories might discourage immigration. But Anti-Catholic and Anti-immigrant sentiments were strong during the years leading up to the War Between the States. These sentiments were responsible for bringing the Know-Nothing or American Party into power during the mid-1850s. There is little doubt that the Republican Party made subtle attempts to limit Catholic immigration to the West but it was not a part of their published platform.

The Mormon Church offered a duel threat to the Republican plan. Not only did they practice what many believed to be a bogus religion but they were well organized and a menacing presence in the West. A request by Church leaders for admitting the State of Deseret to the Union in 1849 became a serious issue. The proposed State would encompass virtually all U. S. Lands between the Rocky Mountains and the Sierra Nevada Range. If statehood had been granted it would be nearly impossible to travel from the eastern United States to California without passing through Deseret. Instead of allowing statehood, the United States Congress established the Utah Territory as a part of the Compromise of 1850; an area which included all of present day Nevada and Utah plus portions of Colorado and Wyoming. Mormon control of the Utah Territory posed a huge problem for Republicans. In addition to controlling thousands of square miles of land that Republicans sought to control, the Mormons were blocking the path chosen by Republicans for the trans-continental railroad. The first attempt by the Republican Party to remove the Mormons from control of the Utah Territory came in 1856. Adopted at convention on June 18, 1856, the 3rd resolution of the Republican Party Platform stated:

"That the Constitution confers upon Congress sovereign powers over the Territories of the United States for their government; and that in the exercise of this power, it is both the right and the imperative duty of Congress to prohibit in the Territories those twin relics of barbarism - Polygamy, and Slavery."

Republicans believed that by tying the Mormon belief in polygamy to the expansion of slavery, the forces of both the public's sentiments and the alleged duties of Congress would drive the Mormons out of Utah. They also believed that they would have the upper hand when their Party nominee, John C. Frémont was elected President in November. They were proven wrong on both counts.

After being pressured for several months by members of the Republican Party, newly elected President James Buchanan decided to replace Utah Governor Brigham Young with Alfred Cumming. Young's refusal to step down as Governor led to an armed confrontation between Mormons and the U. S. Army which lasted well into 1858. After the hostilities ended, Brigham Young stepped down as Governor but Mormons maintained control over much of the land.

The discovery of silver in what is present day Nevada led a small population of non-mormons to the area beginning in 1859. A similar incident had occurred with the discovery of gold in the Pike's Peak region of the Kansas Territory in 1858. As Senators and Representatives began to drop out of Congress due to the secession of Southern States, the Republicans made their move. Under a new Wyandotte Constitution, Kansas was hurriedly admitted to the Union as a Free State. In a four day period from February 28 to March 3, 1861, the Republican controlled Congress had seized more than half of the Utah Territory and created four new territories and effectively surrounding Utah on three sides. Congressional acts in 1862, 1863, 1866 and 1868 reduced the size of the Utah Territory even further. Despite the distractions of a bloody war, the United States Congress passed the Morrill Anti-Bigamy Act on July 8, 1862. Introduced by Republican Representative Justin Smith Morrill, the act banned bigamy in all U. S. Territories and limited property ownership by non-profit organizations in any territory to $50,000. In a private arrangement, Abraham Lincoln suggested that he might allow the Mormons to ignore the act provided that they did not aide the Confederate States. Although the Mormon Church continued their opposition to the Republican controlled government, the last spike in the Trans-Continental Railroad was driven near Promontory Summit in the Utah Territory on May 10, 1869. Even as the Republican Plan began to fall apart, persecution of the Mormon Church did not end. In 1887, an act by the U. S. Congress dis-incorporated the Mormon Church, seized its assets and prohibited the use of sectarian books in Utah schools.

The financial plan of the Republican Party was set into motion long before the 1860 election. It greatly depended on a large increase of tariffs. In 1857, a plan to substantially increase tariffs was proposed by Republican House Representative Justin Smith Morrill and American (Know-Nothing) Party Representative Henry Winter Davis. Both men were members of the powerful House Ways and Means Committee. Because the Committee was controlled by Democrats, the proposal was blocked. After the election of 1860, Davis joined the Republican Party and continued to support the tariff. On February 1, 1860, Republican William Pennington became Speaker of the House and appointed a Republican majority to the House Ways and Means Committee with John Sherman as Chairman. When Ohio Senator Salmon P. Chase resigned to become Secretary of the Treasury, Sherman was elected to fill his seat and was immediately appointed to the Senate Finance Committee chaired by Republican William P. Fessenden. With the absence of Congressmen from Southern States, Republicans were finally able to pass their long awaited Morrill Tariff on March 2, 1861. The fact that they adopted a tariff which depended largely on proceeds from Southern ports and the speed in which they acted, suggests that Republicans did not believe Congressmen from the Southern States would be absent for long. It also suggests that Party leaders neither planned nor anticipated a war with the Southern States.

Early in 1861, it became evident that the seven Southern States which seceded prior to Lincoln's inauguration, had no intentions of returning to the Union. It was a situation that Republicans could not afford to accept. According to the Republican Plan, almost 95% of Federal revenues would be derived from tariffs. Because the tariffs were designed to protect Northern interest, most of the revenue would be generated by Southern Ports. All of the seven States which had already seceded had major seaports; primarily Charleston, Mobile and New Orleans. The City of New Orleans blocked all U. S. trade on the Mississippi River. The State of Texas controlled the major overland mail and stage route to the West Coast. Republicans had control of the money but there was little coming in. If the financial plan was going to succeed, the Southern States would have to be brought back into the Union. Planned or not, the Republicans decided to take military action. As a result, they were not only faced within financing their plan for the West but now had to finance a war. A series of revenue acts were passed in 1861, 1862 and 1864 which included real estate taxes, excise taxes and America's first income tax. None of these efforts were sufficient to finance the war. In reality, it was the money men of the Republican Party which financed the Union war effort; and it came at a high price. Some of these men already controlled much of the nation's wealth. Others used profits from the war to build financial empires that are unmatched in American history. The list of names includes Armour, Carnegie, Chase, Cooke, DuPont, Forbes, Morgan, Rockefeller, and Vanderbilt. Funding the war changed the financial structure of the nation forever. It introduced investment banking and made New York City, the financial capitol of the world. More infamously, it was this group of wealthy financiers and industrialists who forced the continuation of the War Between the States.

Overcoming the obstacle of war was a definite challenge for the Republican Party but it never slowed their plan for a Western Dynasty. Within three weeks of his inauguration, President Lincoln appointed Republican Governors in the newly created Territories of Colorado and Dakota and appointed new Governors in the Nebraska and Utah Territories. Not only had they established the path for the trans-continental railroad but they had created a runaway train.

The first Homestead Act was signed into law by Abraham Lincoln on May 20, 1862. It was a major step in the plan to control the land and the culture of the Western Territories. The Act which was proposed in the 1860 Republican Party platform opened up millions of acres of public lands to immigrants from both the United States and foreign countries. Section one of the Act set the eligibility requirements as:

> "*any person who is the head of a family, or who has arrived at the age of twenty-one years, and is a citizen of the United States, or who shall have filed his declaration of intention to become such, as required by the naturalization laws of the United States, and who has never borne arms against the United States Government or given aid and comfort to its enemies.*"

Applicants could buy 160 acres of land for $1.25 per acre. It was open to both males and females provided they were the head of a family. Because they were required to be a U. S. Citizen or were qualified under the U. S. Naturalization Laws, Blacks and Native Americans were excluded. In addition, persons who gave support to the Confederate States were excluded.

The plan for populating the Western Territories was based on the concept of the *"yeoman farmer"* which essentially created a social class with limited potential. By limiting the amount of land that one family could own, there was little chance that the settlers could gain substantial wealth or reach a high level of social or political prominence. Republicans favored foreign immigration because many immigrants during that era were uneducated and spoke little if any English, making it harder for them to have any influence on society or politics. Republicans also believed that the "yeoman farmer" culture would owe its allegiance to the Party.

On July 1, 1862, the first Pacific Railroad Act was signed into law by Abraham Lincoln. The long title of the Act read: *"An Act to aid in the construction of a railroad and telegraph line from the Missouri River to the Pacific Ocean, and to secure to the government the use of the same for postal, military, and other purposes."* It was the first act by the United States government where grants were made directly to corporations. Previous grants were made to States for the benefit of corporations. The price paid by American citizens was incredible. The amount of land and money that wound up in the hands of the Republican elite was almost unimaginable.

Cornelius Vanderbilt was likely the chief beneficiary of the Republican Plan. By 1860, Vanderbilt was already a wealthy man. He dominated the transportation industry in the United States owning many of the nation's inland steamships, railroads and ocean going vessels which furnished transportation, supplies and mail to the west coast of America. It would be his transportation network which would benefit most from the trans-continental railroad. Vanderbilt is considered by most to be the second wealthiest man in United States history, falling slightly behind the wealth of fellow Republican John Davidson Rockefeller. Although Rockefeller's empire was established by the oil industry, it was the profits which he earned during the War Between the States that provided his investment capital.

The trans-continental railroad created millionaires in the West as well. A group known as the "*Big Four*," composed of Leland Stanford, Collis Potter Huntington, Mark Hopkins, and Charles Crocker became the wealthiest men in California. Virtually all of their wealth was derived from their ownership of the Central Pacific Railroad.

The Pacific Railroad Act of 1862 was the first of several bills which were passed by the Republican controlled Congress to establish a railroad to the West Coast of the United States. After completion of the railroad, similar bills were passed to expand the network of rail lines which supported the trans-continental railroad. The Act provided for the creation of the Union Pacific Railroad Company in the East and the Central Pacific Railroad Company in the West. In addition to funding these projects, millions of acres of land were granted directly to railroad companies. At one point, U. S. railroad companies had been granted more than 175 million acres of land; an area larger than the state of Texas and representing nearly 10% of the entire land mass of the current 48 contiguous States.

Another vital part of the Republican plan was the removal of Native American tribes from the public lands of the Western Territories. Military expeditions, designed to eradicate Native American tribes were launched prior to the War Between the States and continued long after reconstruction. After suffering an embarrassing defeat at the First Battle of Bull Run, the Union Commander, Major General John Pope was transferred to the Department of the Northwest to deal with the Dakota Wars. After Confederate forces withdrew from the Arizona and New Mexico territories, Union forces in the West turned their attention to the removal of Native Americans. On October 12, 1862, Union General James Henry Carlton, Commander of the New Mexico Territory, sent Colonel Christopher "Kit" Carson deep into the Mescalero Apache territory ordering that:

> "*All Indian men of that tribe are to be killed whenever and wherever you can find them.*" [57]

Carleton launched a similar campaign against the Navajo tribe in 1864. Members of the Navajo tribe were captured and forced to march hundreds of miles from their native lands to a make-shift reservation on the Pecos River. Between 1864 and 1866, more than fifty forced marches left thousands of Navajo dead along the trails. In the fall of 1864, Carson entered the Confederate State of Texas to attack Kiowa and Comanche tribes. Just days later, a camp of Cheyenne and Arapahoe was attacked by Union Cavalry in the Colorado Territory. In an event that became known as the "*Sand Creek Massacre*," as many as 200 men, women and children were slaughtered by Union Troops under the Command of Colonel John Chivington. During a Congressional investigation of the event, witness John S. Smith testified:

> *"I saw the bodies of those lying there cut all to pieces, worse mutilated than any I ever saw before; the women cut all to pieces. With knives; scalped; their brains knocked out; children two or three months old; all ages lying there, from sucking infants up to warriors."* [58]

Colonel Chivington is also credited with having said:

> *"Damn any man who sympathizes with Indians! ... I have come to kill Indians, and believe it is right and honorable to use any means under God's heaven to kill Indians. ... Kill and scalp all, big and little; nits make lice.*

It could be contended that Chivington acted on his own authority and that the massacre was no reflection on the Republican controlled government, the Union Army or its Commander-in-Chief Abraham Lincoln but no action was taken against Chivington by Congress or the United States Army. He was allowed to resign without incident. In addition, the Colorado Territory and its militia were controlled by Territorial Governor John Evans. After founding the Republican Party of Illinois, John Evans was appointed Governor of the Colorado Territory by President Abraham Lincoln on March 31, 1862. It was Governor Evans who appointed John Chivington to Colonel in command of the Colorado Cavalry. In the summer of 1864, Evans issued a proclamation to the citizens of Colorado authorizing them to "*go in pursuit of all hostile Indians and to kill and destroy all enemies of the country.*" It should be remembered that the peak of the hostilities against the tribes in the Colorado Territory occurred during the time President Lincoln was being forced to prove to the Radical Republicans that he could hold a hard line against anyone who opposed the policies of the Party.

As a part of the overall plan of the Republican Party, the eradication of Native American tribes was one of their most successful efforts. By the time the party began to lose its control of the nation in the late 1870s, most tribes had been beaten into submission. A large percentage of their population had been killed, starved or placed on reservations. Despite the dwindling numbers of Native Americans, some hostilities continued. Another atrocity occurred in 1890 when an estimated 150 to 300 Lakota men, women and children were massacred by the 7th United States Cavalry near Wounded Knee Creek in South Dakota. Minor conflicts continued until Congress passed the Indian Citizenship of 1924. Republicans were not alone in their prejudice toward Native Americans. Dislike and often hatred toward the Indians was common place and removing them from their lands was almost customary. The aggressiveness of the Republican Party toward Indian removal far exceeded any political faction that preceded them. Their relentless campaign against Native Americans makes it difficult to believe that they could be concerned about the enslavement of one race while attempting to destroy another.

Another deceitful element of the Republican plan is contained in their resolve to silence those who opposed them. Most members were former Whigs who were dedicated to Federalist beliefs. They were convinced that if any form of sovereignty existed, it was transferred to the Federal government when the States ratified the Constitution. While pledging to defend the rights of the States and condemning the use of military forces against them, their actions were completely opposite. It was Republicans who first suggested that even the contemplation of secession amounted to treason. Despite their assertion that the armed invasion of any state was among the gravest of crimes, it is evident that a plan for war was already in place and they would go to any lengths to achieve the goals of the Party.

By July of 1863, the Republicans had all of their initiatives in place. Kansas had been admitted to the Union as a free state and the re-organized territories of the West were under the control of Republican appointed governors. The Republican controlled Congress had passed Homestead and Railroad Acts as planned. Government bonds and the issuance of "Greenbacks" or paper money were providing millions of dollars to support the Federal government but by late 1863, the fortunes of the Republican Party were changing. The war was lasting much longer than they had anticipated. The cost of the war in both dollars and lives was at an astoundingly high level. Americans in the North were beginning believe that the war was no longer worth the price. By 1864, it appeared that a divided Republican Party was going to fall apart; but they were eventually rescued by a diabolical plan to sway the sentiments of the nation.

Overall, the Republican Plan ended in failure. Persecution of the war created a tremendous debt. The removal of Native American tribes from the Western Territories proved to be a monumental task taking decades to complete. Immigration to the United States was slowed by the war and large numbers of badly needed heads of families were forced into military service. Lands which were intended for a society of "*Yeoman Farmers*" fell into the hands of land speculators and cattlemen. Government assistance of railroads opened the door to corruption and misuse of public funds. In 1867, Republicans held some control of the Western Territories and still had a choke hold on the Federal government. At the opening session of the 40th United States Congress in 1867, Republicans held 45 out of the 53 Senate seats and 140 out of the 188 seats in the House of Representatives. In the following years, the Republican's greatest fear became reality and all hopes for the "*Great Western Dynasty*" began to fade. By 1869, as the "*Golden Spike*" was being driven in the final stretch of the Trans-Continental Railroad, the Democratic Party was gaining strength all across the country. In 1875, Democrats took control of the House of Representatives. By 1881, Republicans managed to re-gain a slight majority in the House but lost control of the Senate and in 1892, Grover Cleveland became the first Democrat to be elected in twenty-five years. With the turn of the 20th Century, the Republican Party was back in the White House but their liberal policies began to turn conservative and the "*Party of Lincoln*" was officially dead.

Although the Republicans never realized their dreams for the West, they had re-shaped the nations future. Banking, investing, taxation, immigration, politics and race relations were forever changed by their initiatives.

1860 Republican Convention

The 2nd Republican Party National Convention was held from May 16 to 18, 1860 in Chicago, Illinois at a convention center known as the Wigwam. At the time of the convention the Democratic Party was still a formidable opponent in the arena of Northern Politics. Republicans were well aware that they could not afford another disastrous loss like the 1856 election.

Delegates at the convention were deeply divided over the many issues that plagued the nation. Party membership was dominated by former Whigs. They were interested in continuing Federalist policies and strengthening the Federal government for the support of Northern interests. A clear leader of the Whig faction was New York Senator William H. Seward. In the mid-1830s, Seward joined the Whig Party in opposition to the policies of President Andrew Jackson. Shortly after being re-elected to Senate in 1855, Seward joined the Republican Party. Having a successful 20 year political career as Governor and Senator from New York, Seward was an early front-runner for the Party's Presidential Nomination in 1860.

A second prominent faction within the Republican Party was comprised of former "*Free-Soilers.*" The Free-Soil Party was a single interest party dedicated to preventing slavery from expanding into the Western Territories. While they were opposed to the expansion of slavery, Free-Soilers carefully avoided the subject of slavery in the states where it existed. Republican leaders of Free-Soil faction were Salmon P. Chase, David Wilmot, John P. Hale and Charles Francis Adams. Their leading candidate for the Presidential nomination was Salmon P. Chase but his opposition to protective tariffs made him unpopular among many of the Party members.

A small number of Republicans were former members of the Know-Nothing Party; a Party which was founded in the 1840s to oppose immigration. The Party was also opposed to Catholicism. Due to the strong "*Nativist*" sentiments in antebellum America, Know-Nothings became a prominent political force. In the mid-1850s, they adopted the name "*American Party*" and were the chief opponents to the Democrats in Congress. Former Know-Nothing members in the Republican Party were led by Edward Bates of Missouri and Simon

Cameron of Pennsylvania. During the convention, Bates was supported by the Party founder and leading publicist, Horace Greeley.

Unlike modern elections, in 1860 there were no primary elections. Candidates were nominated and elected during the convention. Before the first ballot, it was popularly assumed that William H. Seward would be the Party nominee for President but that was not to be. It would take three ballots plus corrections to the third to name a winner.

With one exception, the first ballot turned out like most delegates had expected. Seward received the largest number of votes but two major issues had cost him much of his support. In years past, Seward had made several inflammatory statements in favor of abolishing slavery. Most delegates wanted to avoid the issue of slavery as it existed in the Southern States. A more detrimental issue was his association with New York political boss Thurlow Weed.

As expected, a substantial number of votes were given to the leaders of the internal factions.[59] The Whig favorite, William Seward received 173.5 votes but was well short of the 233 needed to secure the nomination. Free-Soiler favorite, Salmon P. Chase finished third, receiving 49 votes and Know-Nothing favorites Simon Cameron and Edward Bates received 50.5 and 48 votes respectively. The surprise candidate was a railroad lawyer and former Illinois Congressman who finished in second place with 102 votes. Lincoln had gained popularity during his debates with his rival Democratic Senator Stephen Douglas but was not considered to be a strong candidate when the convention opened.

When the second vote was cast both front runners gained the favor of delegates with Seward receiving 184.5 votes and Lincoln receiving 181. After a third vote, the nominee was still undecided with Lincoln in the lead receiving 231.5 votes and Seward dropping to 180. Seeing that Lincoln was so close to securing the nomination, four Ohio delegates, led by Robert K. Enos, changed their vote in favor of Lincoln. Their actions led to a flurry of changes by other delegates bringing the corrected ballot to 349 votes for Lincoln and Seward finishing second with 111.5.

143

The Republican Party Platform in 1860 was much like the one adopted in 1856. After an opening statement proclaiming that the delegates were united in their declarations, Republicans adopted seventeen resolutions.

The first resolution proclaimed the necessity of the Party's causes and the demand for its success. A second resolution expressed the importance of maintaining Federalist principles. Out of all the resolutions of the 1860 platform, the third resolution is the most telling. Contained in the first sentence is an expression that the nation owed its success, wealth, honor and its very existence to the principle of perpetual union and goes on to express the Party's abhorrence to any threat of disunion and continued with praise of Republican congressmen for resisting such threats. In the last sentence of the resolution, Republicans revealed their bitter hatred toward Southerners stating:

> *"We denounce those threats of disunion, in case of a popular overthrow of their ascendency as denying the vital principles of a free government, and as an avowal of contemplated treason, which it is the imperative duty of an indignant people sternly to rebuke and forever silence."*

Republicans were clearly united in their contention that even a threat of disunion was an overthrow of the principles of free government and an act of treason. There is little doubt that the principles they were referring to were those principles of the former Federalist Party. The question which remains is what *"free government"* were they referring to? Was it the same free government that declared its independence from Great Britain? The text of the most sacred document in the free government of the United States began with:

> *"When in the course of human events it becomes necessary for one people to dissolve the political bands which have connected them with another and to assume among the powers of the earth, the separate and equal station to which the Laws of Nature and of Nature's God entitle them"* (United States Declaration of Independence)

144

An acknowledgment of Alexander Hamilton's Federalist theory of "*Implied Powers*" embodied in the principles of Republican Party might suggest that the Declaration of Independence defined disunion as a right of the people under the laws of nature. The questionable statements contained in the third resolution were inconsistent with other resolves within the platform and raised more questions about the motives of the Party. Who were the "*indignant people*" and under what authority did it become their duty to "*rebuke*" those who threatened disunion? Perhaps the greatest question of all is how could they be "*forever silenced*?"

Another inconsistency is found in the fourth resolution which stated:

> "*the right of each state to order and control its own domestic institutions according to its own judgment exclusively, is essential to that balance of powers on which the perfection and endurance of our political fabric depends*"

The Party's fourth resolution proclaimed that it was the exclusive right of each State to control its domestic institutions; including the domestic institution of slavery. The fact that the fourth resolution of the Republican Party platform of 1860 defended slavery in the States where it already existed is undeniable. In addition, the fourth resolution stated:

> "*and we denounce the lawless invasion by armed force of the soil of any state or territory, no matter under what pretext, as among the gravest of crimes.*"

Republicans were careful to using the word "*lawless*" in referring to an armed invasion, which suggests that there might be a lawful way for the Federal government to invade a State.

Resolution five accuses the Democrat administration of abusing its power in defending sectional interests. Focusing primarily on events in Kansas, the resolves seem hypocritical considering that Republicans were just as abusive in its attempts to protect the sectional interest of a select group of Northern States. Their attacks on Democrats continue in the sixth resolution charging that fraud and corruption existed in every department of government which demanded change in the entire administration.

Resolutions seven through ten were focused on the Party's opposition to the expansion of slavery. They expressed the

Republican's views on the intent of the Constitution, the supreme authority of the Federal government over the Territories and rejection of the principles of *"Popular Sovereignty."*

Elements of the Republicans plan for a dynasty in the West are expressed in resolutions eleven through sixteen. Resolution eleven demanded the immediate admission of Kansas to the Union as a Free State. The twelfth resolution expressed the need for increasing protective tariffs and stated that these tariffs were to:

> *"encourage the development of the industrial interests of the whole country."*

Since virtually all of the nation's industry was in the Northeastern States and not the whole country, the statement was inherently false.

The Republican plan for settling and controlling the lands in the Western Territories is revealed in the thirteenth resolution. It was a plan that required limiting the amount of land that could be owned by one family and most of all, it required mass immigration. Promoting immigration was a contentious subject even within the ranks of the Republican Party. Most Americans in 1860 were opposed to immigration. Anti-immigrant sentiments allowed the American Party (Know-Nothings) to out pace the Republican Party in the 1850s. Even though the subject posed a threat to the unity and growth of the Republican Party, it was a vital part of the plan. The short but meticulously written resolution protested the sale of public lands to anyone other than actual settlers. Republicans sought to prevent any individual or group of individuals from creating an empire in the West. The resolution included a rebuttal of the Democratic Party contention that such a homestead policy would create a welfare society in the West. It is likely that the Democrats were correct and it is just as likely that the Republicans knew they were correct. The Republican Party was the first American political party to openly and vigorously encourage foreign immigration. A serious flaw in the Republican Party plan was a belief that they would be able to filter out Non-White races and Non-Christian religions. After the Republican dominated Congress had forced its policies into law, the Party touted that the United States of America was an asylum for the oppressed people of all nations. More than any other resolve of the Republican Party of 1860, their policies on immigration redefined liberal politics in America and still exists today. Immigration was further addressed in the fourteenth resolution stating:

146

"That the Republican Party is opposed to any change in our naturalization laws or any state legislation by which the rights of citizens hitherto accorded to immigrants from foreign lands shall be abridged or impaired"

At the time that the United States Constitution was written, immigration was not a major concern. The U. S. Constitution gave Congress the power to establish a uniform rule of naturalization but did not mention immigration. Early acts of Congress allowed the Federal government to determine what races or classes of immigrants could become citizens. By virtue of the Tenth Amendment, powers not delegated to the Federal government by the Constitution are reserved to the States. For the first one hundred years of the nation's existence, immigration laws were written by the States. The first true federal immigration law was sponsored by Republican Representative Horace F. Page in the 1875. Aimed primarily at Asian immigrants, it was the first federal law which classified certain immigrants as *"Undesirables,"* Soon the U. S. Supreme Court would use Alexander Hamilton's theory of *"Implied Powers"* to rule that since the Constitution gave Congress the power to *"to regulate commerce with foreign nations, and among the several States,"* it implied that the federal government had the exclusive right to regulate immigration.

Resolutions fifteen and sixteen were dedicated improvements which provide a vast transportation network leading to the Western Territories. Republicans demanded that improvements in harbors and rivers were required for national security. The true requirement was for the support of the Trans-Continental Railroad expressed in resolution sixteen, stating that:

"A railroad to the Pacific Ocean is imperatively demanded by the interests of the whole country; that the federal government ought to render immediate and efficient aid in its construction; and that, as preliminary thereto, a daily overland mail should be promptly established."

Demand for the railroad had also been included in the 1856 Republican Party platform. Since the 1860 platform made no demand for *"a railroad to the Pacific Ocean by the most central and practicable route,"* it appears that Republicans were confident that they could force the path of the railroad through the center of the

147

Western Territories and they no longer feared that the railroad might take a different route through the Southern States.

The seventeenth and last resolution of the 1860 Republican Party Platform was merely an invitation to other Americans to support their principles. The wants of the Party were clear and concise. They wanted higher protective tariffs, a homestead law, better harbors and a Trans-Continental Railroad. What they clearly opposed was the expansion of slavery into the West, Mormon control of the Utah Territory and the threat of secession. What they accepted was the continuation of slavery in the States where it already existed.

The 1860 National Election

As the last session of the 35th United States Congress ended on March 3, 1859, the Democratic Party was in control of both houses of Congress, the White House and the United States Supreme Court. One year later, they lost control of the House of Representatives and were beginning to splinter amidst sectional differences. The Democratic National Convention held April 23 through May 3, 1860 adjourned in a deadlock without choosing a Presidential nominee. Many of the Southern delegates walked out in protest. A second convention was held at the Front Street Theater in Baltimore, Maryland on June 18. As the convention opened, there was a bitter debate concerning the re-admission of Southern delegates who had bolted during the South Carolina convention. Amidst the turmoil, many of the Southern delegates once again walked out and Illinois Senator Stephen Douglas was nominated for President. In retaliation, the Southern Delegates reconvened at Maryland Institute Hall and nominated Vice- President John Breckinridge,

It is unlikely that having two prominent Democratic nominees was enough to guarantee a Republican Party victory. The Republican Party was primarily sectional and drew most of its support from the areas where Stephen Douglas was still a dominating political figure. In addition, many Americans had considered Vice-President John Breckinridge to be the heir apparent to the office of President. It was conceivable that either or both of the candidates were capable of drawing more votes than Abraham Lincoln but the final vote tally held surprises for everyone.

Perhaps the biggest surprise was the strength of the fourth party candidate John Bell. The first political party to hold a convention and adopt a platform in 1860 was the Constitutional Union Party. The majority of its members were former members of the Whig and Know-Nothing Parties. After their former parties fell apart, they were unwilling to adopt the policies of the Democrats or the Republicans. They were led by a group of Congressmen who were conservative, pro-union and pro-compromise. The Party was organized in December of 1859 through the efforts of U. S. Senator John J. Crittenden of Kentucky. The Constitutional Union Party held its National Convention from May 9 through May 10, 1860 in Baltimore, Maryland. The Party adopted a very simple platform and made no mention of slavery. It attacked the motives of the Democratic and Republican Parties stating:

"Whereas, Experience has demonstrated that Platforms adopted by the partisan Conventions of the country have had the effect to mislead and deceive the people, and at the same time to widen the political divisions of the country, by the creation and encouragement of geographical and sectional parties"

The Party Platform consisted of one simple resolution which read:

"Resolved, that it is both the part of patriotism and of duty to recognize no political principle other than the Constitution of the country, the Union of the States and the enforcement of the laws, and that, as representatives of the Constitutional Union men of the country, in National Convention assembled, we hereby pledge ourselves to maintain, protect, and defend, separately and unitedly, these great principles of public liberty and national safety, against all enemies, at home and abroad; believing that thereby peace may once more be restored to the country; the rights of the People and of the States re-established, and the Government again placed in that condition of justice, fraternity and equality, which, under the example and Constitution of our fathers, has solemnly bound

149

every citizen of the United States to maintain a more perfect union, establish justice, insure domestic tranquility, provide for the common defense, promote the general welfare, and secure the blessings of liberty to ourselves and our posterity."

The Party had substantial support in both the North and South and was particularly strong in Kentucky, Tennessee and Virginia. During the convention, delegates chose former U. S. Senator John Bell of Tennessee over the popular Texas Governor Sam Houston. By voice vote, the Party nominated Edward Everett for Vice-President.

The 1860 election was held on Tuesday, November 6. By percentage, it was one of the largest voter turnouts in American history. When the votes were counted, Abraham Lincoln easily won the electoral vote with 180 out 303 but received only 39.8% of the popular. With the exception of the election of 1824 which had to be decided by the House of Representatives, the percentage of the popular votes received by Abraham Lincoln was the lowest of any President in American history. In contrast to many historical portrayals, Lincoln was a very unpopular President at the time of his election. Northern Democrats viewed Lincoln as a disreputable lawyer representing the interests of the wealthy elite. Members of the new Constitutional Union Party saw Lincoln as a deceitful partisan with little concern for the nation as a whole. Southern Democrats simply viewed Lincoln as a tyrant opposed to the principles of the Constitution. Even within the Republican Party, moderates considered him to be too radical while radicals regarded him as conservative. Lincoln's performance in his role as Commander-in-Chief during the ensuing War Between the States would bring even harsher criticism.

One of the most unique elements of the 1860 election is that it so often portrayed as a contest between slavery and abolitionism. While it is true that the Republican Party opposed the expansion of slavery, its 1860 platform firmly professed that the decision on the future of slavery where it existed was the exclusive right of the States. Northern Democrats further insisted that the extension of slavery was a State's Rights issue. The Constitutional Union Party did not even address the issue of slavery. It is undeniably evident that slavery was an issue which often erupted into fiery debate but when it came to resolving the issue, the United States of America had a long history of side-stepping the problem. The resolve of the political leaders in 1860 was no different.

The outcome of the 1860 Presidential Election was displeasing to most Americans but it is unlikely that a victory by any candidate other than Abraham Lincoln would have prompted Southern States to secede. While sectional differences divided Democrats, they still had a number of common principles and goals. A victory by either Stephen Douglas or John Breckinridge would have produced its share of dissenters but it is unlikely that the divide would be deep enough to inspire disunion. A victory by either Democratic candidate would leave Democrats in control of the Executive Branch, the U. S. Senate and the U. S. Supreme Court. Tariffs would likely remain the same or possibly be reduced and the future of the Western Territories and the Trans-Continental railroad would still be up for debate.

An unlikely victory by the Constitution Union Party candidate John Bell might have been the best solution. The Party platform was dedicated to a conservative interpretation of the Constitution, preservation of the Union, and the peaceful compromise of sectional issues. Bell's election would leave Democrats in control of the U. S. Senate and the Republicans with a plurality in the House. With Democrat Roger Taney as Chief Justice of the United States Supreme Court, it would be difficult to make unreasonable changes in U. S. Laws.

The 1860 election resulted in placing an unpopular candidate in the highest office of the United States government. While Lincoln often professed his empathy for the sentiments of Southerners, he was hated by most of them. For Southerners, Lincoln's election by such a small percentage of popular votes was reminiscent of the "*Corrupt Bargain*" which cost Andrew Jackson the Presidency in 1824. The Republican Party's dedication to sectional interests and the Federalist principles left no room for compromise with the South. The fire which had been smoldering since acceptance of the United States Constitution was now a raging inferno. As Thomas Jefferson stated:

> *"We have the wolf by the ear, and we can neither hold him, nor safely let him go.*

The Secession Crisis

In 1860, the concept of a State seceding from the Union was not a new one. It was a serious consideration in Massachusetts in 1814 and again in South Carolina in 1828. The principle is embodied in the American Revolution and the United States Declaration of Independence. Thomas Jefferson and James Madison clearly believed in the Union of the States but never contended that it was perpetual. They recognized that in the course of human events conditions could develop that require people to separate. Jefferson emphasized both the importance of the Union and a possible cause for disunion by stating:

> *"Separate from our companions only when the sole alternatives left are the dissolution of our Union with them or submission to a government without limitations."*

Over the years, many distinguished historians and political analysts have in engaged in futile debate over the legality or Constitutionality of secession. It is inconceivable that any government could adopt a Constitution that provided a method by which a citizen or a state could remove itself from the authority of that government. It would be much like issuing a marriage license with a divorce decree attached. Abraham Lincoln concurred with that opinion by stating:

> *"It is safe to assert that no government proper ever had a provision in its organic law for its own termination."* [60]

In that respect, the legality of secession is a moot point. A more important debate would be that of patriotism as opposed to treason. The two terms were used by both sides during the American Revolution. Is a revolution an act of patriotism or an act of treason? The answer to the question lies within the bounds of personal opinion but is often represented as historical fact by the victor.

In popular American history, the motives of the Southern States to secede from the Union are defined by a theory labeled as *"The Lost Cause."* Just like the differences between patriotism and treason, the exact nature of that cause is subject to personal opinion and is not supported by historical fact but rather the persuasions of public sentiment. In reality, it would be much easier to count the grains of sand in an hour glass than to establish a single cause of secession.

In recent years a prevalent theory is that the sole motivation of the seceding States was the defense of slavery. Several flaws in that theory are evident. Contending that secession was a defense of slavery suggests that there was action being taken to a abolish slavery. Not only was there no action being taken to abolish slavery, when war first erupted, all major political parties were defending slavery in those States where it existed.

Another flaw in the theory is that rather than a defense, the act of secession was an inherent threat to slavery. Secession meant the end to fugitive slave laws. Southerners were aware that after secession, slaves would have an easy path to freedom by simply making their way to the U. S. Border and there would be little chance of their return. They were also aware that they would be losing their biggest customer. Protective tariffs had created a dependency on New England textile mills to buy their Cotton. Most of all, secession would likely lead to war. Although Republicans had made no threats of using military force, the Southern States were convinced that they would not be allowed to leave the Union peacefully. Texas Governor Sam Houston warned that a war with the United States would lead to a devastating loss of life and property. Much of that property was vested in slaves. Southerners were well aware that if they lost such a war, they would lose everything. In contrast, a decision to remain in the Union would guarantee that any decision concerning slavery would continue to be the exclusive right of the States.

It would be naïve to contend that the Southern leaders were ignorant about their control of slavery. It would be equally as naïve to contend that all Northerners were opposed to slavery. Southern leaders knew that the only way to abolish slavery in the States where it existed was by passage of an Amendment to the Constitution. Any bill proposing an Amendment required a two-thirds vote in both Houses of the U. S. Congress. At the time of Lincoln's election, there were 33 States in the Union. Slavery existed in sixteen of them. In addition, Cotton produced in the Southern States was extremely important to the U. S. economy, especially to the textile mills of Massachusetts and the traders of New York City. These facts plus the racial prejudices which existed in all States made it almost impossible for a bill proposing an end to slavery to receive even a simple majority of the votes in Congress.

Southern leaders were also aware that Republicans were trying to create an imbalance in Congress by controlling the new States as they were admitted to the Union from the Western Territories. They knew that even if the Republicans were able to control all of the new States and gain the favor of all Northern States, it still would not be enough to attain the three-quarters of States necessary to ratify an Amendment. Having 50 U. S. States today, the 14 former Slave States could still block the ratification of a Constitutional Amendment. It is important to remember that even with Southern Representatives absent from Congress on June 15, 1864, the Republican dominated House of Representatives came up a full thirteen votes short of the two-thirds needed to pass the proposed 13th Amendment.

As the 2nd session of the 36th United States Congress convened on December 3, 1860, a flurry of bills defending slavery hit the floors of both Houses. Bills were submitted by Congressmen from all sections of the country and all major political parties.

John J. Crittenden
Brady-Handy Collection
U. S. Library of Congress

Constitutional Unionist Senator John J. Crittenden was one of many Congressmen who believed that a compromise could be reached to save the Union. Crittenden was considered to be a moderate in regard to the issue of slavery. Being a former Whig and having been appointed as Attorney General by two Anti-Slavery Presidents, suggests that he was personally opposed to slavery. In regard to the law, the Constitution and the Union, he was never a moderate. His efforts to establish the Constitutional Union Party demonstrates his staunch support of the Union, strict interpretation of the Constitution and enforcement of the law as it was written. On December 18, 1860, Crittenden proposed six Constitutional amendments and four Congressional resolutions. Known as the Crittenden Compromise, the package of bills re-established the 36°30' parallel boundary of 1820, enforcement remedies for the Fugitive Slave Laws and allowed for popular sovereignty in the Western Territories. The compromise also denied Congress the authority to abolish slavery where it existed, interfere with the slave trade and prohibited any future bills which would change the proposed amendments. Republicans generally accepted the proposal but opposed any act which would allow slavery to extend into the Western Territories.

Continued Republican opposition would eventually cause the compromise to be tabled. Both the wording of the Republican Party's 1860 Platform and their refusal to compromise on the expansion of slavery in the West suggests that most Republican Congressmen had little fear that the Southern States would make good on their threats of secession. South Carolina proved them wrong by declaring their independence on December 20, 1860. Six other Southern States would do the same before the end of January in 1861.

The Corwin Amendment

Prior to the close of the final session of the 36th U. S. Congress, more than fifty bills had been presented which proposed a Constitutional Amendment to preserve the rights of the States. They were designed to end the continued secession of Southern States and draw those States which had already seceded back into the Union. Only one of these bills was approved by Congress and sent to the States for ratification. Most publications which deal with War Between the States make mention of the proposed amendment, they seldom include more than a short paragraph on the subject.

Perhaps the primary reason that some authors exclude what became known as the "Corwin Amendment" is that it totally contradicts what many Americans would like to believe about the War Between the States. In contrast to all theories that the War was caused by slavery, it reveals a part of America's past that most authors and historians are uncomfortable with exposing. In addition, it presents the frightening realization that slavery almost became a permanent part of the Constitution. Another painful realization is that America's "*Great Emancipator*" was complicit in drafting the proposal.

The proposed Amendment was named for Thomas Corwin; a Republican Representative from Ohio. He was neither the author nor the original sponsor of the bill. Corwin was chairman of a special

House Committee known as the Committee of Thirty-Three. It was created to handle the enormous number of bills being presented to end the secession crisis. Corwin presented the bill to the House of Representatives which read:

> *"No amendment shall be made to the Constitution which will authorize or give to Congress the power to abolish or interfere, within any State, with the domestic institutions thereof, including that of persons held to labor or service by the laws of said State."* [61]

A similarly worded bill was presented in the Senate by Republican William H. Seward. A letter from President-Elect Abraham Lincoln to Republican Senator Lyman Trumbull of Illinois, suggests that it might have been Lincoln who actually authored the Bill. The letter dated December 21, 1860 read:

> *"Thurlow Weed was with me nearly all day yesterday & left at night with three short resolutions which I drew up and which, or the substance of which, I think would do much good, if introduced, and unanamously supported by our friends. They do not touch the territorial question. Mr. Weed goes to Washington with them; and says he will, first of all, confer with you and Mr. Hamlin. I think it would be best for Mr. Seward to introduce them, & Mr. Weed will let him know that I think so. Show this to Mr. Hamlin; but beyond him, do not let my name be known in the matter."* [62]

In the letter, Lincoln clearly expresses his belief that a guarantee of the perpetual right to slavery in the States where it existed could be acceptable, provided that it did not extend to the Territories. Such a policy would be consistent with the 1860 platform of the Republican Party. Other details of the letter raise some curious questions. Why would Lincoln risk losing political support by associating himself with Thurlow Weed and why would he trust Weed with confidential information? Thurlow Weed was a man with strong political influence but was considered by many to be unethical or even corrupt. William H. Seward's close association with Weed was a contributing factor in his loss of the Republican Presidential nomination to Abraham Lincoln. Did Lincoln form a bond with Weed because he was afraid of Weed's political influence or was he using Weed to influence William Seward to take a strong stand in support of the proposed

156

amendment? Another curious detail in Lincoln's letter to Trumbull was his desire to remain anonymous. He was actively involved in all measures regarding the secession crisis yet in his first inaugural address he suggested that he had little knowledge of the proposed amendment, stating:

> "*I understand a proposed amendment to the Constitution - which amendment, however, I have not seen - has passed Congress, to the effect that the Federal Government shall never interfere with the domestic institutions of the States, including that of persons held to service.*"

Lincoln's contention that he had not seen the amendment is highly questionable. He continues his address by offering his approval of the amendment saying:

> "*I have no objection to its being made express and irrevocable.*"

The word "*irrevocable*" was unique to the Corwin Amendment. If ratified, it would have become the first Constitutional Amendment that could not be reversed or overturned. It is unlikely that Lincoln could have known that the proposed amendment would be irrevocable if he had not read it. Even more unlikely is the possibility that he would approve of the proposal without knowing what was in it. His words are strong contradictions to the popular nickname given to him as "*Honest Abe.*"

With or without Lincoln's acknowledged awareness, the proposed amendment was approved by a Joint Resolution of Congress on March 2, 1861 and submitted to the States for ratification. It is important to remember that Representatives and Senators from seven seceding States had left the halls of Congress by the time the resolution was approved. Republicans held 26 of the 53 seats in the Senate and 116 out of 209 House seats. The Amendment was drafted solely by Republicans who were able to secure the two-thirds vote required for passage.

The Amendment was first ratified by Kentucky on April 4, 1861, followed by Ohio on May 13, 1861, Rhode Island on May 31, 1861, Maryland, January 10, 1862 and Lincoln's home State of Illinois on February 14, 1862. The validity of the Illinois ratification is questionable. Ohio rescinded its ratification on March 31, 1864 and oddly enough, the State of Maryland rescinded its ratification of the Amendment on April 7, 2014. As of 2016, the Corwin Amendment was one of six proposed Constitutional Amendments which had been ratified by a number of States but never became law.

The obvious willingness by Republicans to support the Corwin Amendment leaves a burning question. Why was it allowed to simply and quietly die? One answer would be that the Amendment had no impact on the secession crisis. Another possibility is that in a hurried attempt to resolve the secession crisis, they overlooked the dangerous precedent that they were setting.

The Amendment stated that Congress would have no power to interfere with domestic institutions within the States and that laws pertaining to persons held to labor or service were included. Slavery was only a small part what was about to be perpetual and irrevocable. If ratified, the Amendment would give voice to the very principle they had vowed to silence. Sovereignty would once again be given to the States. Federalists fought fiercely against State Sovereignty in opposing a bill of rights just as the Republicans fought the concept of Popular Sovereignty in the Kansas-Nebraska Act. Accepting any form of sovereignty other than that vested in the Federal government would re-admit the debates over States' rights to nullification. Republicans could not afford to acknowledge sovereignty of the States or the people.

Lincoln's War

The belief that the War Between the States was initiated by the firing on Fort Sumter is widely accepted but it obviously was not the first military actions taken by the Confederate States. During President James Buchanan's administration, United States Military installations were being seized in seven former States. The Confederate bombardment of Fort Sumter on April 12, 1861 was not the first time shots had been fired in Charleston Harbor. A Union supply vessel named "*Star of the West*" attempted to enter Charleston Harbor to carry supplies to Fort Sumter on January 9, 1861. The vessel was fired upon by cadets from the Citadel Military College stationed at Morris Island. Although the ship was not seriously damaged, it was struck several times and forced to return to port in New York.

Despite the acts by Confederate military forces, President James Buchanan refused to retaliate. His convictions concerning the use of military force against one or more of the States in the Union were clear and concise. Buchanan expressed his convictions in his fourth and final State of the Union address to Congress on December 3, 1860. His address included some ominous warnings. After opening his address with praise of the nation's prosperity, Buchanan began detailing the agitations which were threatening the Union. Concerning the possibility of war, Buchanan stated:

> *"It may be safely asserted that the power to make war against a State is at variance with the whole spirit and intent of the Constitution."*

He questioned the wisdom of making war by stating:

> *"But if we possessed this power, would it be wise to exercise it under existing circumstances? The object would doubtless be to preserve the Union. War would not only present the most effectual means of destroying it, but would vanish all hope of its peaceable reconstruction. Besides, in the fraternal conflict a vast amount of blood and treasure would be expended, rendering future reconciliation between the States impossible. In the meantime, who can foretell what would be the sufferings and privations of the people during its existence?"*

As Buchanan continued his lengthy address, he expressed that the Union only exists in the hearts of its citizens and that they cannot be forced into a Union that they will not accept, saying:

> *"The fact is that our Union rests upon public opinion, and can never be cemented by the blood of its citizens shed in civil war. If it can not live in the affections of the people, it must one day perish."*

159

He further denies that the government has the right or authority to force such a Union by stating:

> *"Congress possesses many means of preserving it by conciliation, but the sword was not placed in their hand to preserve it by force."*

In an urgent plea to both those who favored secession and those who opposed it, Buchanan said:

> *"But may I be permitted solemnly to invoke my countrymen to pause and deliberate before they determine to destroy this, the grandest temple which has ever been dedicated to human freedom since the world began? It has been consecrated by the blood of our fathers, by the glories of the past, and by the hopes of the future. The Union has already made us the most prosperous, and ere long will, if preserved, render us the most powerful, nation on the face of the earth. In every foreign region of the globe the title of American citizen is held in the highest respect, and when pronounced in a foreign land it causes the hearts of our countrymen to swell with honest pride. Surely when we reach the brink of the yawning abyss we shall recoil with horror from the last fatal plunge. By such a dread catastrophe the hopes of the friends of freedom throughout the world would be destroyed, and a long night of leaden despotism would enshroud the nations. Our example for more than eighty years would not only be lost, but it would be quoted as a conclusive proof that man is unfit for self-government."*

Lincoln's assessment of the secession crisis was much different than that of President Buchanan. It was derived from a legal point of view. He expressed that his duty as President of the United States was to uphold the Constitution. Lincoln's dedication to his perceived duty was also demonstrated in his handling of the slavery issue.

On March 4, 1861, Lincoln opened his first inaugural address by acknowledging that he was taking an oath prescribed by the Constitution of the United States. He also acknowledged that there were apprehensions among Southerners concerning the newly elected Republican administration. Lincoln addressed those apprehensions by a personal offering:

160

"I have no purpose, directly or indirectly, to interfere with the institution of slavery in the States where it exists. I believe I have no lawful right to do so, and I have no inclination to do so."

He then reassured the people that other Republicans shared the same sentiments by reading the fourth resolution of the 1860 Republican Party Platform which defended *"the right of each State to order and control its own domestic institutions according to its own judgment exclusively."*

During his address, Lincoln refers to the Constitution no fewer than thirty-four times. In his boldest assertion of Constitutional principles, he stated:

"I hold that, in contemplation of universal law and of the Constitution, the Union of these States is perpetual."

In all of American history, the most contentious debate in the interpretation of the United States Constitution is the subject of perpetuity. It began with the delegates at the Constitutional Convention and is still debated today. Lincoln's view was vested in the Federalist principles of Alexander Hamilton which asserted that once the States were united, they became one Republic and indivisible. In contrast, most Southerners held to the Anti-Federalist principles of Thomas Jefferson which demanded that the Union of States was an act whereby the States had entered into a *"firm league of friendship"* and that each State retained their sovereignty and all rights not expressly delegated to the United States Congress by the Constitution.

In modern times, this argument has become the dividing line between liberal and conservative politics. In the 21st Century, many States have attempted to re-assert their sovereignty through resolutions passed by their conservative legislatures and have even suggested secession. Liberal politicians contend that the sovereignty of a State is neither expressed nor implied by the Constitution.

The divisiveness of the argument is demonstrated by the contrast between the two Presidents in 1861. President James Buchanan refused to wage war against a State because he believed the Union could only be perpetuated in the hearts and minds of American citizens and that the Constitution did not place *"the sword"* in the hands of the Federal government. President Abraham Lincoln contended the perpetuity was embodied in the Constitution and that the Federal government had both the right and the duty to use whatever means necessary to preserve the Union.

Why did Lincoln wait so long to take action? He clearly had the support in Congress to take whatever action he felt necessary. Federal property had been seized in seven States. A vessel under the United States flag had been fired upon. Was he waiting on public sentiment to shift in his favor or did he believe that he could reach a compromise? In any case, any hope of resolving the crisis required immediate action. With each passing day, Confederate military defenses were growing stronger. It is possible that a withdrawal of Union troops from Fort Sumter would have allowed more time for negotiations. Was Lincoln really trying to negotiate or just waiting for the right time to strike? Why did he send an armed flotilla to Charleston, knowing they would be fired upon? If Lincoln was trying to reach a peaceful resolution, it was a serious mistake.

As expected, the approach of Union ships prompted Confederate batteries to open fire on Fort Sumter on April 12, 1861. Pounded by continuous cannon fire, the fort was surrendered the next day. At the time that Abraham Lincoln became Commander-in-Chief, the entire United States military consisted of about 16,000 men. On April 15, 1861, Lincoln issued a proclamation requesting another 75,000 men. The proclamation relied on early militia acts which allowed for the President to call for a maximum 75,000 men when in his judgment, the laws of the United States were obstructed by:

> *"combinations too powerful to be suppressed by the ordinary course of judicial proceedings, or by the powers vested in the marshals by law."*

Lincoln justified his request by asserting that it was:

> *"An effort to maintain the honor, the integrity, and the existence of our National Union, and the perpetuity of popular government; and to redress wrongs already long enough endured."*

This one sentence demonstrates that Lincoln had shifted his stance from one of compromise to one of aggression. He implies that the Southern States had insulted the honor and integrity of the nation and threatened its very existence. Once again, he expounds on his contention that perpetuity is a major component of the Constitution. His phrase *"redress wrongs already long enough endured"* is clearly another way of saying it is time to *"Rebuke and Forever Silence"* the traitors.

Lincoln would soon learn that the 75,000 troops would not be nearly enough. Before its end, the War Between the States would require the Union to enlist more than 2.6 million soldiers and sailors, leaving an estimated 600,000 dead or wounded. Lincoln would never concede that there was a war or revolution; to him it was a rebellion. A problem with that contention is that many of Lincoln's actions could only be legally justified as acts of war but Lincoln denied the existence of a war.

His initial call for troops further enraged Southerners. In less than eight weeks, four more States had seceded. Missouri, Kentucky and Maryland were threatening to follow.

On July 16, 1861, a Union army of almost 35,000 men under the command of Brigadier General Irvin McDowell left Washington in full confidence that they would easily force their way through Confederate lines all the way to the Confederate capitol in Richmond. Twenty-five miles southwest of Washington, they encountered a Confederate force of equal size near a Virginia stream known as Bull Run. The ensuing battle ended in a total rout of the Union army sending soldiers on a hurried retreat back to the Nation's Capitol. The devastating defeat sent a shock wave through the Northern States with civilians fearing that Confederate forces would take Washington.

Four days later McDowell was relieved of his command and replaced by Major General George McClellan. At the same time, Abraham Lincoln appointed John C. Frémont commander of the Department of the West. A few months later, President Lincoln named McClellan General-in-Chief of the Union Army. In a very short time, both Frémont and McClellan would feel the wrath of the impatient President and were eventually added to a long list of Generals who were relieved of duty by Lincoln.

Despite the many assertions that Lincoln was a brilliant strategist, these views rest almost entirely on conjecture. For more than half of Lincoln's first term in office, the President's initiatives as Commander-in-Chief, ended in failure. Although Lincoln claimed victory at the Battle of Antietam, the bloody confrontation was little more than a stalemate and only temporarily halted the Confederate invasion of the North. Prior to Antietam, the Union army lost every major battle in the Eastern Theater. Lincoln's most successful plan was derived through collaboration with General Winfield Scott. What was known as the "*Anaconda Plan*" was an initiative to divide that Confederate States and choke them into submission by taking control of the Mississippi River and blockading every Confederate seaport. Overall, the plan was a success but brought with it some unforeseen troubles. Texas was virtually impenetrable. Several attempts to invade Texas were easily rejected. Texas maintained its trade routes in and through Mexico. It continued to provide men and supplies for the Confederate war effort west of the Mississippi River and by 1864 had virtually eliminated any threat by Union forces in Texas, Arkansas and Western Louisiana. In addition to being repelled in the three Confederate States, attempts to build the Eastern leg of the Trans-Continental Railroad were stifled and the Republican's treasured Western Territories were becoming a violent lawless frontier.

Even worse than Lincoln's military failures was his inability to draw support from foreign powers. Many of the failures of Lincoln's foreign policy had been inherited from previous administrations or unrelated events in Europe.

In 1861, the United States had no independent bordering nations. Canada was still a British Colony. Many of the Canadian colonists were still at odds with their neighbors to the South. The discovery of gold in British Columbia in the late 1850s was creating hostilities between Canadians and the encroaching miners from Oregon and California. To the South, French emperor Napoleon III was preparing to establish a puppet government in Mexico.

The first European power to refuse aid to the United States was Spain. While there were several reasons for Spain to refuse aid to the United States, one of the leading causes of opposition is found in a document known as the "*Ostend Manifesto*." In October of 1854, three American diplomats, Pierre Soulé -Minister to Spain, James Buchanan - Minister to Great Britain and John Young Mason - Minister to France, held a secret meeting in Ostend, Belgium. They drafted a document which suggested that it would be in the best interest of all nations for the United States to purchase Cuba from Spain. The document also expressed that in the event that Spain refused to sell Cuba, the United States would be justified in taking Cuba by force. The trio professed the need for such action by stating:

"We should, however, be recreant to our duty, be unworthy of our gallant forefathers, and commit base treason against our posterity, should we permit Cuba to be Africanized and become a second St. Domingo, with all its attendant horrors to the white race, and suffer the flames to extend to our own neighboring shores, seriously to endanger or actually to consume the fair fabric of our Union."

When word of the document reached the U. S. House of Representatives, they demanded that the document be published. The portion of the document which addressed a possible refusal by Spain to sell Cuba, stated:

"by every law, human and divine, we shall be justified in wresting it from Spain."

Queen Isabel II of Spain
photo by L. Mouton 1868

The obvious threat of military force was not taken well by Spain's monarch, Queen Isabel II. Republicans attempted to quiet the situation by including a condemnation of the manifesto in their 1856 platform. The Republican's condemnation did little to sway the Queen's views concerning the United States. Fortunately for the Union, she distrusted the newly formed Confederate States government as well. In addition to threats against Cuba, the Queen had other pressing issues in North America. The government of Mexico, under President Benito Juárez had created massive debts to Spain, France and Great Britain. The Juárez government ceased payments on the loans in July of 1861. The three nations entered into an agreement in October to collect the debts. Upon signing the agreement, the Spanish fleet carried troops to Mexico's major port of Vera Cruz. After discovering that France had plans to seize all of Mexico, both Spain and Great

165

Britain withdrew from the coalition. Fears that Spain might offer support to the Confederate States was well warranted. Diplomatic relations between the United States and Spain had always been awkward at best. At the time of the war, Spain was pro-slavery. The close proximity of Cuba to the Confederate States would contribute to a strong trade relationship were it not for the Union blockade of Southern ports. Although it remained a worrisome threat, Spain adopted a wait-and-see attitude and remained neutral throughout the war.

Emperor Napoleon III of France
painting by Alexandre Cabanel

Public sentiments concerning the War Between the States was mixed in France but sympathies among the political factions were more easily defined. French President Louis-Napoléon Bonaparte established the Second French Empire by dissolving the French National Assembly and declaring himself the emperor with the title of Napoleon III. Being the nephew of Napoleon Bonaparte, he claimed to be the rightful heir to the French throne. He was opposed by a group or royalists who believed that Prince Philippe, Count of Paris was the rightful heir. Napoleon III, was also opposed by several revolutionist factions which demanded that the French Republic be restored. Two of the more prominent revolutionists were philosopher Karl Marx and French activist Édouard de Laboulaye. To the disatisfaction of Napoleon III, most of the leaders who opposed him were supporters of Abraham Lincoln. Prince Philippe and his brother Robert traveled to the United States and for a short period, served on the staff of Union Major General George McClellan. Communist theorist Karl Marx was a close friend and former employee of Republican Horace Greeley. Marx was a loyal supporter of Lincoln. Because unpaid labor in the form of slavery conflicted with his theory, Marx praised the President for opposing the expansion of slavery. Édouard de Laboulaye had a passion for American history. His extraordinary admiration for Abraham Lincoln inspired a campaign which would eventually lead to the construction of the Statue of Liberty. The close association of the United States with the French leaders, who opposed Napoleon III, presented an obstacle to French support of the United States. In addition, Napoleon III favored an alliance with the Confederate States. Cotton was important to the French economy and to the

166

puppet government established by the French regime in Mexico. The U. S. blockade of Southern ports was hostile to French interests but Napoleon III was reluctant to take action that might result in out right war with the United States. Officially, France remained neutral and did not formally acknowledge the legitimacy of the Confederate States, but the emperor offered covert support to the South. One of the emperor's schemes was exposed when it was discovered that he secretly supported the construction of two ironclad ships to be delivered to the Confederate navy. In June of 1863 John Slidell, the Confederate commissioner to France, met secretly with Napoleon III, to discuss building warships in France. Soon after the meeting, shipbuilder Lucien Arman entered into a contract with Confederate

CSS Stonewall
Washington Navy Yard, 1865-67
U.S. Naval History and Heritage Command

agent James D. Bulloch to build two massive ironclad steamers. To avoid suspicion, the ships being constructed in Bordeaux, France were named Cheops and Sphynx and it was purposely rumored that they were intended for the Egyptian navy. After the scheme was exposed by a shipyard clerk, the United States pressured the French government to block the sale of the ships but Arman managed to illegally sell them to Denmark and Prussia. The Confederate government was able to negotiate a purchase of the ship that was delivered to Denmark. They took possession of the vessel on January 6, 1865. The ship was re-commissioned as the "*CSS Stonewall*." Several U. S. warships attempted to intercept the *Stonewall* but were no match for the 1,300 ton super-ironclad and were content to watch from a safe distance as it steamed into Havana Harbor on May 6, 1865. After discovering that the war was over, the *CSS Stonewall* was turned over to the Spanish government in Cuba.

The British government was quick to react to the War Between the States. One month after the firing on Fort Sumter, Queen Victoria issued a "*British Proclamation of Neutrality*." British sentiments offered little hope of gain or fear of loss from the war in America. Grieving from the death of her mother in March of 1861 and the death of her husband in December of 1861, Queen Victoria entered into a self-imposed isolation from the public. Affairs of government were handled by British Prime Minister, Henry John Temple, 3rd Viscount Palmerston. Lord Palmerston had long been openly hostile toward the United States; believing they would not cease their expansion efforts until they had seized all of North America. He believed that dissolution of the Union might be a benefit to Great Britain by diminishing the power of the United States. He also believed that the British economy would better benefit from having the Confederate States as a trade partner without the influence of the U. S. protective tariffs. Both Palmerston and British Foreign Secretary Lord Russell distrusted Lincoln but their distrust of United States Secretary of State William Seward was even greater. Lord Richard Lyons was appointed as the British minister to the United States in April of 1859. Even before Seward became Secretary of State, Lyons wrote a letter to Lord Russell stating:

Lord Palmerston 1863
photo by W & D Downey

"I cannot help fearing that he will be a dangerous foreign minister. His view of the relations between the United States and Britain had always been that they are a good material to make political capital of. He thinks at all events that they may be safely played with - without any risk of bringing on a war. . . I do not think Mr. Seward would contemplate actually going to war with us, but he would be well disposed to play the old game of seeking popularity here by displaying violence toward us." [63]

Lord Lyons was correct in his assessment of William Seward. After becoming Secretary of State, Seward often acted arrogantly and without fear of retaliation from foreign nations. He warned Great Britain that recognition of Confederate States as an independent nation might be considered as an act of war.

168

An act committed by the United States in late 1861 did in fact bring the two nations to the brink of war. Union officials were well aware that the Confederate States government was planning to send diplomats to Great Britain. They learned that Confederate commissioners James Murray Mason and John Slidell were scheduled to leave Havana, Cuba on November 7, 1861 aboard the British mail ship "*RMS Trent*," bound for England by way of St.

Thomas. On November 8, 1861, the "*USS San Jacinto*" approached the vessel in international waters and fired two warning shots which brought the "*Trent*" to a halt. A U. S. Navy officer boarded the ship and arrested Mason and Slidell. Upon receiving word of the incident Lord Palmerston was enraged. The British navy was readied for war and thousands of additional troops were sent to Canada with plans for a possible invasion of the United States. A demand for the release of the two diplomats was sent to Washington but the U. S. was slow to respond. Knowing that war was imminent, the U. S. agreed to British demands on

"*USS San Jacinto*" stops "*RMS Trent*"
By Edward Sylvester Ellis

December 27, 1861. Mason and Slidell were released and boarded the Royal Navy's "*HMS Rinaldo*" in route to England. Relations between the Lincoln administration and Great Britain were beyond repair. Throughout the war, Great Britain remained neutral and did not officially recognize the legitimacy of the Confederate government but they never ruled out the possibility of intervention.

Another dispute arose over the construction of the "*CSS Alabama*." The infamous Confederate raider was secretly built in 1862 by British shipbuilders John Laird Sons & Company near Liverpool. To disguise her identity, the ship was constructed as "*hull number 290*" and launched under the name "*Enrica*." During her 2 year career the "*CSS Alabama*" won no fewer than 65 engagements and took and estimated six-million dollars in bounty. After the war, the United States filed claims against Great Britain for losses caused by the "*CSS Alabama*" and was eventually awarded 15.5 million dollars by a joint arbitration commission.

After failing to receive the support of Great Britain, France or Spain, it appeared that the United States would be without allies in the War Between the States. Even worse, the U. S. foreign policy had created fears among European nations that their interests in North American might be at risk. It was very clear that Great Britain was hostile toward Lincoln's administration and France favored an alliance with the Confederate States. Even Spain feared that the U. S. might attempt to seize Cuba while claiming it was an attempt to prevent the expansion of slavery. There was a continual threat that foreign powers might support the Confederate States but Lincoln had been nurturing another alliance early on. In the end, it was Russia that became the only country to offer support to the cause of the Union. That support was one of several tools that Lincoln used to save his Presidency in 1863 and 1864.

The Emancipation Proclamation

In American history, the name Abraham Lincoln is synonymous with the *"Emancipation Proclamation."* Although it is the best remembered, Lincoln's proclamation was hardly the first act which included emancipation. In fact, one of the earliest acts was repealed by Lincoln.

On August 6, 1861, Congress passed the first of two *"Confiscation Acts."* The act titled *"An Act to confiscate Property used for Insurrectionary Purposes,"* allowed through federal court rulings, the confiscation of the property, including slaves, belonging to anyone who offered support to the rebellion. Knowing the views and temperament of Supreme Court Chief Justice Roger Taney, President Lincoln was reluctant to sign the act for fear that it would be ruled unconstitutional thereby setting a precedent affecting future acts. Powerful Republicans persuaded him to sign the act in spite of his fears.

In Missouri, Major General John C. Frémont declared the State to be under Martial Law. On August 30, 1861, Frémont issued his own proclamation declaring that the slaves of those bearing arms in the rebellion would be confiscated and subsequently declared to be free.

He acted without notifying the President or members of Congress. The President and many of his Republican supporters were outraged. In a letter to Orville H. Browning, Republican Senator from Illinois, Lincoln stated:

> *"General Frémont's proclamation . . . is not within the range of military law, or necessity. . . If the General needs them, he can seize them and use them; but when the need is past, it is not for him to fix their permanent future condition."* [64]

Ironically, it would be exactly one year from the date of his letter to Browning, that Lincoln would announce a similar proclamation. On November 2, 1861, Lincoln repealed and publicly denounced Frémont's proclamation and relieved him of his command in the Department of the West. Lincoln's brash firing and public humiliation of Frémont accompanied by an insulting report prepared by Montgomery Blair would come back to haunt the Commander-in-Chief in the fall of 1863.

On March 13, 1862, Congress passed a "*Law Enacting an Additional Article of War*" which prevented Union army officers from returning confiscated slaves to their owners. Despite the 1857 Supreme Court ruling which stated that Congress was powerless to regulate slavery in U.S. territories, a bill was passed which prohibited slavery in all current and future United States territories. The bill made no reference to States where slavery existed. On July 17, 1862, a second confiscation act was passed which added punishments for anyone who had sworn an oath of allegiance to the Confederacy.

By July of 1862, Lincoln was preparing a draft of his emancipation proclamation. He was persuaded that the proclamation could only be effective if it were supported by a decisive military victory. An attempt to take the Confederate capitol at Richmond, known as the "*Seven Days Battles*" had ended in failure. Feeling that General McClellan was acting too timidly, Lincoln relieved McClellan as General-in-Chief of the Union Army but left him in command of the Union Army of the Potomac. The new General-in-Chief, Major General Henry Halleck ordered McClellan to withdraw his army from the assault on Richmond and move to support General Popes Union Army of Virginia.

171

On August 30, 1862, a second battle at Bull Run in Virginia ended in a worse defeat than the first, causing more than 14,000 Union casualties and leaving the Confederate Army only a few miles from the nation's capitol. Lincoln was desperate for a Union Victory. In September, the Confederate army crossed the Potomac River into Maryland.

September 17, 1862 turned out to be the bloodiest single day in American military history. The Union army under the command of Major General George McClellan clashed with General Robert E. Lee's Confederate army along Antietam Creek near Sharpsburg, Maryland. Although Lincoln claimed a Union victory, the battle which resulted in a combined total of almost 23,000 casualties resulted in no more than a draw. The Confederate army moved quietly across the Potomac and prepared for another invasion of the North. With the Union having a two to one advantage over the Confederates, Commanding General George McClellan's failure to crush the Confederate army prompted Lincoln to replace him with Major General Ambrose Burnside. This was the second demotion for McClelland and his abrupt firing would be yet another move that would come back to haunt Lincoln in the fall of 1863.

On September 22, 1862, Lincoln announced that on January 1, 1863, he would emancipate the slaves in any State that remained in rebellion but offering that States which ceased hostilities and returned to the Union prior to that date would not be affected. Both Lincoln and leaders of the Radical Republican faction believed that emancipation of slaves in the Southern States would cause a slave uprising and lead to an economic collapse in the Southern States. Lincoln also believed that it would sway sentiments in Great Britain. Union military efforts continued to decline as Lincoln's army under his newly appointed commander. General Ambrose Burnside was soundly defeated at the Battle of Fredericksburg, Virginia on December 13, 1862. The Confederate States were still unaffected by Lincoln's threat of emancipation. Despite his continued military failures, Lincoln issued his emancipation proclamation on January 1, 1863. Not only did it have no impact on the Confederate States but the relatively minor number of slaves which received word of the proclamation offered little response. Great Britain responded quite the opposite of what Lincoln expected. British leaders viewed the proclamation as both hypocritical and dangerous. They knew that the intent of the proclamation was to weaken the Confederate States and they believed that the most likely result of the proclamation would be to incite a race war. A letter published in the *London Times* read:

> *"It is a matter of very serious import that the grand old cause of the Anti-Slave-trade and Anti-Slavery movement should be thought to have degenerated into a mere cat's-paw to Mr. Seward, and that one of the most glorious bands of disinterested philanthropists which this or any other country has produced, should be thought to have sunk into a few dupes of President Lincoln, advocating a measure which is not freedom to the blacks, but is, as far as possible, massacre to the women and children of the whites."* [65]

At home, anti-administration newspapers proclaimed that Lincoln was a tyrant. In Lincoln's home state of Illinois, The Chicago Times printed an editorial stating:

> *"We have here an assumption that the President, who is a creature of the constitution, may, by proclamation, fasten upon the people an irrevocable law which subverts the Constitution. If the proclamation cannot be retracted, then every provision in the constitution pertaining to slavery is abrogated. . . If it cannot be retracted any more than the dead can be brought back to life, then the soul of the Constitution has been murdered - assassinated - by him who solemnly swore to preserve, protect and defend it."* [66]

Even more troublesome was the strong disapproval voiced by some of Lincoln's most ardent supporters. Union loyalists in Lincoln's hometown of Springfield, Illinois, planned a rally to take place on September 3, 1863. Many of the planners were dissatisfied with Lincoln's administration and his emancipation proclamation. They invited President Lincoln to attend the meeting and address their concerns. The invitation was extended by Lincoln's one-time friend and supporter, James C. Conkling. As a member of the Illinois State Central Committee and Presidential elector, Conkling was among the most influential Republicans in the State and one that Lincoln could ill afford to ignore. September of 1863 was a month of severe turmoil for Lincoln and he knew that he could not risk taking time to travel to Illinois. He replied to Conkling's invitation with a letter stating:

> "*I cannot leave here now. Herewith is a letter instead. You are one of the best public readers. I have but one suggestion. Read it very slowly. And now God bless you, and all good Union-men.*"

The letter went into great detail to explain the President's actions and motives and acknowledged he was aware of his unpopularity. A portion of the letter stated:

> "*There are those who are dissatisfied with me. To such I would say: You desire peace; and you blame me that we do not have it. But how can we attain it? There are but three conceivable ways. First, to suppress the rebellion by force of arms. This I am trying to do. Are you for it? If you are, so far we are agreed. If you are not for it, a second way is to give up the Union. I am against this. Are you for it? If you are, you should say so plainly. If you are not for force, nor yet for dissolution, there only remains some imaginable compromise. I do not believe any compromise, embracing the maintenance of the Union, is now possible.*
>
> *But to be plain, you are dissatisfied with me about the Negro. . . Yet I have neither adopted, nor proposed any measure, which is not consistent with even your view, provided you are for the Union.*
>
> *You dislike the emancipation proclamation; and, perhaps, would have it retracted. You say it is unconstitutional--I think differently. I think the constitution invests its Commander-in-chief, with the law of war, in time of war. The most that can be said, if so much, is, that slaves are property. Is there - has there ever been - any question that by the law of war, property, both of enemies and friends, may be taken when needed? And is it not needed whenever taking it, helps us, or hurts the enemy?*
>
> *You say you will not fight to free Negroes. Some of them seem willing to fight for you; but, no matter. Fight you, then exclusively to save the Union. I issued the proclamation on*

174

purpose to aid you in saving the Union. Whenever you shall have conquered all resistance to the Union, if I shall urge you to continue fighting, it will be an apt time, then, for you to declare you will not fight to free Negroes.

I thought that in your struggle for the Union, to whatever extent the Negroes should cease helping the enemy, to that extent it weakened the enemy in his resistance to you. Do you think differently? I thought that whatever Negroes can be got to do as soldiers, leaves just so much less for white soldiers to do, in saving the Union." [67]

After the meeting, Conkling reported to Lincoln that his message had been well received. A few days later Conkling reported to Lincoln that a convention was being planned to replace him as nominee for President. Little did Lincoln know that things were about to get much worse.

Despite its unpopularity, Lincoln held firm to his defense of his emancipation proclamation. There is little doubt that Lincoln was aware that his proclamation might not hold up if tested by the Supreme Court but he also knew that by the time the proclamation was revoked, his intended results would already be attained. To the President's disappointment, the proclamation produced very few of the results that he had intended. Perhaps the only success realized from the emancipation proclamation was that for the few slaves that received word of it, the document presented a ray of hope in a dream that had long been anticipated. It was the first prospect of a freedom that once seemed impossible. In that aspect, the proclamation was a success. In other aspects, the "*Great Emancipator*" would soon reveal that he was the "*Great Manipulator.*"

The Story Changes

From the earliest days of the War Between the States, a handful of Radical Republicans insisted that the war should be prosecuted on the pretence that it was a war to end slavery. At the time the war began, no such pretence had ever been asserted by the Republican Party. The 1860 Republican Party Platform defended slavery as the exclusive right of the States where it existed. Republicans only objected to slavery being expanded into the Western Territories.

Defending those objections, they insisted that the Territories were owned and controlled by the Federal government and had no right to "*Popular Sovereignty.*" President Abraham Lincoln and the Republican Party as a whole made it clear that any use of military force would be solely for the purpose of maintaining the Union.

By the summer of 1863, sentiments in the United States were changing. What was supposed to be a simple act of suppressing a rebellion, evolved into the bloodiest war in American history. The concept of forcing the Southern States to remain in a Union that they no longer wanted was beginning to lose all reason. The hundreds of thousand of grieving parents, broken hearted brothers and sisters and despairing widows and orphans had taken its toll. The cries for ending the war at any cost were growing louder.

For the Lincoln administration and the Republican Party, only the total subjugation of the Confederate States would be acceptable. They had many reasons to continue the war, not all of which were honorable. One of the less honorable aspects was the calloused view that big wars meant big money. Although it is difficult to accept that part of America's history, it remains a reality. The fortunes of a few were derived by the blood of thousands. For the President and his Party, a premature end to the war would present an array of problems. It would mean that their efforts had failed, the blood was on their hands and they would never be able to silence the threat of secession. Their only salvation would be defeating the Confederate States so severely that no State would ever revolt against the authority of the Federal government again. President Lincoln knew more than anyone that the only way to accomplish their goals was to sway the sentiments of the American people.

Continued Struggles

The first six months of 1863 were particularly trying for President Lincoln and the Union. General Burnside's defeat at the Battle of Fredericksburg in December of 1862 had prompted Lincoln to replace him with Major General Joseph Hooker. Heavy losses prompted Congress to pass the Civil War Military Draft Act in March.

As fighting resumed in the spring of 1863, Lincoln's emancipation proclamation was becoming increasingly unpopular, both at home and abroad. It still failed to have any impact on the Confederate army or the Southern economy. Long before military activities began to escalate in the spring, President Lincoln found himself fighting another war; the war of public opinion.

The fact the President Abraham Lincoln committed many acts that were in conflict with the United States Constitution is indisputable. Lincoln justified his actions by claiming that the Constitution gave him the authority to commit these acts as Commander-in-Chief in a time of war. The problem with Lincoln's claim is that he continuously asserted that the War Between the States was not a true war but only a rebellion.

Among the gravest of Lincoln's unconstitutional acts was the suspension of the privilege of a *"writ of habeas corpus."* The Constitution does allow the suspension when in *"cases of rebellion or invasion the public safety may require it,"* but only by an act of Congress. Lincoln was not given that authority until March 3, 1863. Historians disagree on the number of citizens that were arrested under Lincoln's orders prior to that date but some estimates suggest that the number was as many as 35,000. Despite the absence of an exact number of arrests, it can easily be asserted that the number of arrests was very large. Included in those numbers were Mayors, Councilmen, State Militia Officers and State Legislators acting under their authority as elected or appointed officials. In one of his boldest and most arrogant moves, Lincoln ordered the arrest of members of the Maryland General Assembly for considering secession. Arrests were made in defiance of the ruling by Supreme Court Chief Justice Roger Taney in the case of *"ex parte Merryman"* in 1861. While *"Habeas Corpus Suspension Act 1863"* gave Lincoln the authority to continue his arrests, the act also required that an actual indictment be made; something often ignored by Lincoln and his generals. Many of the arrests were clearly made for the purpose of suppressing criticism of the Presidents policies and his acts as Commander-in-Chief.

Lincoln was not the first President who attempted to suppress free speech and freedom of the press. The Hamilton Federalists attempted to suppress criticism of President John Adams' administration through passage of the Alien and Sedition Acts in 1798. President Lincoln attempted to suppress criticism of his administration by closing newspapers that printed articles thought to be critical of Lincoln or the Union war effort. Although there is no accurate count of the number of newspapers closed by Abraham Lincoln and his Generals, there may have been as many as 300 closings.

After being relieved of duty as the commander of the Union Army of the Potomac, General Ambrose Burnside was appointed commander of the Department of Ohio which consisted of the states of Ohio, Michigan, Indiana, Illinois, Wisconsin, and part of Kentucky. On April 13, 1863, General Burnside issued General Order No. 38, which stated:

> *"Hereafter all persons found within our lines who commit acts for the benefit of the enemies of our country, will be tried as spies or traitors and if convicted, will suffer death. . .*
>
> *The habit of declaring sympathies for the enemy will no longer be tolerated in the department. Persons committing such offences will be at once arrested, with a view to being tried as above stated, or sent beyond our lines into the lines of their friends."*

On May 5, 1863, anti-war Democrat Clement Vallandigham was arrested and charged with *"Publicly expressing, in violation of General Orders No. 38, from Head-quarters Department of the Ohio, sympathy for those in arms against the Government of the United States, and declaring disloyal sentiments and opinions, with the object and purpose of weakening the power of the Government in its efforts to suppress an unlawful rebellion."*

Arrest of Hon. C.L. Vallandigham May 5.1863.
U. S. Library of Congress

Vallandigham was tried, convicted and sentenced to confinement in a military prison for the remainder of the war. An application for a writ of habeas corpus was filed on his behalf in a U. S. Circuit Court on May 11, 1863. Stating that Vallandigham's arrest and military trial was valid under the war powers of the President, a Federal Judge upheld the military court's ruling. The incident caused an angry uproar across the Northern

States. Fearing further reprisal, Lincoln ordered Vallandigham to be transported across enemy lines into the Confederacy where Confederate officials ordered him to be placed under guard at Wilmington, North Carolina. On June 29, 1863, Lincoln replied to the demands of a group of Ohio Democratic Congressmen stating that he would revoke the order if Vallandigham supported the polices of the administration. The Congressmen promptly replied that they had not requested revocation of the order as a favor but rather as the right of the people of Ohio. Vallandigham was released by the Confederate authorities and traveled to the Bahamas and then to Canada. He returned to Ohio in time to attended the 1864 Democratic National Convention in Chicago and become a District Delegate for Ohio in support of George McClellan for President. Federal authorities kept a watchful eye on him but made no attempt to arrest him.

Lincoln's attempts to maintain public approval did him more harm than good. He could only hope that a strong military victory would boost his approval rating. In early May, the Union Army of the Potomac was soundly defeated by Confederate General Robert E. Lee's Army of Northern Virginia at the Battle of Chancellorsville. Journalist Noah Brooks was at the White House when President Lincoln received word of the Union defeat at Chancellorsville and noted:

> *"Never as long as I knew him, did he seem to be so broken, so dispirited, and so ghostlike. Clasping his hands behind his back, he walked up and down the room, saying 'My God! My God! What will the country say! What will the country say! He seemed incapable of uttering any other words than these, and after a little time he hurriedly left the room. Dr. Henry, whose affection for Lincoln was deep and tender, burst into a passion of tears. I consoled him as best I could, and while we were talking and trying to find a gleam of sunshine in this frightful darkness, I saw a carriage drive up to the entrance of the White House, and looking out, beheld the tall form of the President dart into the vehicle, in which sat General Halleck, and drive off. Immediately after, an attendant came to tell us that the President and General Halleck had gone to the Army of the Potomac, and that Mr. Lincoln would return next day, and would like to see me in the evening."* [68]

Throughout Abraham Lincoln's political career, he was obsessed with the powers of public sentiment. As indicated by his reaction to the Union defeat at Chancellorsville, the incredible loss of life or the defeat of his army was much less a concern as his fear of how the public would react to it. Although General Grant was having success in the West, Lincoln's army was being humiliated in the East. In June of 1863, the Confederate army moved northward and began crossing the Potomac River near Hagerstown, Maryland. By the end of the month, the Confederate army had moved deep into Pennsylvania.

Frustrated that General Hooker had allowed the Confederate army to invade the North, Lincoln once again changed the command of his army by replacing General Hooker with Major General George Meade on June 27, 1863.

The High Water Mark

Around dawn on the morning of July 1, 1863, soldiers from General Robert E. Lee's Confederate Army of Northern Virginia and General George Meade's Union Army of the Potomac collided near the sleepy little town of Gettysburg, Pennsylvania. The encountered marked the beginning of a bloody three day struggle which is remembered as the greatest battle in the history of the Western Hemisphere. It was here that General Robert E. Lee made the ill-fated decision that Gettysburg would be the place where he would decide the outcome of the war with his greatest victory. On the third and final day of the battle, Lee ordered an assault on the center of the Union line along a low stone wall on the Western slope of Cemetery Ridge. Preceded by a barrage of approximately 170 Confederate cannons, more than 12,000 Confederate troops under the command of General George Pickett advanced three-quarters of a mile across an open field toward the Union defenses on Cemetery Ridge. As ordered by General Lee, the attack was focused on a *"copse of trees"* at a portion of a stone wall. Because of the heavy numbers of casualties, the spot would later become known as the *"Bloody Angle."* At the end of the assault, Confederate troops under the command of General Lewis Armistead were able to breach the stone wall but were overwhelmed by a Union counterattack. The point where Armistead's men broke through

Union defenses is recorded in history as the *"High-Water Mark of the Confederacy."* While the spot marked the end of the last major offensive by the Confederate army, it was the high-water mark for more than just the Confederacy. If the Confederate army had been successful, they would be able to surround the nation's capitol at Washington. It is likely that the victory would have led to support for the Confederate States from other countries and would force the United States to accept the Confederacy as a free and independent nation. In that respect, the spot along the *"Bloody Angle"* was the high-water mark for the Union. It was also the high-water mark for the Presidency of Abraham Lincoln. Already unpopular over his

"The High Water Mark" Gettysburg, Pennsylvania - published by Detroit Publishing Company, about 1900.
Source: U. S. Library of Congress

emancipation proclamation and his leadership as Commander-in-Chief, a Confederate victory at Gettysburg would have put an end to Lincoln's political career.

In addition to being a turning point in the war, the Confederate defeat at Gettysburg had a profound impact on the United States as a nation. Among the dead, scattered across the battlefield, were the dying dreams of Jefferson and Madison. Their hopes for a *"league of friendship"* among the States were being transformed into the one thing that Jefferson feared most; a despotic republic with a central government of uncontrollable strength. It was the Federalist principles of Hamilton and Adams which claimed the greatest victory at Gettysburg on that day.

181

On July 4, 1863, President Lincoln celebrated the nation's birthday with the surrender of Confederate forces at Vicksburg, Mississippi. The last Confederate stronghold on the Mississippi River at Port Hudson, Louisiana, surrendered on July 9th. At long last, the President's *"Anaconda Plan"* had succeeded; dividing the Confederacy and giving the Union control of the Mississippi River. For a brief moment, the beleaguered President was able to bask in the glory of victory.

Lincoln's Dilemma

Most significantly, the Union victory at Gettysburg was a turning point for the sentiments of the American people. Compared to previous engagements, the uniqueness of the Battle of Gettysburg was that it was the first time that the war had traveled so deep into northern territory. For the first time, the horrors of war had fallen upon the doorsteps of citizens in the North. The people of Gettysburg were witness to the largest military engagement ever seen on the North American continent. They sheltered in horror while hearing the Confederate army conduct what was at the time, the largest artillery barrage in the history of the world. The countryside quaked from gunfire and was covered with the soot of black powder. It was also covered with the lifeless bodies of thousands of men, horses and mules. The city was overwhelmed by the stench of death. Citizens assisting in the cleanup after the battle, used peppermint oil around their noses to lessen the smell of rotting flesh. Many of the buildings in town were transformed into make-shift hospitals. The desperate cries of the wounded and dying could be heard all around town. Residents of the area quickly adopted the view that no cause could be worth that degree of carnage. It was a view that would continue to grow all across the Northern States demanding an immediate end to the war.

To most foreign leaders, Gettysburg was just another senseless battle in a war of futility. British Prime Minister Lord Palmerston still distrusted Lincoln and his cabinet members. In France, Emperor Napoleon III still waited for an opportunity to officially recognize the Confederacy and form a trade alliance. With the threat of British and French intervention still looming, Lincoln reluctantly turned to Russian Tsar Alexander II for support.

Anti-war sentiments were stronger in New York City than any other city in the United States. The city's economy had strong ties to the Southern States. As the Southern States began to secede, New York City Mayor Fernando Wood urged City Aldermen to declare New York a free and independent city and continue trade with the Confederacy. Wood was a leader in New York's Democratic Party political machine known as *"Tammany Hall."* He asserted that President Lincoln's administration was made up of *"Black Republicans"* and that their war goal was not to save the Union but to emancipate Blacks. In the 1850's, a wave of Irish immigrants hit the City of New York. Many of them feared that freed slaves would infiltrate the city and cause them to lose their jobs. A combination of Lincoln's emancipation proclamation and an attempt to enforce draft laws incited a riot in New York City on July 13, 1863. What started as a protest against the Military Draft Act turned into a race riot which left approximately 120 dead and over 2,000 injured. Led primarily by Irish immigrants, rioters burned or destroyed several public buildings and churches along with many black homes and the Colored Orphan Asylum. With assistance from New York State militia and several Union Army units, the riot ended after four days of hostilities. The riot was highly publicized, causing more criticism of President Lincoln's administration.

For President Lincoln, an end to the war without a total defeat of the Confederate army was unacceptable. His Democratic rivals used his uncompromising position as a weapon against him and his popularity among Republicans was declining rapidly. Lincoln began hearing rumors that his nemesis and former General George McClellan was planning to enter politics seeking the Democratic nomination for President.

By September of 1863, President Lincoln's approval rating had reached an all time low but the situation would get worse. Although rumors were being cast from all directions, Lincoln had not come to the realization that a group led by his former supporter Horace Greeley, was searching diligently for his replacement. It seemed that Lincoln believed that a military triumph would solve all of his political woes. Beginning on September 19, 1863, along Chickamauga Creek in Georgia, General William Rosecrans Union Army of the Cumberland was engaged a Confederate force under the command of Confederate General Braxton Bragg. The two day battle resulted in one of the worst defeats of a Union army over the entire course of the war. After the Army of the Cumberland retreated to Chattanooga, Tennessee, Rosecrans was replaced as commander by Major General George Thomas.

The Russian Fleet in New York Harbor
Published in "*Harper's Weekly*." October 17. 1863

To Lincoln's good fortune, he was spared much of the public humiliation from Rosecrans' defeat when the Russian Navy's Baltic Fleet arrived in New York Harbor on September 24, led by its flagship, "Alexander Nevsky." The Imperial Russian Navy Pacific Fleet arrived in San Francisco Harbor two months later. It is likely that both Lincoln and Russian Tsar Alexander II knew that they were using each other and that the expedition was simply a show of force for the benefit of Great Britain and France. For the United States, the expedition gave the impression of an alliance of the two powers to discourage foreign intervention on behalf of the Confederacy. For the Russians, it offered a safe winter port for the Russian Fleet. In New York City, Russian sailors were treated to parades and grand balls. The two fleets remained in American waters for seven months. At one point, a portion of the Baltic Fleet dropped anchor in the Potomac River near Washington. The awesome spectacle of the Russian fleet was only one of many tactics that Lincoln would use to sway public sentiment.

Russian Tsar Allexander II
(Public Domain)

Lincoln's military efforts were still troubled. In perhaps one of his best military decisions, he assigned General Ulysses S. Grant to the command of the newly formed Division of the Mississippi, which included the Armies of the Cumberland, Tennessee, and Ohio. By December, the Union forces under Grants command had driven the Confederate army back into Georgia.

184

After the promotion of General Grant, Lincoln's armies were making progress but his political efforts continued on a downward spiral. By late September, 1863, Lincoln learned that Republicans would likely select a new nominee for President. In October, George McClellan confirmed his intention to run for President as a Democrat. The Democrats were insisting on an end to the war by any means possible. McClellan was not particularly anti-war but was definitely anti-Lincoln. George McClellan was everything that Abraham Lincoln was not. He was young, handsome, well educated, a decorated veteran and immensely popular. He was supported by a group of New York City businessmen with deep pockets and was also backed by two of New York's most popular newspapers; a situation which troubled former Lincoln supporter Horace Greeley. From the time that McClellan announced his candidacy until the very day of the Presidential election in 1864, Lincoln was convinced that he would lose the election. Many Republicans held the same view.

Knowing that the armies would soon go to winter quarters and it was still months away from convention time, Lincoln escalated his attempts to sway public sentiments about the war. Realizing that the people would have the final voice in the election, Lincoln had to convince the people of the North that a continuation of the war was necessary.

On October 3, 1863, President Abraham Lincoln issued his "Thanksgiving Proclamation."

> *"The year that is drawing towards its close, has been filled with the blessings of fruitful fields and healthful skies. To these bounties, which are so constantly enjoyed that we are prone to forget the source from which they come, others have been added, which are of so extraordinary a nature, that they cannot fail to penetrate and soften even the heart which is habitually insensible to the ever watchful providence of Almighty God. In the midst of a civil war of unequalled magnitude and severity, which has sometimes seemed to foreign States to invite and to provoke their aggression, peace has been preserved with all nations, order has been maintained, the laws have been respected and obeyed, and harmony has prevailed everywhere except in the theatre of military conflict; while that theatre has been greatly contracted by the advancing armies and navies of the Union. Needful*

diversions of wealth and of strength from the fields of peaceful industry to the national defense, have not arrested the plough, the shuttle or the ship; the axe has enlarged the borders of our settlements, and the mines, as well of iron and coal as of the precious metals, have yielded even more abundantly than heretofore. Population has steadily increased, notwithstanding the waste that has been made in the camp, the siege and the battle-field; and the country, rejoicing in the consciousness of augmented strength and vigor, is permitted to expect continuance of years with large increase of freedom. No human counsel hath devised nor hath any mortal hand worked out these great things. They are the gracious gifts of the Most High God, who, while dealing with us in anger for our sins, hath nevertheless remembered mercy. It has seemed to me fit and proper that they should be solemnly, reverently and gratefully acknowledged as with one heart and one voice by the whole American People. I do therefore invite my fellow citizens in every part of the United States, and also those who are at sea and those who are sojourning in foreign lands, to set apart and observe the last Thursday of November next, as a day of Thanksgiving and Praise to our beneficent Father who dwelleth in the Heavens. And I recommend to them that while offering up the ascriptions justly due to Him for such singular deliverances and blessings, they do also, with humble penitence for our national perverseness and disobedience, commend to His tender care all those who have become widows, orphans, mourners or sufferers in the lamentable civil strife in which we are unavoidably engaged, and fervently implore the interposition of the Almighty Hand to heal the wounds of the nation and to restore it as soon as may be consistent with the Divine purposes to the full enjoyment of peace, harmony, tranquility and Union."

It is difficult to determine if the proclamation was intended to be a prayer or a political address. In fairness to Lincoln, these are the words of a man struggling with the most stressful events of his political career but his Thanksgiving Proclamation was clearly an attempt to turn the attentions of a grief stricken nation away from the horrors of war. It was also an attempt to persuade Americans that the War Between the States was an act of God rather than an act of the President.

Lincoln opens with the assertion that the year had been filled with the blessings of divine providence. He then explains that despite the threat of foreign aggression, peace with the nations of the world had been preserved. Next, Lincoln contends that other than on the field of battle, laws had been honored and obeyed and that harmony prevailed. With many parts of the nation under martial law, citizens being arrested without due process and riots in the streets, you would have to believe that Lincoln was fully aware that he was telling a lie. Lincoln justifies the cost of the war with the words *"needful diversions of wealth"* and contended that it had not interfered with farming, transportation or trade. He offered a reminder that the country gained great wealth from the mining of iron, coal and precious metals. His final sentences show the clever manipulative ability of a deceitful politician. With a few closing words, Lincoln lays the blame of his administration's failures on the people of the South. In claiming that God was angered by the nation's sins, he pleads for the American people, united as one heart and one voice, to repent for America's perverseness and disobedience. Lincoln commends to God's care all those who had become widows, orphans, mourners or sufferers due to the unavoidable war. He ends his proclamation with plea for the hand of God to heal the nation and restore it the divine principles of peace, harmony, tranquility and Union. It is possible that President Lincoln's proclamation included a sincere offering of hope and comfort to a troubled nation but the primary objective of the proclamation was to address the issues that were threatening his re-election.

Lincoln's Gettysburg Address, November 19, 1863
Published by Sherwood Litho. Co., Chicago
U. S. Library of Congress Prints and Photographs Div.

On November 19, 1863, Lincoln was provided with the setting to deliver what would become his best remembered speech. The timing and location could not have been better for the beleaguered President. Just seventeen days before the dedication ceremony of the Gettysburg National Cemetery, David Wills, the cemetery committee chairman, sent a somewhat rude invitation to President Lincoln to attend the event. Considering that the invitation was sent with much shorter notice than many of the

187

other attendees, it seemed to be almost an after-thought. Wills bluntly informed the President that the dedication was a State funded event and that Edward Everett would be the orator. He carefully expressed to the President that after Everett's oration, he would be allowed to make only *"a few appropriate remarks."* The short notice given along with President Lincoln's limited role in the ceremony suggests that some of the Gettysburg residents still held Lincoln responsible for the carnage which was brought to their community. President Lincoln was eager and willing to accept his part. At about 2:00 P.M on the afternoon of the 19th, facing thousands of on-lookers, President Lincoln began his short but concise address:

"Four score and seven years ago our fathers brought forth on this continent, a new nation, conceived in Liberty, and dedicated to the proposition that all men are created equal.

Now we are engaged in a great civil war, testing whether that nation, or any nation so conceived and so dedicated, can long endure. We are met on a great battle-field of that war. We have come to dedicate a portion of that field, as a final resting place for those who here gave their lives that that nation might live. It is altogether fitting and proper that we should do this.

But, in a larger sense, we can not dedicate; we can not consecrate; we can not hallow this ground. The brave men, living and dead, who struggled here, have consecrated it, far above our poor power to add or detract. The world will little note, nor long remember what we say here, but it can never forget what they did here. It is for us the living, rather, to be dedicated here to the unfinished work which they who fought here have thus far so nobly advanced. It is rather for us to be here dedicated to the great task remaining before us; that from these honored dead we take increased devotion to that cause for which they gave the last full measure of devotion; that we here highly resolve that these dead shall not have died in vain; that this nation, under God, shall have a new birth of freedom and that government of the people, by the people, for the people, shall not perish from the earth."

The first sentence is well remembered but the phrase *"dedicated to the proposition that all men are created equal"* is an expression which conflicts with America's history and with Lincoln's personal views. Even as Lincoln was delivering his famous address, the Union army was vigorously removing Native Americans from their homelands. Union Colonel Christopher H. *"Kit"* Carson was engaged in a campaign against the Navajo tribes; their homes, food and supplies being destroyed by his scorched earth tactics; capturing them whenever it was possible and killing them when it was not. History records that Abraham Lincoln was a man of strong and unwavering convictions. He was always opposed to slavery and never recanted his statements about the issue but he often expressed his belief that whites were superior and never recanted those statements. So why did Lincoln state that *"all men are created equal?"* In typical Lincoln fashion, he was testing the waters in preparation of his next move. He would soon assert that the war was a glorious endeavor, ordained by God. The intent of his speech at Gettysburg was to convince the people that despite the destruction and incredible loss of life, the war must be continued. He proclaimed that the cemetery was a final resting place for the men who *"gave their lives that that nation might live"* suggesting that the nation would die if the Southern States were allowed to secede from the Union. As he proceeded with his address, Lincoln proved once again that he could shift the blame of the war to the people. He proclaimed that sacrifices made on the battlefield were part of *"unfinished work"* and that the people should be *"dedicated to the great task remaining"* before them. Lincoln also asserted that the guilt would fall upon the people if they allowed the war to end because the Union soldiers would have *"died in vain"* and the government would *"perish from the earth."*

Lincoln's address was interrupted several times by applause. After delivering his speech, he expressed to friends that he believed that the oration was a total failure. It received mixed reviews in Northern newspapers but to Lincoln's advantage, it was widely published. The influence of Lincoln's Gettysburg address had a far greater impact than he could have ever expected. Due to his persuasiveness, the war would eventually be viewed as a *"battle cry of freedom."*

The Election of 1864

In all of American history, the story of the 1864 Presidential Election is probably the most distorted. A popular version is that Republican candidate Abraham Lincoln defeated Democratic candidate George McClelland and that John C. Fremont entered the race as a third party candidate but withdrew. In truth, it could just as easily be contended that Lincoln was a third party candidate and Fremont was the Republican choice or possibly that there was no Republican candidate at all.

In 1864, as the New Year rang in, President Abraham Lincoln was a man without a party. Both Lincoln and Republican Party leaders believed that he was incapable of being re-elected. Not yet nominated, General George McClellan was the most popular candidate for President. Republican membership was still divided into three distinct groups; the communicators, the legislators and the financiers. The communicators, led by Horace Greeley, were the first to abandon Abraham Lincoln as a Republican candidate for the Presidency. Greeley, founder and editor of the *New-York Tribune*, was continuously embarrassed by the anti-Lincoln images and articles published by his chief competitor; Manton Marble's *New York World* newspaper. Horace Greely had political aspirations of his own and felt that Lincoln's failures would hinder his political future.

In the early days of Lincoln's presidency, the legislators of the Republican Party had little choice other than to support him. From the very beginning of the war, Radical Republicans in Congress insisted that prosecuting the war for sole purpose of saving the Union would never be enough to gain public support and would threaten the success of Party candidates in future elections. By 1864, radicals were demanding that the Republican Party's resolve to continue the war must include a demand for an end to slavery. President Lincoln's apprehension about supporting that position was a major cause of the Republican Party split. In keeping with radical demands, Senator John B. Henderson of Missouri submitted a resolution for a constitutional amendment to abolish slavery on January 11, 1864. With Republicans holding two-thirds of the Senate seats, the resolution was easily passed by the Senate on April 8, 1864. It was the first time in American history that either House of Congress had passed bill that would attempt to bring an end to slavery. It is difficult to understand how Radical Republicans expected to convince the American people that the War Between the States was caused by slavery after enduring three long years of death and destruction before addressing the issue in Congress. Having waited until election year, especially an election they feared they would lose made their motives extremely questionable. Despite success in the Senate, a House version of the bill was defeated on June 15, 1864.

For his first three years as President, Lincoln opposed the radical demands for portraying the war as a struggle to free the Black race from the bonds of slavery; for two very good reasons. First, Lincoln new that such a pretence would be a lie. He knew that he would have to recant every claim that he had made about the necessity of war and feared that he would be viewed as a liar. Second, Lincoln knew that the use of military force to change the laws of the United States would be in effect, an act of treason. His quandary was; how could he convince the American people that the war was now and always had been a struggle to end slavery and at the same time, save his reputation and stay within the confines of the Constitution? The Radical Republican faction in Congress was tired of waiting for Lincoln to find an answer; they wanted him replaced with a more forceful leader.

As always, the financiers of the Republican Party operated behind the scene. In 1864, President Lincoln found his salvation in the form of the Republican Party's wealthy elite. Most of these men were members of a secret society known as the Union League.

The Union League

In America's early days, it was common for the wealthy and socially prominent men of their respective cities and communities to gather at private men's clubs. Their discussions and their meetings were held in secret. What happened in the club, stayed in the club. Many of these organizations still exist. One of the oldest of the gentleman's clubs was the Philadelphia Club. A main topic of discussion among members was politics. With the coming of the War Between the States, the Club began to splinter along conservative and liberal political lines. Much like the sentiments of the nation, conservatives concerned themselves with the rights of the states while liberals dedicated themselves to the preservation of the Union. Republicans and Democrats began meeting in separate areas of the club. Because of the hostile environment, some Republicans split away to form a league of loyalists which became known as the "*Loyal League*" or "*Union League*." A similar situation occurred with the Union Club of the City of New York. One group held to the name "*Club*" and remained predominantly anti-war Democrats while the second group adopted the name "*League*" and consisted mainly of Republicans who supported the war effort. The three largest Union Leagues were in Philadelphia, New York and Chicago. During the reconstruction era, the Union Leagues were responsible for mobilizing the Freedman's Bureau and seizing control of politics in the Southern States for the Republican Party. The membership in New York and Philadelphia included some of the wealthiest men in America. More importantly, its members would have the most to lose by an early end to the war. The war effort was very profitable for them. In Philadelphia, League members were concerned about Lincoln's failures as Commander-in-Chief but they had close ties with the President. Jay Cooke, a prominent member of the Union League of Philadelphia and confidant of Treasury Secretary Salmon Chase, was the chief financier of the war. Cooke made his fortune selling bonds and is considered by most to be the father of investment banking in America.

Two prominent newspaper men, John Weiss Forney and Morton McMichael, arranged a meeting where President Lincoln could address the Philadelphia Union League in February of 1864. No accounts of Lincoln's address to the League were every published during his lifetime. Efforts by the Philadelphia Union League to insure Lincoln's nomination for President were conducted quietly without gaining public attention. The radical members of the Republican Party continued their search for a candidate to replace Lincoln. Soon rumors were circulating that another of President Lincoln's enemies, John C. Fremont would be nominated by the Republicans.

The Hard Hand of War

With the arrival of spring, Union and Confederate forces broke from their winter camps. Believing that he would be facing two of his former Generals in the Presidential election, Lincoln was sure that his record as Commander-in-Chief would become a prominent issue during the campaign. Lincoln also knew that radicals wanted blood and revenge. If he had any chance of gaining their support he would have to demonstrate that he was capable of crushing the Southern resistance in brutal fashion. As the war resumed in 1864, President Lincoln pitted his most successful General, Ulysses S. Grant against General Robert E. Lee's Army of Northern Virginia. General Grant's success in the Western theater had been much more than just military conquests. It was Grant that taught his Generals to forage for their needs and destroy everything else. By 1864, Grant and his subordinates had a reputation for leaving a trail of devastation behind them. They had taken the city of Vicksburg by surrounding the town for more than six weeks and starving the citizens and the soldiers into surrender. Perhaps the most aggressive of Grant's Generals was William T. Sherman; well known for burning towns and destroying property in Tennessee and Mississippi. Sherman demonstrated the type of combativeness that President Lincoln needed. In Georgia, Union General William T. Sherman was ordered to commence a campaign which would become known as "*Sherman's march to the sea.*" The scorched earth tactics of the expedition included the destruction of buildings, homes, barns, crops, killing of livestock and the burning of the City of Atlanta. There has long been a debate as to whether the violence was an act of war or an act of terror. Some historians contend that the acts were war crimes. Historically, Lincoln defenders often contend that the President was unaware of the atrocities and brutality during the Sherman's campaign. Since the President was famous for micro-managing the war and known to fire any General who acted against his orders there is little doubt that the President was fully aware and approved of General Sherman's actions. With the President being complicit in the atrocities, serious question remain; were these actions a necessity of war or necessary to win an election? Did President Lincoln want triumphs or trophies? The fall of Atlanta on September 2, 1864, proved to be a great prize leading into the election in November. The precedent set by the Atlanta Campaign was that for the first time, the United States army was engaged in a war against private citizens. After burning the City of Atlanta and leaving a trail of destruction through the center of Georgia, Sherman reported:

> *"We are not only fighting hostile armies, but a hostile people, and must make old and young, rich and poor, feel the hard hand of war, as well as their organized armies."* [69]

The Great Lie

Anyone who is a fan of misinformation would be thrilled by United States Presidential Election of 1864. Like magic, the Republican Party disappeared in the spring and re-appeared in the fall. On May 31, 1864, a group of Radical Republicans held a convention in Cleveland, Ohio. Very few detailed accounts of the Convention have ever been published. Depending on which version of the story you accept, there were as few as 200 or as many as 500 delegates at the convention. Newspaper accounts suggest that the Republican group adopted the name, Radical Democracy Party but that fact can neither be confirmed nor denied. The delegates selected John C. Frémont as the Party's nominee for President. Some historians contend that he was a third party candidate while others insist that he was the true Republican nominee.

On June 7, 1864, a group calling themselves the National Union Party began their convention in Baltimore, Maryland. The National Union Party consisted of moderate Republicans and Democrats who were in favor of continuing the war. By a vote of 484 to 22, delegates chose Abraham Lincoln over Ulysses Grant as their Presidential Nominee. They then selected Democrat Andrew Johnson as his Vice-Presidential running mate. With the National Union Party being a mixture of Republicans and Democrats there were likely more Republicans in the Radical Democracy Party. This again raises the argument about who was the third party candidate; Frémont or Lincoln? Ironically, both parties had almost identical platforms. The only difference between the two was the Presidential nominees. It has long been the preference of most historians to down-play the split in the Republican Party. The fact that the Republican Party was

194

bitterly divided during the early months of 1864, is undeniable. The object of their division was Abraham Lincoln. While both groups demanded the continuation of the war, the main issue was how the party should represent the necessity of war to the American people.

It was during the National Union Party convention in Baltimore that the *"Great Lie"* was born. The National Union Party platform contained eleven resolutions. The first resolved that it was the duty of every American Citizen to maintain the Union and the paramount authority of the Constitution and laws of the United States. It further resolved that Party favored *"quelling by force of arms the Rebellion now raging against its authority, and in bringing to the punishment due to their crimes the Rebels and traitors arrayed against it."* The principle was continued in the second resolution, demanding that no compromise be offered to the Rebels and that no offer of peace could be made other than unconditional surrender.

While seldom noted, the third resolution of the National Union Party's 1864 platform changed the history of the War Between the States forever. Prior to June of 1864, there had been no resolve or any utterance by a major political party in American that the war was even remotely related to the issue of slavery. Now as the nation continued to suffer from three years of war and as its citizens grieved the loss of hundreds of thousand of lives, the delegates of the National Union Convention resolved:

> *"That as slavery was the cause . . . "*

The combined delegates of two political parties chose to proclaim to the American people that slavery was suddenly *"hostile to the principles of Republican government,"* and that the United States government, in its own defense, had prosecuted the war to end the gigantic evil. The resolution amounted to a rebuttal of the Republican Party's 1860 resolution which resolved:

> *"the rights of the states, and especially the right of each state to order and control its own domestic institutions according to its own judgment exclusively, is essential to that balance of powers on which the perfection and endurance of our political fabric depends"*

More importantly, the 1864 resolution was in total conflict with prior statements made by party nominee Abraham Lincoln. Lincoln stated in his inaugural address of March 4, 1861:

> *"I have no purpose, directly or indirectly, to interfere with the institution of slavery in the States where it exists. I believe I have no lawful right to do so, and I have no inclination to do so."*

The question as to whether slavery was a cause of the War Between the States or to what if any degree it contributed to the War has been debated since the first shots were fired. Not knowing the thoughts or convictions of the men who were engaged in the conflict, it is unlikely that any answer to the question could be conclusive. What can be concluded is that the decision to use military force against the Southern States was ultimately made by one man; President Abraham Lincoln. He was a man who was never bashful about expressing his views or convictions. He firmly asserted that his only intent in using military force was to preserve the Union. In Lincoln's second inaugural address on March 4, 1865, he seemed reluctant to defend the Republican resolve as to the cause of the war by stating:

> *"slaves constituted a peculiar and powerful interest. All knew that this interest was somehow the cause of the war. To strengthen, perpetuate, and extend this interest was the object for which the insurgents would rend the Union even by war, while the Government claimed no right to do more than to restrict the territorial enlargement of it."*

The use of a word such as *"somehow"* was totally out of character for Lincoln. This statement during his address suggests that it was the powerful interest created by slavery rather than the evils of slavery that concerned Lincoln most. It also suggests that Lincoln believed that the Southerners had misunderstood his intent. Regardless of the true meaning of his statement, it is clear that Lincoln was reluctant to conclude that slavery, in the States where it existed, was the true cause of the war.

Lincoln was aware that delegates were treading on thin ice with their third resolution. It stated that the party was in favor of a Constitutional Amendment to abolish slavery but it did not clearly state that the Amendment would be the only means used to end slavery. Lincoln

196

had already been condemned by many for over-throwing the Constitution. He fully understood that slavery, in the States where it already existed, was protected by U. S. Law and use of the military to usurp those laws could be construed as an act of treason.

Resolutions four through seven dealt with support and praise for the military, the President and his administration and resolutions eight and nine called for promoting immigration and further support for the Trans-Continental Railroad.

Resolution ten dealt with the National debt. The war was more costly than anyone could have anticipated and the resolution called for a new system of taxation plus asserted that it was the duty of each state to assist with the debt and promote the use of the National currency. This is the only resolution in the platform that uses the word "*state*." Unlike previous political platforms, no mention is made of "*State's Rights*," only the "*State's duties*" to the Federal government.

While not specifically naming names, the eleventh and final resolution of the 1864 platform dealt with French intervention in Mexico. Napoleon III had established his puppet government in Mexico and obviously had intentions of conducting trade with the Confederate States across the border with Texas.

During the last week of August, 1864, the Democrats held their national convention in Chicago. As expected, George McClellan was chosen as the Democratic presidential candidate. This was likely the lowest point in Lincoln's political career and perhaps the lowest point in his life. The fanfare of his nomination in June had died down. He was still unsure if his attempts to sway public sentiment had been successful. His armies were still struggling. In mid-July, Confederate forces commanded by General Jubal Early attacked Union defenses at Fort Stevens on the outskirts of Washington; causing a panic in the nation's capitol. General Grant's attempt to take the Confederate capitol at Richmond had stalled. Three Union Armies under the command of General Sherman were making progress in Georgia but were facing fierce opposition from the Confederate forces now under the command of General John Bell Hood. Every attempt to invade Texas had ended in failure. Losses by Union Generals Frederick Steele and Nathanial Banks left Confederate forces virtually unmolested in Texas, Arkansas and most of Louisiana. The State of

Missouri was in total chaos, eliminating any chance for construction on the east end of the Trans-Continental Railroad. As desperate as the military situation was, Lincoln's political situation was even worse. He was facing two prominent political opponents who hated him. In addition to firing General's John Fremont and George McClellan, Lincoln had publicly humiliated them and now they wanted revenge. Republicans were deeply divided and Horace Greeley was blasting Lincoln in the New York press. More than ever, Lincoln was convinced that he would loose the election.

In September, the President's political fortunes began to change. On September 3, 1863, Lincoln received a message from General Sherman reading, "*Atlanta is ours, and fairly won.*" The fall of Atlanta was not the most significant battle of the war but it was Abraham Lincoln's greatest prize. It was a trophy that he flaunted in front of his enemies and opponents. Coming just two months before the election, no military victory did more for Lincoln's political career.

It is likely that the victory also influenced the decisions of John Fremont. The Radical's nominee for President knew full well that he had little chance of winning the election but wanted revenge against Lincoln. He also knew that every vote for him would amount to a vote for George McClellan. As an abolitionist and a former out-cast from the Democratic Party, Fremont was opposed to George McClellan's election as well. His desire to embarrass Lincoln yet save the election for the Republican Party resulted in a compromise. Through a deal that was supposedly brokered by Michigan Senator Zachariah Chandler, Fremont agreed to withdraw from the Presidential race in exchange for the firing of Postmaster General Montgomery Blair. Since Lincoln and Blair had both been responsible for his public humiliation, the deal would effectively serve as revenge against both men.

Montgomery Blair was a moderate and had long been a target of Radical Republicans but Lincoln staunchly defended him. To fire him at the demand of radicals would be a great embarrassment to the President; a situation that would bring great satisfaction to John Fremont. On September 22, 1864, John C. Fremont officially withdrew from the Presidential race. On September 23, President Lincoln wrote to Montgomery Blair saying:

"My dear sir - you have generously said to me more than once, that whenever your resignation could be a relief to me, it was at my disposal. The time has come. You very well know that this proceeds from no dissatisfaction with you, personally or officially. Your uniform kindness has been unsurpassed by that of any friend."

There is little to suggest that the President was complicit in negotiating the deal but it clearly shows that he was willing to sacrifice friendship and loyalty in order to win the election. Blair immediately submitted his resignation and the President replaced him with William Dennison.

The Lincoln Presidency received an unexpected boost on October 12, 1864 by way of the death of Chief Justice Roger Taney. Unlike some of the Radical Republicans such as Charles Sumner, Lincoln made no public comment. Not wanting to offend anyone so close to the election, Lincoln made no attempt to replace the Chief Justice. Still scrambling to gain all possible support, Lincoln turned his attention to the Territory of Nevada which was applying for Statehood and where he had strong support. While admitting Nevada into the Union would only allow him two additional electoral votes, Lincoln believed that the two votes might be the deciding factor. Fearing that the Nevada Constitution would not reach Washington in time for the election, the entire document was sent by telegraph. Containing more than 16,000 words, the Constitution took two days to transmit at a cost of more than $4,300. This was yet another demonstration of Lincoln's desperation in his attempt at re-election.

The vote tally in the 1864 Presidential election revealed that Lincoln had underestimated his efforts. He easily won the electoral vote by a total 212 to 21. There were three key elements to his success. First, drawing War Democrats into the National Union Party divided the Democratic Party much deeper than anyone had anticipated. Second, Sherman's sacking of Atlanta supplied new hope that the war would soon end with a grand Union victory. Third and most importantly, Fremont's withdrawal from the race left Radicals with no alternative but to vote for Lincoln. After the election, like a stroke of magic, the Republican Party re-appeared.

As President-elect, one of Lincoln's earliest initiatives was to solve a serious problem within his cabinet. His former supporter and Secretary of the Treasury, Salmon Chase had sided with the

Radicals against Lincoln. Knowing that Chase still had political ambitions of his own; Lincoln removed Chase from both his cabinet and the political arena by appointing him to the office of Chief Justice of the United States Supreme Court. Although Lincoln remained unpopular, he was in control again. He could now proceed with a Republican agenda that had been badly neglected but first he had to insure that the Confederacy was destroyed. Just one week after the Presidential election, General William T. Sherman torched the City of Atlanta and continued his devastating march to the sea.

Lincoln's Final Term

With the arrival of the New Year in 1865, it was time for the President-elect and the Republican Party to get back to business. The President and his Party had been successful in passing legislation to support finance, immigration, homesteads and the Trans-Continental Railroad but they had not anticipated the magnitude or the impact of the war. The war had been costly and the government was virtually mortgaged to wealthy bankers and financiers. A once rapidly increasing wave of immigration had been dissuaded by hostilities across the country. What few homesteaders that settled in the Western Territories found themselves unprotected and poorly supplied, forcing many of them to abandon their dreams of a new home. While the Central Pacific Railroad broke ground in California on January 8, 1863, the eastern leg of the railroad had not begun construction. The great plan of the Republican Party had been frustrated by a four year delay.

On February 17, 1865, Union General William T. Sherman burned the South Carolina Capitol City of Columbia. Many historians deny Sherman's responsibility in the act. Fearing a similar fate, citizens in Charleston, South Carolina evacuated the city.

As one of the final acts of the 38th United States Congress, the Freedmen's Bureau bill was passed on March 3, 1865. The bill created the Bureau of Refugees, Freedmen, and Abandoned Lands, commonly known as the Freedmen's Bureau. Created as a part of the United States War Department, the Freedmen's Bureau was intended to deal with the problems associated with the growing number of Black refugees in addition to supporting the seizure lands once held citizens of the Southern States.

On March 4, 1865, President Abraham Lincoln delivered his second inaugural address. After a brief opening paragraph, the President offered a remembrance of his address four years earlier; stating:

> *"While the inaugural address was being delivered from this place, devoted altogether to saving the Union without war, insurgent agents were in the city seeking to destroy it without war - seeking to dissolve the Union and divide effects by negotiation. Both parties deprecated war, but one of them would make war rather than let the nation survive, and the other would accept war rather than let it perish, and the war came."*

In his subtle deceitful manner, Lincoln acquitted himself of any guilt relating to the war. He asserted that his only intent had been to save the Union without war. As he had done so many times before, Lincoln conveyed the guilt to the people by alleging that the South initiated a war that the North was forced to accept in order to save the nation. In contrast to his previous speeches, Lincoln included a new contention but one that he could not or simply chose not to explain. Expressing that the enormous number of slaves localized in the Southern States constituted a peculiar and powerful interest, he now contended that this interest was "*somehow*" the cause of the war. In his reference to his first inaugural address, he did not admit to saying that he had no purpose, inclination or right to interfere with the institution of slavery in the States where it existed. Lincoln also failed to mention that he had prefaced his emancipation proclamation with a promise to the Southern States that they could keep their slaves if they returned to the Union.

As the President continued his address, his contentions went far beyond the influences of a peculiar interest. On March 4, 1865, on the steps of the U. S. Capitol building, the President of the United States of America proclaimed to the American people that the War Between the States was an act of God; stating:

"He gives to both North and South this terrible war as the woe due to those by whom the offense came"

In his evangelical tone, the President proclaimed that a defeat of the South would be the righteous judgment of God saying:

"if God wills that it continue until all the wealth piled by the bondsman's two hundred and fifty years of unrequited toil shall be sunk, and until every drop of blood drawn with the lash shall be paid by another drawn with the sword, as was said three thousand years ago, so still it must be said - the judgments of the Lord are true and righteous altogether."

Abraham Lincoln's elaborate use of references to God in the last months of his life has been a subject of intense debate. Some claim that Lincoln became very religious before his death. Others claim that he had long been an atheist and remained that way until he died. Religious conjecture aside, Lincoln's second inaugural address could easily be viewed in today's society as the *"rants of a mad man."* His address includes several signs of narcissistic and sociopathic behavior associated psychological disorders. In any case, his address was successful in swaying public sentiment toward continuing the war. Many claim that the address was Lincoln's greatest work. Lincoln was also pleased with his speech.

In response to compliments paid to the President by New York's infamous Thurlow Weed, Lincoln replied in a letter:

"Everyone likes a compliment. Thank you for yours on my little notification speech, and on the recent Inaugural address. I expect the latter to wear as well as - perhaps better than - anything I have produced"

One sentence in the short letter reflects on Lincoln's assertion that the war was God's punishment; saying:

"Men are not flattered by being shown that there has been a difference of purpose between the Almighty and them." [70]

The month of April in 1865, brought a number of great successes for President Lincoln, It was also the month when Abraham Lincoln's life would end. On April 2, after being warned by General Lee that he could no longer defend Richmond, Confederate President Jefferson

Davis and his staff began evacuating the capitol city. The day after the evacuation, General Robert E. Lee surrendered the Confederate Army of Northern Virginia to Union General Ulysses Grant.

On Good Friday, April 14, 1865, President Abraham Lincoln was struck in the head by a bullet fired from the gun of Confederate sympathizer John Wilkes Booth. After nine hours in a coma, the President died at 7:22 AM the next morning. For at least a short period, news of the President's death brought shock to the entire nation. He was the first American President to be killed in office. The irony that General Robert E. Lee surrendered on Palm Sunday and that President Abraham Lincoln was shot on Good Friday adds a religious overtone to Lincoln's words:

> "*until every drop of blood drawn with the lash shall be paid by another drawn with the sword*"

In a similar religious metaphor, the man who had once "*lived by the sword*" had now "*died by the sword.*"

Chapter 5

The Aftermath

(1865 to Present)

The life and death of Abraham Lincoln, along with the aspirations and resolves of his Republican Party, re-shaped the United States of America forever. What began as a *"league of friendship"* among thirteen States, evolved into a consolidated republic which was declared to be indivisible. Almost a quarter of a century of Republican Party domination left its mark on the Constitution, American law, immigration, politics, taxation, government finance, banking and race relations.

Fulfilling their resolves of 1860, the Republicans had clearly *"rebuked"* those claiming State and popular sovereignty. The challenge before them now; could they be *"forever silenced*?" In their desperate attempt to win an election, Lincoln's followers had allowed a Southern Democrat to enter the White House. Their frustrations led to impeachment proceedings against President Andrew Johnson.

From the very beginning of hostilities, President Lincoln and the Republican controlled Congress contended that the Southern States could not and did not secede from the Union and that the War Between the States was a rebellion rather than a revolution. Interestingly enough, Congress spent twelve grueling years in the process of re-admitting States to a Union that they supposedly never left. Radical Republican Thaddeus Stevens, Chairman of the Joint Committee on Reconstruction, suggested that the Southern States be kept under military rule and never re-admitted to the Union. The destructive and divisive period referred to as the *"reconstruction era,"* officially ended in 1877. The era was filled with graft, corruption and government abuses. Many Northerners, commonly referred to as *"Carpetbaggers,"* raced to the Southern States to take advantage of impoverished people with no rights or legal remedies to protect themselves. Blacks were often placed in positions of authority to punish Southerners for what was perceived by many Northerners to be treasonous and immoral wickedness. With little notoriety,

Congress and the United States Army continued the process of removing Native Americans from their tribal homelands. War profiteers, primarily financiers and railroad owners, continued to amass their fortunes. Efforts to feed, house and educate the millions of Black Americans freed by the Thirteenth Amendment, proved to be inadequate and in many cases declined. In 1868, a Freedmen's Village which had been established on the confiscated property of Robert E. Lee, began evicting residents to expand Arlington National Cemetery. By 1872, the entire Freedmen's Bureau was closed down. As if the devastation of war had not been enough, Republican reconstruction policies created a bitter divide that would extend well into the 20th century and in many ways remains in American society today.

Lincoln the Martyr

The shocking assassination of Abraham Lincoln exalted him to a level of fame unmatched by any American President. He became much larger in death than he had ever been in life. He was revered by many as a near God-like figure and numbered among the country's greatest President's. He has been adorned with titles such as "*Honest Abe, the Ancient One, the Great Emancipator and the Liberator*" and as President and Commander-in-Chief, he has been credited with saving the nation. While being loved by many he was hated and demonized by others.

There is little need to analyze the life of Lincoln. He was a man of strong will and resolve. His own words and actions give a far greater testimony than any historian could ever present; to quote Lincoln, "*we hold these truths to be self-evident.*" His opposition to the institution of slavery was consistent. His willingness to interfere with slavery was not. Lincoln's assertion that the White race was superior to that of Blacks was unwavering. His wisdom can easily be attributed to his awareness of the power of public sentiment and knowing that for most Americans, perception was reality. Praise of Lincoln's honesty is not only presumptuous but unfounded. The President's statements were often conflicting; leading to the conclusion that only one version of those conflicts could be statements of truth. Lincoln's emancipation proclamation, by his own admission, was issued only by his authority as Commander-in-Chief during at time of war; an act which offered freedom to slaves in States where the Federal government had no power to enforce the act, and left slavery intact in those States where the government could enforce it. He began his Presidency in support of slavery in the States where it existed. He evaded all suggestions of a Constitutional amendment which would legally end slavery until the moment that he felt he would lose an election. The President demonstrated the willingness to accept any demand by the Southern States other than the demand for disunion. His true legacy is often distorted in history. Lincoln was not the first President to face rebellion or secession but he was the first President to make the decision to "*forever silence*" those who he portrayed to be traitors. Neither time nor the persuasions of history can erase Lincoln's abuses of the Constitution or his actions which lead to the death of three-quarters of a million Americans. Among the questions that require a truthful answer are; did President Abraham Lincoln save the Union or did he re-create it? Did saving the Union save the nation or did it replace the nation with a new Republic?

On May 4, 1865, the coffins of Abraham Lincoln and his son William *"Willie"* Lincoln were placed in a receiving vault at Oak Ridge Cemetery in Springfield, Illinois. The journey of the 16th President of the United States was at an end but his legend was only beginning. As the nation grieved, Republicans continued their plans; but now they had a martyr. With calloused indifference, Republicans hailed their fallen leader as the *"Savior of the Union"* and the *"Great Emancipator."* Suddenly, a man who was one of the most unpopular Presidents of all time had risen to a glorious position as equal or superior to Presidents such as George Washington, Thomas Jefferson, James Madison and Andrew Jackson. A massive monument resembling the Temple of Zeus was dedicated to Abraham Lincoln on May 30, 1922. Another resemblance to the Temple of the Greek God Zeus is portrayed inside the monument by the 19 foot statue of Lincoln sitting on what resembles a thrown. Behind the statue is inscribed the phrase:

IN THIS TEMPLE

AS IN THE HEARTS OF THE PEOPLE

FOR WHOM HE SAVED THE UNION

THE MEMORY OF ABRAHAM LINCOLN

IS ENSHRINED FOREVER

Abraham Lincoln is the only U. S. President whose memory is enshrined in a temple.

The Thirteenth Amendment

The Thirteenth Amendment to the U. S. Constitution was the first of three amendments passed by the Republican controlled Congress during the era of reconstruction. The original intent of all three amendments was clearly aimed at the rights of the Black race. The final text of the Thirteenth Amendment was simple and straight forward, stating:

> *"Section 1. Neither slavery nor involuntary servitude, except as a punishment for crime whereof the party shall have been duly convicted, shall exist within the United States, or any place subject to their jurisdiction."*

> *"Section 2. Congress shall have power to enforce this article by appropriate legislation."*

A bill proposing the amendment was passed by the U. S. Senate on April 8, 1864. With Republicans having only a plurality, passage of a similar bill in the House of Representatives would prove to be difficult. Even in the North, abolishing slavery was a sensitive subject. Many Northerners feared that masses of freed slaves would flee to the Northern States; taking jobs away from white laborers. Others simply did not want blacks within their white society. The House version of the bill was defeated on June 15, 1864, falling 13 votes short of the required two-thirds by a vote of 93 in favor and 65 against. More than seven long months elapsed before enough votes could be accumulated to pass the House bill. Most historians agree that those votes were acquired by way of political favors, bribes and other corrupt acts. Because these acts were committed in secret, many of them are hard to prove. Some historians contend that the votes were generated by the persuasiveness of Abraham Lincoln and Radical Republican Representative Thaddeous Stevens but it is important to note the time period associated with the acts. The House bill had been defeated during the lowest point in Abraham Lincoln's career. The Radicals who supported the bill were Lincoln's opponents. Lincoln knew that he had no chance of re-election without gaining the support of the Radicals. He had consistently proven that he was willing to go to any extreme to gain their support. Lincoln also knew that passage of the bill would require support from the anti-war

Democrats who hated him. Many books, movies and articles related to the events contained unsubstantiated accounts and inaccurate quotes. Ironically, even Lincoln admirers credit him with unfavorable statements which he probably never made. Whether proven are not, it would be hard to contend that there was no corruption involved. What has been proven is that Secretary of State William Seward hired a distinguished group of lobbyist to assist in getting the bill passed. Correspondence between the lobbyists and politicians, newspaper publishers and the wealthy elite includes references to political appointments and cash; one mentioning as much as $10,000.[71]

The bill was finally passed by the U. S. House of Representatives on January 31, 1865 by a vote of 119 for and 56 against. The required number for passage would have been 122 but eight Democrats were mysteriously absent, lowering the requirement to 117 votes. President Lincoln did not live to see the Thirteenth Amendment become law. Eight months after the end of the War Between the States, Secretary of State Seward, declared the Amendment ratified on December 18, 1865.

The Fourteenth Amendment

The Fourteenth Amendment is one of the most important yet most abused Amendments in the U. S. Constitution. Its original intent was to reverse the U. S. Supreme Court decision in Dred Scott v. Stanford which stated that African slaves and their descendents were not and could not be American citizens. The impact of the Amendment stretched far beyond the original intent of its authors. To fully understand the impact of the Amendment requires an examination of the events leading up to the drafting of the Amendment and an understanding of the principles which lead to the founding of the Republican Party.

The primary principles upon which the Republican Party was founded were those of the former Federalist Party. Led by Alexander Hamilton, the Federalists were bitterly opposed to Amending the Constitution to include a bill of rights, especially those which limited the power of the Federal government. It was Hamilton who led the delegation calling for a Constitutional convention deceitfully implying that the intent of the convention was to reform the Articles of Confederation when in reality, the secret meeting was designed to replace the Articles with a government of his own design. The Federalists depended upon Article 1, Section 8, Clause 18 for the strength of their new government; it states:

> "*The Congress shall have power to make all laws which shall be necessary and proper for carrying into execution the foregoing powers, and all other powers vested by this Constitution in the Government of the United States, or in any department or officer thereof.*"

This provision is often referred to as the "*Necessary and Proper Clause*" or sometimes more accurately described as the "*Elastic Clause.*" Hamilton and his followers were fully aware that anything can be deemed necessary and that depending on the sentiments of the people; everything can be viewed as proper. To the dissatisfaction of the Federalists, the 10th Amendment limited those powers. To over-ride the Amendment, Hamilton presented the Federalist theory of "*Implied Powers.*" It was this theory that has allowed the Supreme Court to distort the 14th Amendment in a way that would affect the nation forever.

The precursor to the 14th Amendment was the "*Civil Rights Act of 1866.*" Introduced in the Senate by Lyman Trumbull and in the House by James F. Wilson, the Act was clearly intended to protect the rights of the newly freed slaves while excluding the rights of Native Americans; and nothing else. Wilson explained to the House that the Act provided for:

> "*the equality of citizens of the United States in the enjoyment of civil rights and immunities.*"

In theory, parts of that Act are still in effect today. Fully titled as "*An Act to protect all Persons in the United States in their Civil Rights, and furnish the Means of their Vindication,*" the opening text contained two very important phrases. The first is:

> *"all persons born in the United States and not subject to any foreign power, excluding Indians not taxed, are hereby declared to be citizens of the United States"*

The words *"not subject to any foreign power"* are consistent with current immigration law which states that a child born on American soil to a foreign ambassador, head of state, or foreign military prisoner is not an American citizen but the implications of the entire phrase are much broader. Native Americans on reservations or under tribal authority were not taxed because they were considered as aliens rather than citizens. The words *"excluding Indians not taxed"* implies that children born to all aliens are excluded from citizenship.

The second important phrase is one which guarantees equal protection under the law, including the words:

> *"as is enjoyed by white citizens, and shall be subject to like punishment, pains, and penalties."*

Many Congressmen and other Americans contended that current *"Hate Crime"* legislation is unconstitutional because it provides for different prosecution and punishment for a like crime. The Civil Rights Act of 1866 clearly expressed that punishment for a crime was to be the same for all citizens.

Claiming that Congress had insufficient authority to enforce the Civil Rights Act, President Andrew Johnson vetoed it but his veto was overridden by Congress. Several Republicans agreed with President Johnson and presented proposals for a Constitutional Amendment. The wording of the proposed Amendment was slightly changed to address the issue of both aliens and Indians in a single phrase, stating:

> *"All persons born or naturalized in the United States and subject to the jurisdiction thereof are citizens of the United States and of the State wherein they reside."*

The phrase *"and subject to the jurisdiction thereof"* continues to be the focus of intense debate. Two very prominent opinions have been offered by the U. S. Supreme Court in regard to the intent of the 14th Amendment.

John Elk was a Winnebago Indian, born on a reservation. Later in life, he resided among whites and renounced his tribal allegiance. He attempted to vote on April 5, 1880 and was denied by registrar Charles Wilkins. In the ensuing 1884 U. S. Supreme Court case Elk v. Wilkins, the issue was whether or not an Indian, born as a member of one of the Native American tribes is, merely by reason of his birth within the United States, a citizen within the meaning of the first section of the Fourteenth Amendment of the Constitution. The Court determined that while reservations were within the Territorial limits of the United States, members of Indian tribes were aliens and an Indian could not make himself a citizen of the United States without the consent and cooperation of the government. This is a clear statement that the authors of the Fourteenth Amendment had not intended for birth-right citizenship to apply to aliens.

Another important Supreme Court Case gave a slightly different interpretation of the phrase *"and under the jurisdiction thereof."* The 1898 case of The United States v. Wong Kim Ark, resulted in the opinion that children born on American soil to alien parents who were permanently domiciled in the United States were American citizens. The ruling added a new element to citizenship equation by establishing the requirement of permanent domicile; leaving yet another issue that required interpretation. Even though it offered a new opinion concerning jurisdiction, the ruling did not clearly establish that birthright citizenship was mandated by the 14th Amendment. Use of the phrase *"permanent domicile"* did however eliminate any contention that birthright citizenship could apply to aliens who had entered the country illegally.

Following the ratification of the 14th Amendment, a bill prohibiting Federal and State governments from denying a citizen the right to vote based on that citizen's race, color, or previous condition of servitude, became the 15th Amendment to the U. S. Constitution on February 3, 1870. It was the third and final Amendment directed at securing the rights former slaves. The fact that it took three separate amendments over the course of five years to secure those rights, suggests that Republicans were uncertain about how many rights should be given to Blacks. Failure to extend those rights to women or Native Americans further suggest that there motives were purely political.

Railroads

The long awaited Trans-Continental Railroad opened to traffic on May 10, 1869. Just like the War Between the States, the railroad proved to be more costly than anyone had anticipated. In addition to cash loans and grants for construction, the total of lands granted to the to the Union Pacific and Central Pacific railroads, amounted to more than 200 million square miles; an area larger than the State of Texas.

In conjunction with poor supervision of the project, the incredible amount of wealth involved led to corruption. One scandal involving several prominent Republican politicians came to public attention in 1872. Republican Vice-President Schuyler Colfax and future Republican President James Garfield were implicated in the scandal but were never charged.

Despite a financial panic in 1873 which forced several railroad companies into bankruptcy, the transportation industry was one of the greatest sources of wealth during the post war years of the nineteenth century. Railroad magnates such as J. P. Morgan, Jay Gould and Cornelius Vanderbilt were among the richest men in the world but for Republicans, the Trans-Continental Railroad did not produce the results that they had anticipated. They quickly lost control of the railroad and they never gained complete control of the Western Territories.

Fate of Native Americans

It is disturbing to realize that the American people and the Federal government maintained and supported an institution which treated a race of people like property; importing, selling, buying and trading them with little compassion. It is even more disturbing to realize that the entire nation was complicit in the wholesale slaughter of Native Americans; driving them from their native lands and confining them to reservations like wild animals.

Lincoln's words *"With malice toward none, with charity for all"* are well known among Americans. Republicans used those words as a slogan for their efforts to re-shape the nation but it is hard to find evidence that any charity was ever broadly extended and their malice toward Native Americans was obvious and well documented. With God having placed his mighty sword in the hands of the Union Army, many of America's native tribes were brought to near extinction. It is clear that not just the Republicans were responsible for the hostilities directed at Native Americans. Just as the case was with slavery, the entire nation had been guilty throughout its history. Colonists were driving Native Americans from their homeland long before the first slave ship reached the Colonies. Every President prior to and including Abraham Lincoln had been complicit in Indian removal acts. All administrations made promises to Native Americans that were never kept.

Lincoln knew before taking office that the only U. S Lands where Indians could live, hunt and roam free were in the Western Territories and they would have to be removed. He kept a close watch on the actions of his armies and was fully aware of the assaults on women and children at Bear River in Idaho and Sand Creek in Colorado. Lincoln was well known for his attitude toward the inferiority of Mexicans and Blacks. There is little to suggest the he felt any differently about Native Americans.

Republican efforts to eradicate Native tribes did not end with the death of Abraham Lincoln. After the war, the most applauded Union Cavalry General in the War Between the States, General Philip Sheridan, was placed in Command of the Union Army on the Western Plains. Sheridan's tactics were often brutal. Whether or not he actually said that *"the only good Indian is a dead Indian"* is questionable but his actions clearly supported that sentiment. General Sheridan's tactics included surprise attacks on unprotected Indian villages which resulted in the death of women and children. He also supported the mass slaughter of Buffalo to starve Indians off of the land.

While a number of Indian Wars continued well into the twentieth century, Republicans had effectively eliminated Native American resistance prior to losing their control of the Federal government in the mid-1880s. They had begun a program of assimilation which was based on the theory that Native Americans could only be civilized by adapting them to the social and psychological characteristics of the white race. A major component of the forced assimilation was the Indian Boarding Schools whereby Native American children were taken from their parents and forced to learn the ways of the white race. The flagship of the program, the Carlisle Indian Industrial School, was founded in 1879. One of America's greatest athletes, Jim Thorpe attended the Carlisle school from 1907 to 1912. In all more than 100 boarding schools were created, the last of which closed in the 1940s.

Most Americans are shocked to discover that the vast majority of Native Americans did not become U. S. Citizens until 1924. Some did not receive full rights of citizenship until the 1950s. Because Indian tribes were defined by U. S. law to be alien nations, Native Americans were not granted citizenship under the Fourteenth Amendment. The first Indian Citizenship Act was signed into law by President Calvin Coolidge on June 2, 1924. It had been created in part to give recognition to thousands of Native Americans for their service to the United States military during World War I. The act stated:

> *"That all non citizen Indians born within the territorial limits of the United States be, and they are hereby, declared to be citizens of the United States: Provided That the granting of such citizenship shall not in any manner impair or otherwise affect the right of any Indian to tribal or other property."*

Because Native Americans living on reservations were still considered to be members of "*domestic dependent nations*," their rights were often confused and abused until passage of the Indian Civil Rights Act of 1968.

Immigration

Of all the influences left behind by Abraham Lincoln and the Republican leaders of that era, it is their impact on immigration that remains the most notable. Immigration was a key factor in their plan for the Western Territories. In Lincoln's words:

> *"an outlet for free white people everywhere - the world over"*

The Republicans' inability to control and transform immigration into a useful tool was also a key factor in the downfall of the Party.

From the time that the Colonies declared their independence in 1776, up to the year 1830, there was very little immigration to the United States. In 1830, more than 99% of the citizens of the United States were native born. It was so much a non-issue in the eighteenth century that the Constitution gave no express authority to the Federal government to regulate immigration. In the 1840s and 1850s, war and famine caused many to flee Europe and the British Isles. The discovery of gold in California and the vast amounts of land ceded to the United States after the War with Mexico attracted even more immigrants. It was during this period that the Republican Party was born. The sudden wave of immigrants was a very unpopular event for most of America but Republicans saw immigration as an opportunity; a view shared by liberal politicians in today's society.

It is important to realize that the Republican Party's interest in the new arrivals from Europe was not based on compassion for the immigrants. Their plan to offer land and support to the newcomers also included a plan for limiting their prosperity. Party leaders knew that they could not maintain a sense of loyalty among people of wealth and political influence. The ideal immigrant needed to be white, poorly educated and have language barriers which would deter them from gaining a prominent status in society but the immigrants needed the determination and physical ability to assume the role of yeomen farmers. They were restricted to small tracts of land which would prevent them from developing agrarian empires like the wealthy planters of the South. Their defense, maintenance and success depended on government support; a government that the Republican Party intended to control.

The success that the Republican Party hoped to gain through the promotion of immigration was never fully realized. The hostilities of war interrupted mass immigration and Native Americans proved to be a more formidable foe than expected. The Western frontier was harsh and challenging. Protecting and supplying settlers was a difficult task. Many of the early settlers abandoned their dreams and returned to the East. Lands that were intended for small farms soon fell into the hands of corrupt railroad investors and land speculators.

Post-war years proved to be even more difficult. An unexpected boom in the cattle industry turned quiet communities into to rowdy cow-towns. Former Confederate soldiers still bitter over the war roamed the Western Territories; often engaging in violent conflicts

217

with those who fought for or supported the Union. Some became notorious outlaws attacking anything that represented the Federal government, including banks, railroads and U. S. Marshals. Republicans lost control of the West long before it lost control of the government.

Although the Republican plan for immigration was a failure, the influences of their actions lived on. Article 1, Section 8, of the Constitution enumerates the powers delegated to the Federal government. Among those numerated, is the power to establish a uniform rule of naturalization. Because there is no mention of immigration in the Constitution, the power to regulate immigration is delegated to the States by the 10th Amendment. For the first 100 years of the United States' existence, immigration laws were State laws. This is where the Republican Party forever changed U. S. immigration laws by the use of Alexander Hamilton's theory of "*implied powers.*" The first federal immigration law was the Page Act of 1875. It was designed to prevent Chinese aliens, which were considered to be "*undesirable,*" from entering the United States. While continuing to vigorously promote immigration, the Republican controlled Congress attempted to filter out immigrants which did not meet their qualifications. While no authority to regulate immigration had been expressed by the Constitution, the U. S. Supreme Court has repeatedly ruled that the authority of Congress to regulate immigration was "*implied*" by both the "*Naturalization Clause*" and the "*Commerce Clause*" of the Constitution. The 1875 Act sparked a flurry of restrictive immigration laws based on ethnic origin. The Immigration Act of 1891, established the Office of Superintendent of Immigration within the Treasury Department. By 1893 the newly created bureaucracy employ 180 people with two-thirds of them stationed at Ellis Island in New York. The Ellis Island facility was strategically placed adjacent to the newly dedicated Statue of Liberty. Since March 1, 2003, the bureau has operated as United States Citizenship & Immigration Service under the Department of Homeland Security. In 2016, the agency had more than 19,000 employees and contractors working at 223 offices around the world.

The use of immigrants to gain political control was not unique to the Republican Party of the 19th century but they did set the standard which is supported by modern day politics. Voting rights have been given to non-citizens on and off throughout U. S. History and remains a controversial issue in current politics. Looking at the examples set by the Republican Party of old, many questions arise. Are American immigration policies concerned with human rights or a part of a political agenda? Would the extension of voting rights to non-citizens be a testimony to fairness or a deceitful attempt by a political party to gain control of government?

Republicans and Race Relations

Perhaps the most damaging effects of the original Republican Party's resolve, was the role that it played in the evolution or race relations in the United States. As the War Between the States came to a close, Republicans contended that the sole cause of the war was slavery; an issue that they had made no attempt to address until the election of 1864. As the victorious Generals led their Union Armies in Grand Review down the streets of Washington on May 23 and May 24, 1865, the nearly 200,000 Black veterans who had defended the Union cause were excluded from the festivities. From 1865 to 1870, Republican Congressmen slowly enacted legislation that they claimed to be in support of civil rights for the newly freed slaves. While reflecting on their proclaimed benevolent acts, it is difficult to find any evidence that Party leaders were truly intent on defending or supporting the civil rights that they proclaimed. In addition to slavery, women's rights were serious issues in the 19th century. Not only did the Republican Party have members who were abolitionists, they had women's rights activists as well. Despite a twenty-five year choke-hold on the Federal government, women's rights were never addressed by the Republicans. Women were not guaranteed the right to vote until 1920. In addition to the Party's failure to address the rights of women, the rights of Native Americans were not addressed until 1924.

Although certain rights were guaranteed to Blacks by way of the 13th, 14th, and 15th Amendments to the Constitution, few clear provisions were made for the support of millions of people who were essentially condemned to a life of homeless share-croppers. The Freedmen's Bureau, the only agency created by Congress to offer assistance to the newly freed slaves, lost most of its funding by 1869 and was abandoned in 1872. During its short existence, the Freedman's

Bureau accomplished the election of Blacks to State elected positions in the South during a period that many White Southerners were not allowed to vote. A racial divide, resulting from these acts was unavoidable. Republican leaders clearly intended to promote racial hatred and punish Southerners. This combined with the contention that Southerners had waged a war to maintain slavery were clear contributions to racial unrest in the South.

In the 21st century, many historians contend that the actions of the Republican controlled government during the "*Reconstruction Era*" were necessary and justified. That has not always been the accepted opinion of scholars and theorists. Until the 1930s, the most widely accepted historical views of the era were those of Columbia University professor William Archibald Dunning. The large contingency of noted scholars who concurred with his opinions became known as the "*Dunning School.*" The Dunning School of thought was that military rule of Southern State governments by the Republican controlled Congress manipulated Blacks and that their corrupt, extravagant, unrepresentative, and oppressive acts were the very root of racial hatred in America.

Other scholars who were not considered to be members of the Dunning School, offered similar opinions; among the most noted of which was Ellis Merton Coulter. Serving for four decades as professor at the University of Georgia, Coulter was the author of 26 published books on the War Between the States and the era of Reconstruction. In addition to supporting many of the theories of Dunning scholars, Coulter was particularly critical of the practice of forcing blacks into a position of leadership before they were fully prepared. In recent times, Coulter has been labeled as a racist and a Southern apologist but some of his assertions contained undeniable truths. In one of his many writings, Coulter stated:

> "*As each generation feels constrained to rewrite the past, points of view and methods of approach necessarily change, and so revisionists arise. If they remain within the reasonable bounds of established facts, they may well make lasting contributions in fresher interpretations and in the presentation of new information; but if they depart from the old channels to attract attention in novel and unsubstantiated points of view, they themselves may soon be revised.*"

While Coulter offered that revised theories of history can be acceptable if they are bound by established facts, he reflects on the reconstruction era with the unwavering contention that:

"no amount of revision can write away the grievous mistakes made in this abnormal period of American history." [72]

W. E. B. Du Bois
by C. M. Battey
U. S. Library of Congress

One of the earliest and most noted critics of the Dunning School was William Edward Burghardt "W. E. B." Du Bois. His many titles and accomplishments included American historian, sociologist, civil rights activist, Pan-Africanist, author, and editor. While attending Harvard University in 1895, Du Bois became the first African American to earn a Ph.D. In 1909, he was one of the co-founders of the National Association for the Advancement of Colored People. His views on Reconstruction were as deeply criticized by conservatives as Dunning's views were criticized by liberals but he was one of the first true civil rights champions in America. He was among the earliest activists to point out that the Republican Party's actions did not embrace the needs of African Americans and that government policies did not fully include them as citizens. Reflecting on a return trip from Europe, Du Bois expressed his feelings as he passed the Statue of Liberty, stating that *"he was unable to imagine the same sense of hope he assumed some immigrant arrivals had felt"*[73] as they passed the statue and that the hope and liberty represented by the statue did not apply to his race. Du Bois was clearly a leader rather than a follower. He was well known for his opposition to the views of Booker T. Washington. Du Bois was also known for his interest in socialism. His views on socialism were clearly his own rather than those of theorists such as Karl Marx. He considered that socialism might be a better path to racial equality than capitalism. His belief that socialism would contribute to racial equality was similar to a contemporary belief that socialism would benefit the American economy; a theory promoted by Vermont Senator Bernie Sanders in his 2016 Presidential campaign.

In 1911, Du Bois joined the Socialist Party of America but was forced to resign a year later for supporting Democratic candidate Woodrow Wilson for President. During the Progressive Era of the twentieth century, Du Bois played a major role in persuading Black voters to withdraw their support for the Republican Party in favor of the Democratic Party.

The Republican Party that was founded in 1854 essentially disappeared with the turn of the twentieth century. Today, the Party and its first President, Abraham Lincoln, are touted for their leadership in the struggle for racial equality. America's recorded history does not support that legacy. More devastating than the failure of the Republican Party to achieve racial equality in America, is the cruel and deceitful manner in which they perpetrated the lie which gave a false hope to millions of former slaves.

Dr. Martin Luther King, Jr.,
Speech in Washington, D. C., August 28, 1963
National Archives & Records Administration

1963 marked the 100th anniversary of the emancipation proclamation. In that same year, Dr. Martin Luther King, Jr. delivered his "*I have a dream*" speech. His words professing that dream are well remembered but the ominous condemnation that was embedded in that speech goes virtually unnoticed. On August 28, 1963, Dr. King stood in the shadow of a shrine dedicated to the man who issued the emancipation proclamation. Peering down on him from behind was the 19 foot marble sculpture of Abraham Lincoln; a man who proclaimed that the Black race was inferior to Whites; a man who offered to withdraw his sacred proclamation in exchange for the allegiance of those who were fighting desperately to free themselves from his tyranny.

After offering a single sentence proclaiming his happiness to be present at the momentous event, Dr. King described the great hope that by the emancipation proclamation by stating:

> *"Five score years ago a great American in whose symbolic shadow we stand signed the Emancipation Proclamation. This momentous decree was a great beacon of hope to millions of Negro slaves who had been seared in the flames of withering injustice. It came as a joyous daybreak to end the long night of their captivity."*

222

It was at that moment that Dr. King delivered the most truthful account of the devastation caused by a century of perpetuating a lie. Continuing his speech, Dr. King asserted:

> *"But 100 years later the Negro still is not free. 100 years later the life of the Negro is still badly crippled by the manacles of segregation and the chains of discrimination. 100 years later the Negro lives on a lonely island of poverty in the midst of a vast ocean of material prosperity. 100 years later the Negro is still languished in the corners of American society and finds himself in exile in his own land."*

Few words could greater describe the pain of a race of people who were promised a new tomorrow, only to discover 100 years later that it was a heart breaking repeat of yesterday. The willingness of Dr. King to refer to Abraham Lincoln as a great American is an incredible testament to the persuasiveness of the late President. After 100 years of lies, broken promises and demeaning insults, Lincoln remains a near God like figure in the hearts and minds of many; including the race that he so badly deceived and manipulated. Many Lincoln apologists contend that his words were often taken out of context or that his opinions changed during his last days but most of those contentions are baseless and unsubstantiated.

As professor Coulter had stated, no amount of revision can write away that portion of our history. It cannot be denied that Lincoln and many of his Party leaders were willing to trade the freedom of Blacks for the preservation of the Union. They were also willing to lie about their intent in order to win an election. The sentiments of the American people can often be swayed to view their actions as honorable but their impact on race relations in America will be hard to erase.

Evolution of the Party

By the end of President Ulysses S. Grant's second term, Republicans could feel their power slipping away. Their dreams for the Western Territories better resembled a nightmare. The Trans-Continental railroad had been completed but control of the empire was seized by corrupt investors and the wealthy elite, commonly referred to as the *"Robber Barons."* By the time that hostilities had ceased between the

Union Cavalry and Native American tribes, Republicans had lost control of Congress. Their fear that after reconstruction, Southern Democrats would gain enough political influence to launch a campaign of revenge against the Party proved to be unfounded. Their fiercest opposition during the post-war nineteenth century came from Northern Democrats who had been agitated by the Republicans ruthless twenty-five year reign. New York Governor Grover Cleveland won the Presidential election of 1884 becoming the first Democrat to be elected President in 28 years. In 1885 Democrats controlled the House but Republicans managed to gain control of the Senate. During the Presidential election of 1888, Republicans regained the White House only to lose it again to Grover Cleveland in 1892. During the final years of the nineteenth century, Republicans were haunted by the actions in their past. The careless waste and corruption by the previous Republican administrations contributed to an era so reckless and out of control that writer Mark Twain referred to it as "*The Gilded Age*." It was also an era when immigration began to spiral out of control.

As the twentieth century arrived, Republicans were once again in control of the White House and both Houses of Congress but the sentiments among Party members were rapidly changing. Just as the Republican Party had been exalted to its highest level of prominence by an assassin's bullet, another presidential assassination would mark the end of their dominant political influence. On the afternoon of September 6, 1901, William McKinley became the third Republican President to fall victim to an assassination. After his death on September 14, the Vice-President Theodore Roosevelt was sworn in as President of the United States; it was a day that ushered in a reversal of roles within the Democratic and Republican Parties.

The Republican Party of the nineteenth century, founded on the liberal Federalist principles of Alexander Hamilton transformed into the conservative Democratic principles of the Thomas Jefferson in the twentieth century. Likewise, the Democratic Party made a complete reversal in ideologies. The defining years of that transition began with the administration of President Theodore Roosevelt and ended with the administration of President Franklin Roosevelt.

While Theodore Roosevelt was the catalyst for major changes in Republican philosophies the Party was already demanding lower tariffs and stronger immigration restrictions. Theodore Roosevelt is most often associated with the period of social activism and political reform known as the "*progressive era*." He muddied the political waters by asserting that:

"*wise progressivism and wise conservatism go hand in hand*"

The problem with Roosevelt's assertion is that progressivism and conservatism are conflicting philosophies. The platform of his progressive "*Bull Moose Party*" was equally conflicted; causing many Republicans to distance themselves from him.

While Republicans were dealing with the confusion caused by Roosevelt's ideologies, Democrats were dealing with the rise in socialism. While having no direct link to the Democrats, the growing popularity of socialism in the late nineteenth and early twentieth century, had a major impact on Party policies; especially among liberals. The growing phenomenon gained strong support from trade unions, social reformers and immigrants. Francis Bellamy, author of the "*Pledge of Allegiance*," considered himself to be a "*Christian Socialist*" proclaiming that capitalism was a sin. His cousin Edward Bellamy contributed to the organization of a large network of socialist political groups known as the "*Nationalist Clubs*." Former Democrat Eugene Debs was a founding member of the Socialist Party of America in 1901 and was a five time Presidential candidate for the Socialist Party. His last presidential campaign was conducted from the Atlanta Federal Penitentiary after he was convicted of violating the 1918 Sedition Act by undermining the government's conscription efforts during World War I.

Roosevelt mixing spicy ingredients
cartoon by Karl K. Knecht
published in the Evansville Courier 1912

Theodore Roosevelt's continued trend toward progressivism caused the Republican Party to abandon him prior to the 1912 Presidential election; an election where Roosevelt received only 88 electoral votes as compared to Democrat Woodrow Wilson's 435 votes. The Party's separation from progress polices was the beginning of a transition toward conservatism. The events occurring during the 28 year period between 1917 and 1945 changed the fortunes and political views of virtually every American. It began with the United States' entry into World War I, included America's greatest economic depression and concluded with the end of World War II. The most defining event during the political transition was Franklin D. Roosevelt's election as a Democrat in 1932. The administration of Franklin Roosevelt was responsible for the realignment of the Democratic Party and became the very definition of liberal politics. It set new standards for taxation, deficit spending, entitlements, social programs and big government. While elements of liberalism and conservatism could be found in both political parties at the end of the Roosevelt administration, the persuasions of the two parties were more clearly defined during the mid-1960s; Democrats were progressive liberals and Republicans were staunch conservatives.

Although the names of political parties have changed many times over the years, two dominant political principles have remained the same. The Federalist principles of Alexander Hamilton are still prevalent among liberals while the Democratic principals of Thomas Jefferson are still dominant among conservatives. Burning questions still remain; is the nation "*The*" United States or is it "*These*" United States? Are there any rights which or still delegated to the States? Does the Constitution still guarantee certain rights to the People?

Despite popular contentions, the Constitution of the United States is not a living, breathing entity. It is a contract between the government and the people who created it. It was created in a manner that in the case of errors or omissions, it could be amended by the People. Nothing within the Constitution was ever intended to be "*implied*." The Constitution has no value unless it represents the expressed wishes of the American People. While the "*league of friendship*" was destroyed by the Republican Party in the 1860s, the principles upon which the sovereign states were united still live but it is difficult to establish a direction for the country's future while denying where it has been.

Appendices

Republican Party Platform of 1856

This Convention of Delegates, assembled in pursuance of a call addressed to the people of the United States, without regard to past political differences or divisions, who are opposed to the repeal of the Missouri Compromise; to the policy of the present Administration; to the extension of Slavery into Free Territory; in favor of the admission of Kansas as a Free State; of restoring the action of the Federal Government to the principles of Washington and Jefferson; and for the purpose of presenting candidates for the offices of President and Vice-President, do

Resolved: That the maintenance of the principles promulgated in the Declaration of Independence, and embodied in the Federal Constitution are essential to the preservation of our Republican institutions, and that the Federal Constitution, the rights of the States, and the union of the States, must and shall be preserved.

Resolved: That, with our Republican fathers, we hold it to be a self-evident truth, that all men are endowed with the inalienable right to life, liberty, and the pursuit of happiness, and that the primary object and ulterior design of our Federal Government were to secure these rights to all persons under its exclusive jurisdiction; that, as our Republican fathers, when they had abolished Slavery in all our National Territory, ordained that no person shall be deprived of life, liberty, or property, without due process of law, it becomes our duty to maintain this provision of the Constitution against all attempts to violate it for the purpose of establishing Slavery in the Territories of the United States by positive legislation, prohibiting its existence or extension therein. That we deny the authority of Congress, of a Territorial Legislation, of any individual, or association of individuals, to give legal existence to Slavery in any Territory of the United States, while the present Constitution shall be maintained.

Resolved: That the Constitution confers upon Congress sovereign powers over the Territories of the United States for their government; and that in the exercise of this power, it is both the right and the imperative duty of Congress to prohibit in the Territories those twin relics of barbarism--Polygamy, and Slavery.

Resolved: That while the Constitution of the United States was ordained and established by the people, in order to "form a more perfect union, establish justice, insure domestic tranquility, provide for the common defense, promote the general welfare, and secure the blessings of liberty," and contain ample provision for the protection of the life, liberty, and property of every citizen, the dearest Constitutional rights of the people of Kansas have been fraudulently and violently taken from them. Their Territory has been invaded by an armed force; Spurious and pretended legislative, judicial, and executive officers have been set over them, by whose usurped authority, sustained by the military power of the government,

227

tyrannical and unconstitutional laws have been enacted and enforced; The right of the people to keep and bear arms has been infringed. Test oaths of an extraordinary and entangling nature have been imposed as a condition of exercising the right of suffrage and holding office. The right of an accused person to a speedy and public trial by an impartial jury has been denied; The right of the people to be secure in their persons, houses, papers, and effects, against unreasonable searches and seizures, has been violated; They have been deprived of life, liberty, and property without due process of law; That the freedom of speech and of the press has been abridged; The right to choose their representatives has been made of no effect; Murders, robberies, and arsons have been instigated and encouraged, and the offenders have been allowed to go unpunished; That all these things have been done with the knowledge, sanction, and procurement of the present National Administration; and that for this high crime against the Constitution, the Union, and humanity, we arraign that Administration, the President, his advisers, agents, supporters, apologists, and accessories, either before or after the fact, before the country and before the world; and that it is our fixed purpose to bring the actual perpetrators of these atrocious outrages and their accomplices to a sure and condign punishment thereafter.

Resolved: That Kansas should be immediately admitted as a state of this Union, with her present Free Constitution, as at once the most effectual way of securing to her citizens the enjoyment of the rights and privileges to which they are entitled, and of ending the civil strife now raging in her territory.

Resolved: That the highwayman's plea, that "might makes right," embodied in the Ostend Circular, was in every respect unworthy of American diplomacy, and would bring shame and dishonor upon any Government or people that gave it their sanction.

Resolved: That a railroad to the Pacific Ocean by the most central and practicable route is imperatively demanded by the interests of the whole country, and that the Federal Government ought to render immediate and efficient aid in its construction, and as an auxiliary thereto, to the immediate construction of an emigrant road on the line of the railroad.

Resolved: That appropriations by Congress for the improvement of rivers and harbors, of a national character, required for the accommodation and security of our existing commerce, are authorized by the Constitution, and justified by the obligation of the Government to protect the lives and property of its citizens.

Resolved: That we invite the affiliation and cooperation of the men of all parties, however differing from us in other respects, in support of the principles herein declared; and believing that the spirit of our institutions as well as the Constitution of our country, guarantees liberty of conscience and equality of rights among citizens, we oppose all legislation impairing their security.

Republican Party Platform of 1860

Resolved: That we, the delegated representatives of the Republican electors of the United States in Convention assembled, in discharge of the duty we owe to our constituents and our country, unite in the following declarations:

1. That the history of the nation during the last four years, has fully established the propriety and necessity of the organization and perpetuation of the Republican party, and that the causes which called it into existence are permanent in their nature, and now, more than ever before, demand its peaceful and constitutional triumph.

2. That the maintenance of the principles promulgated in the Declaration of Independence and embodied in the Federal Constitution, "That all men are created equal; that they are endowed by their Creator with certain inalienable rights; that among these are life, liberty and the pursuit of happiness; that to secure these rights, governments are instituted among men, deriving their just powers from the consent of the governed," is essential to the preservation of our Republican institutions; and that the Federal Constitution, the Rights of the States, and the Union of the States must and shall be preserved.

3. That to the Union of the States this nation owes its unprecedented increase in population, its surprising development of material resources, its rapid augmentation of wealth, its happiness at home and its honor abroad; and we hold in abhorrence all schemes for disunion, come from whatever source they may. And we congratulate the country that no Republican member of Congress has uttered or countenanced the threats of disunion so often made by Democratic members, without rebuke and with applause from their political associates; and we denounce those threats of disunion, in case of a popular overthrow of their ascendency as denying the vital principles of a free government, and as an avowal of contemplated treason, which it is the imperative duty of an indignant people sternly to rebuke and forever silence.

4. That the maintenance inviolate of the rights of the states, and especially the right of each state to order and control its own domestic institutions according to its own judgment exclusively, is essential to that balance of powers on which the perfection and endurance of our political fabric depends; and we denounce the lawless invasion by armed force of the soil of any state or territory, no matter under what pretext, as among the gravest of crimes.

5. That the present Democratic Administration has far exceeded our worst apprehensions, in its measureless subserviency to the exactions of a sectional interest, as especially evinced in its desperate exertions to force the infamous Lecompton Constitution upon the protesting people of Kansas; in construing the personal relations between master and servant to involve an unqualified property in persons; in its attempted enforcement everywhere, on land and sea, through the intervention of Congress and of the Federal Courts of the extreme pretensions of a purely local interest; and in its general and unvarying abuse of the power entrusted to it by a confiding people.

6. That the people justly view with alarm the reckless extravagance which pervades every department of the Federal Government; that a return to rigid economy and accountability is indispensable to arrest the systematic plunder of the public treasury by favored partisans; while the recent startling developments of frauds and corruptions at the Federal metropolis, show that an entire change of administration is imperatively demanded.

7. That the new dogma that the Constitution, of its own force, carries slavery into any or all of the territories of the United States, is a dangerous political heresy, at variance with the explicit provisions of that instrument itself, with contemporaneous exposition, and with legislative and judicial precedent; is revolutionary in its tendency, and subversive of the peace and harmony of the country.

8. That the normal condition of all the territory of the United States is that of freedom: That, as our Republican fathers, when they had abolished slavery in all our national territory, ordained that "no persons should be deprived of life, liberty or property without due process of law," it becomes our duty, by legislation, whenever such legislation is necessary, to maintain this provision of the Constitution against all attempts to violate it; and we deny the authority of Congress, of a territorial legislature, or of any individuals, to give legal existence to slavery in any territory of the United States.

9. That we brand the recent reopening of the African slave trade, under the cover of our national flag, aided by perversions of judicial power, as a crime against humanity and a burning shame to our country and age; and we call upon Congress to take prompt and efficient measures for the total and final suppression of that execrable traffic

10. That in the recent vetoes, by their Federal Governors, of the acts of the legislatures of Kansas and Nebraska, prohibiting slavery in those territories, we find a practical illustration of the boasted Democratic principle of Non-Intervention and Popular Sovereignty, embodied in the Kansas-Nebraska Bill, and a demonstration of the deception and fraud involved therein.

11. That Kansas should, of right, be immediately admitted as a state under the Constitution recently formed and adopted by her people, and accepted by the House of Representatives.

12. That, while providing revenue for the support of the general government by duties upon imports, sound policy requires such an adjustment of these imports as to encourage the development of the industrial interests of the whole country; and we commend that policy of national exchanges, which secures to the workingmen liberal wages, to agriculture remunerative prices, to mechanics and manufacturers an adequate reward for their skill, labor, and enterprise, and to the nation commercial prosperity and independence.

13. That we protest against any sale or alienation to others of the public lands held by actual settlers, and against any view of the free-homestead policy which regards the settlers as paupers or suppliants for public bounty; and we demand the passage by Congress of the complete and satisfactory homestead measure which has already passed the House.

14. That the Republican party is opposed to any change in our naturalization laws or any state legislation by which the rights of citizens hitherto accorded to immigrants from foreign lands shall be abridged or impaired; and in favor of giving a full and efficient protection to the rights of all classes of citizens, whether native or naturalized, both at home and abroad.

15. That appropriations by Congress for river and harbor improvements of a national character, required for the accommodation and security of an existing commerce, are authorized by the Constitution, and justified by the obligation of Government to protect the lives and property of its citizens.

16. That a railroad to the Pacific Ocean is imperatively demanded by the interests of the whole country; that the federal government ought to render immediate and efficient aid in its construction; and that, as preliminary thereto, a daily overland mail should be promptly established.

17. Finally, having thus set forth our distinctive principles and views, we invite the co-operation of all citizens, however differing on other questions, who substantially agree with us in their affirmance and support.

1864 National Union Party Platform

1. Resolved: That it is the highest duty of every American citizen to maintain against all their enemies the integrity of the Union and the paramount authority of the Constitution and laws of the United States; and that, laying aside all differences of political opinion, we pledge ourselves, as Union men, animated by a common sentiment and aiming at a common object, to do everything in our power to aid the Government in quelling by force of arms the Rebellion now raging against its authority, and in bringing to the punishment due to their crimes the Rebels and traitors arrayed against it.

2. Resolved: That we approve the determination of the Government of the United States not to compromise with Rebels, or to offer them any terms of peace, except such as may be based upon an unconditional surrender of their hostility and a return to their just allegiance to the Constitution and laws of the United States, and that we call upon the Government to maintain this position and to prosecute the war with the utmost possible vigor to the complete suppression of the Rebellion, in full reliance upon the self-sacrificing patriotism, the heroic valor and the undying devotion of the American people to the country and its free institutions.

3. Resolved: That as slavery was the cause, and now constitutes the strength of this Rebellion, and as it must be, always and everywhere, hostile to the principles of Republican Government, justice and the National safety demand its utter and complete extirpation from the soil of the Republic; and that, while we uphold and maintain the acts and proclamations by which the Government, in its own defense, has aimed a deathblow at this gigantic evil, we are in favor, furthermore, of such an amendment to the Constitution, to be made by the people in conformity with its provisions, as shall terminate and forever prohibit the existence of Slavery within the limits of the jurisdiction of the United States.

4. Resolved: That the thanks of the American people are due to the soldiers and sailors of the Army and Navy, who have periled their lives in defense of the country and in vindication of the honor of its flag; that the nation owes to them some permanent recognition of their patriotism and their valor, and ample and permanent provision for those of their survivors who have received disabling and honorable wounds in the service of the country; and that the memories of those who have fallen in its defense shall be held in grateful and everlasting remembrance.

5. Resolved: That we approve and applaud the practical wisdom, the unselfish patriotism and the unswerving fidelity to the Constitution and the principles of American liberty, with which ABRAHAM LINCOLN has discharged, under circumstances of unparalleled difficulty, the great duties and responsibilities of the Presidential office; that we approve and indorse, as demanded by the emergency and essential to the preservation of the nation and as within the provisions of the Constitution, the measures and acts which he has adopted to defend the nation against its open and secret foes; that we approve, especially, the Proclamation of

Emancipation, and the employment as Union soldiers of men heretofore held in slavery; and that we have full confidence in his determination to carry these and all other Constitutional measures essential to the salvation of the country into full and complete effect.

6. Resolved: That we deem it essential to the general welfare that harmony should prevail in the National Councils, and we regard as worthy of public confidence and official trust those only who cordially indorse the principles proclaimed in these resolutions, and which should characterize the administration of the government.

7. Resolved: That the Government owes to all men employed in its armies, without regard to distinction of color, the full protection of the laws of war—and that any violation of these laws, or of the usages of civilized nations in time of war, by the Rebels now in arms, should be made the subject of prompt and full redress.

8. Resolved: That foreign immigration, which in the past has added so much to the wealth, development of resources and increase of power to the nation, the asylum of the oppressed of all nations, should be fostered and encouraged by a liberal and just policy.

9. Resolved: That we are in favor of the speedy construction of the railroad to the Pacific coast.

10. Resolved: That the National faith, pledged for the redemption of the public debt, must be kept inviolate, and that for this purpose we recommend economy and rigid responsibility in the public expenditures, and a vigorous and just system of taxation; and that it is the duty of every loyal state to sustain the credit and promote the use of the National currency.

11. Resolved: That we approve the position taken by the Government that the people of the United States can never regard with indifference the attempt of any European Power to overthrow by force or to supplant by fraud the institutions of any Republican Government on the Western Continent and that they will view with extreme jealousy, as menacing to the peace and independence of their own country, the efforts of any such power to obtain new footholds for Monarchical Government, sustained by foreign military force, in near proximity to the United States.

Bibliography

Basler, Roy P.: "*The Collected Works of Abraham Lincoln, Volume 4,*" Rutgers University Press, 1953.

Beckert, Sven: "*The Monied Metropolis: New York City and the Consolidation of the American Bourgeoisie, 1850-1896,*" Cambridge University Press, 2003.

Bennett, Lerone, Jr.: "*Forced Into Glory: Abraham Lincoln's White Dream,*" Johnson Publishing Company, 2007.

Berwanger, Eugene H.: "*The Frontier Against Slavery: Western Anti-Negro Prejudice and the Slavery Extension Controversy.*" University of Illinois Press, 1967.

Bonomi, Patricia U.: "*Under the Cope of Heaven : Religion, Society, and Politics in Colonial America,*" Oxford University Press, 2003.

Boorstin, Daniel J.: "*The Americans: The Colonial Experience.*" Knopf Doubleday Publishing Group, 2010.

Brooks, Noah: "*Washington in Lincoln's Time.*" Century Company, 1895.

Brown, Charles Raymond: "*The Northern Confederacy: According to the Plans of the Essex Junto 1796-1814.*" Princeton University Press, 1915.

Churchill, Ward: "*A Little Matter of Genocide: Holocaust and Denial in the Americas 1492 to the Present.*" City Lights Books, 1997.

Conyngham, David: "*Sherman's March Through the South: With Sketches and Incidents of the Campaign*" Applewood Books, 2001.

Coulter, E. Merton: "*The South During Reconstruction, 1865-1877: A History of the South.*" LSU Press, 1947.

DiLorenzo, Thomas: "*The Real Lincoln: A New Look at Abraham Lincoln, His Agenda, and an Unnecessary War.*" Crown Publishing Group, 2009.

Du Bois, W. E. B.: "*The Autobiography of W.E.B. Du Bois: A Soliloquy on Viewing My Life From the Last Decade of Its First Century.*" New York International Publishers, 1968.

Escott, Paul D.: "*Lincoln's Dilemma: Blair, Sumner, and the Republican Struggle over Racism and Equality in the Civil War Era.*" University of Virginia Press, 2014.

Gienapp, William E.: "*The Origins of the Republican Party, 1852-1856.*" Oxford University Press, 1987.

Greeley, Horace: "*Proceedings of the Republican National Convention held at Chicago, May 16, 17 & 18, 1860.*" Weed, Parsons and Company, 1860.

Green, Michael S.: "*Freedom, Union, and Power: Lincoln and His Party During the Civil War.*" Fordham University Press, 2004.

Hammond, Bray: "*Banks and Politics in America from the Revolution to the Civil War.*" Princeton University Press, 1991.

Hinton, John Howard: "*History of the United States of America, from the First Settlement of the Country, Volume 1.*" Samuel Walker and Company, 1875.

Howe, Julia Ward: "*A Trip to Cuba.*" Ticknor and Fields, 1860.

Jordan, John H. "*Black Americans 17th Century to 21st Century: Black Struggles and Successes*" Trafford Publishing, 2013.

Kroll, C. Douglas: "*Friends in Peace and War: The Russian Navy's Landmark Visit to Civil War San Francisco.*" Potomac Books, Inc., 2007.

Remini, Robert V.: "*Andrew Jackson: The Course of American Democracy, 1833-1845.*" JHU Press, 2013.

Rhoades, Richard N.: "*Lady Liberty: The Ancient Goddess of America.*" iUniverse, 2013.

Richard, Carl J.: "*The Battle for the American Mind: A Brief History of a Nation's Thought.*" Rowman & Littlefield, 2006.

Saler, Bethel: "*The Settlers' Empire: Colonialism and State Formation in America's Old Northwest.*" University of Pennsylvania Press, 2014.

Sears, Stephen W.: "*George B. McClellan: The Young Napoleon.*" Da Capo Press, 1999.

Sharp, James Roger: "*American Politics in the Early Republic: The New Nation in Crisis.*" Yale University Press, 1993.

Singer, Allen J.: "*New York and Slavery: Time to Teach the Truth.*" State University of New York Press, 2008.

Snay, Mitchell: "*Horace Greeley and the Politics of Reform in Nineteenth-century.*" America Rowman & Littlefield, 2011.

Sora, Steven: "*Secret Societies of America's Elite: From the Knights Templar to Skull and Bones.*" Destiny Books, 2003.

Thornton, Russell: "*American Indian Holocaust and Survival: A Population History Since 1492.*" University of Oklahoma Press, 1987.

Wilder, Craig Steven: "*Ebony and Ivy: Race, Slavery, and the Troubled History of America's Universities.*" Bloomsbury Publishing USA, 2014

Wilentz, Sean: "*The Rise of American Democracy: Jefferson to Lincoln.*" W. W. Norton & Company, 2006.

Zinn, Howard: "*A People's History of the United States, 1492-Present.*" Harper Perennial, 2003.

End Notes

[1] U. S. National Park Service; *"The French Connection: Statue of Liberty Nation Monument, New York."*

[2] U. S. Library of Congress: *"Thomas Jefferson's Letter to the Danbury Baptist association in the state of Connecticut,"* January 1, 1802.

[3] United States Supreme Court: *"Reynolds v. United States,"* 98 U.S. 145 (1878)

[4] U. S. Library of Congress: *"Laws and Orders Concluded by the Virginia General Assembly, March 05, 1624, Virginia Records Manuscripts. 1606-1737"*

[5] Thorpe, Frances Newton: *"The Federal and State Constitutions Colonial Charters, and Other Organic Laws of the States, Territories, and Colonies Now or Heretofore Forming the United States of America Compiled and Edited Under the Act of Congress of June 30, 1906,"* U. S. Government Printing Office, Washington, DC,1909.

[6] Henning, William Waller: Statutes at Large of Virginia, vol. 12 (1823): pages 84-86.

[7] Thorpe, Frances Newton: *The Federal and State Constitutions Colonial Charters, and Other Organic Laws of the States, Territories, and Colonies Now or Heretofore Forming the United States of America Compiled and Edited Under the Act of Congress of June 30, 1906,"* U. S. Government Printing Office, Washington, DC,1909.

[8] Lindman, Janet Moore and Tarter, Michele Lise: "*A Centre of Wonders: The Body in Early America*," Cornell University Press, 2001, pages 152-153.

[9] O'Halloran, Sharyn: "*The Future of the Voting Rights*," Russell Sage Foundation, 2006, p. 192.

[10] Kingsbury, Susan Myra, ed: *"Letter from John Rolfe to Sir Edwin Sandys, January, 1619/1620,"* Records of the Virginia Company of London, Volume 3. P. 243. Washington, D.C.: Government Printing Office, 1906-1933.

[11] *"The Founders' Constitution,"* Volume 1, Chapter 15, Document 53, The University of Chicago Press, Collections of the Massachusetts Historical Society.

[12] Clark, George L., "*A history of Connecticut*", G.P. Putnam's Sons; 2nd edition (1914). p. 156

[13] Jordan, John H.: *"Black Americans 17th Century to 21st Century: Black Struggles and Successes*". Trafford Publishing, Nov 7, 2013. p. 504

[14] *"Minutes of the Common Council of the City of New York, vol. II,"* p. 458, December 13, 1711 (New York Historical Society),

[15] Singer, Allen J.: "*New York and Slavery: Time to Teach the Truth,*" State University of New York Press, Albany, NY, 2008, p. 58.

[16] McManus, Edgar J.: *"A History of Negro Slavery in New York,"* Syracuse University Press, 2001, p. 115-116.

[17] *"The Concession and Agreement of the Lords Proprietors of the Province of New Caesarea, or New Jersey, to and With All and Every the Adventurers and All Such as Shall Settle or Plant There – 1664."* The Avalon Project, digital collections, Lillian Goldman Law Library, Yale University.

[18] "Journals of the House of Burgesses, April 1, 1772," p.131, as cited in the Collections of the Virginia Historical Society.

[19] *"Report of Proceedings in Congress; February 21, 1787"* Documents Illustrative of the Formation of the Union of the American States. Edited by Charles C. Tansill. 69th Cong., 1st sess. House Doc. No. 398. Washington, D.C.: Government Printing Office, 1927.

[20] *"Resolution No. 2, Declaration and Resolves of the First Continental Congress adopted October 14, 1774."* Documents Illustrative of the Formation of the Union of the American States.Government Printing Office, 1927. House Document No. 398. Selected, Arranged and Indexed by Charles C. Tansill

[21] Letter from John Adams to Abigail Adams, 3 July 1776, Original manuscript from the Adams Family Papers, Massachusetts Historical Society.

[22] Rulings of the United States Supreme Court, *"Texas v. White,"* et al.74 U. S. 700, Decided April 12, 1869.

[23] Article I, Treaty of Paris (1783).

[24] Hamilton, Alexander: *"Federalist No. 84,"* from McLean's Edition, New York. April 4, 1788.

[25] *"The Founders' Constitution. Volume 3, Article 1, Section 8, Clause 18, Document 11."* http://press-pubs.uchicago.edu/founders/documents/a1_8_18s11.html. The University of Chicago Press

[26] Patrick Henry addressing the Virginia Ratifying Convention, June, 1788.

[27] John Jay, in a letter to President John Adams, Jan. 2, 1801

[28] Thomas Jefferson's letter to Judge Spencer Roane, Sept. 6, 1819.

[29] Thomas Jefferson's letter to Judge Spencer Roane, 1821.

[30] Thomas Jefferson's Sixth Annual Presidential Message to Congress, December 2, 1806.

[31] Letter by Thomas Jefferson to John Holmes, April 22, 1820. From the digital collections of the U. S. Library of Congress.

[32] South Carolina Ordinance of Nullification, November 24, 1832: An ordinance to nullify certain acts of the Congress of the United States, purporting to be laws laying duties and imposts on the importation of foreign commodities.

[33] Letter from John Marshall to William Gaston, December 20, 1832.

[34] Ellis, Richard E.: *"The Union at Risk: Jacksonian Democracy, States' Rights and the Nullification Crisis."* Oxford University Press, 1987. p. 78

[35] Zinn, Howard: *"A People's History of the United States, 1492-Present"* Harper Perennial, 2003, p. 143

[36] Clark, Carmen E.: *"Garrison, William Lloyd,"* Encyclopedia of American Journalism, edited by Stephen L. Vaughn. Routledge, 2007. p. 195.

[37] Letter from William Lloyd Garrison to Rev. Samuel J. May, July 17, 1845.

[38] Emerson, Ralph Waldo, from his lecture "*Courage*," delivered in Boston on November 8, 1859.

[39] Howe, Julia Ward: "*A Trip to Cuba*" Ticknor and Fields, 1860. p. 12

[40] Spooner, Lysander: Essay No. VI, "*The Constitution of No Authority*" 1867.

[41] Woodburn, James Albert: "*The life of Thaddeus Stevens: a study in American political history, especially in the period of the civil war and reconstruction.*" Bobbs-Merrill Company, 1913. p. 519.

[42] Hinton, John Howard: "*History of the United States of America, from the First Settlement of the Country, Vol. 1,*" Samuel Walker and Company, 1875. p. 608

[43] O'Sullivan, John L.: "*Manifest Destiny*" editorial, New York Morning News, December 27, 1845.

[44] Berwanger, Eugene H.: "*The Frontier Against Slavery: Western Anti-Negro Prejudice and the Slavery Extension Controversy.*" University of Illinois Press, 1967. p. 125-126.

[45] Abraham Lincoln's speech at Springfield, Illinois, June 26, 1857.

[46] President Franklin Pierce, Special Message to the United States Senate and House of Representatives on January 24, 1856.

[47] President James Buchanan's Second Annual Address to Congress on the State of the Union. December 6, 1858.

[48] Resolution 4 of the 1860 Republican Party Platform of 1860, adopted and approved at convention, May 17, 1860

[49] Inaugural Address of President Franklin Pierce, Friday, March 4, 1853.

[50] Lincoln-Douglas debate at Alton, Illinois, October 15, 1858.

[51] Lincoln Douglas Debate, Ottawa, Illinois, August 21, 1858.

[52] Abraham Lincoln's lecture on "*Discoveries and Inventions*" first delivered on April 6, 1858 in Bloomington, Illinois.

[53] Abraham Lincoln's Fourth Debate with Stephen Douglas at Charleston, Illinois on September 18, 1858.

[54] Meeting at the White House on August 14, 1862 between President Abraham Lincoln and Committee of 5 black ministers, E. M. Thomas, Chairman.

[55] Speech of Abraham Lincoln at Peoria, Illinois, October 16, 1854.

[56] Abraham Lincoln's seventh debate with Stephen Douglas, Alton, Illinois, October 15, 1858.

[57] Letter from Brigadier General James H. Carleton, Commanding the Department of New Mexico, to Colonel Christopher Carson, 1st New Mexico Volunteers, October 12, 1862.

[58] From the Congressional testimony of John S. Smith, Joint Committee on the Conduct of the War, Massacre of Cheyenne Indians, 38th Congress, 2nd Session Washington, D. C., March 14,1865.

[59] Greeley, Horace: "*Proceedings of the Republican National Convention held at Chicago, May 16, 17 & 18, 1860.*" Weed, Parsons and Company, Albany, 1860.

[60] Abraham Lincoln's First Inaugural Address, March 4, 1861.

[61] Joint resolution to amend the Constitution of the United States, March 2, 1861. United States Statutes at Large, Volume 12, Page 251, U. S. Library of Congress.

[62] Basler, Roy P.: "*The Collected Works of Abraham Lincoln, Volume 4,*" Rutgers University Press, New Brunswick, New Jersey, 1953. p. 159

[63] Barnes, James J. & Patience P.: "*Private and Confidential: Letters from British Ministers in Washington to the Foreign Secretaries in London, 1844-67.*" Susquehanna University Press, 1993. p. 239.

[64] Letter from Abraham Lincoln, to Senator O. H. Browning, September 22, 1861.

[65] Anonymous letter published in The London Times newspaper on March 5, 1863.

[66] Guelzo, Allen C.: "*Abraham Lincoln as a Man of Ideas*" SIU Press, Jan 26, 2009. p. 171. Article reprinted in the Plymouth Weekly Democrat, Plymouth, Indiana, Thursday, September 10, 1863.

[67] Letter from President Abraham Lincoln to James C. Conkling, August 26, 1863.

[68] Brooks, Noah: "Washington in Lincoln's Time" Century Company, 1895, Washington, D.C. p. 58

[69] Letter from General William T. Sherman to General Henry Halleck, written in the field near Savannah, Georgia, December 24, 1864.

[70] Letter from President Abraham Lincoln to Thurlow Weed, March 15, 1865.

[71] Cox, LaWanda and John H.: "*Politics, Principle & Prejudice 1865-66: Dilemma of Reconstruction America*" . The Free Press of Glencoe, New York, 1963.. pages 1 - 30.

[72] Coulter, E. Merton: "*The South During Reconstruction, 1865 - 1877: A History of the South*" LSU Press, June 1, 1947. p. xi.

[73] Du Bois, W. E. B.: "*The Autobiography of W.E.B. Du Bois: A Soliloquy on Viewing My Life From the Last Decade of Its First Century*" New York International Publishers, 1968.

www.ingramcontent.com/pod-product-compliance
Lightning Source LLC
Chambersburg PA
CBHW032043080426
42733CB00006B/171